ReFocus: The Films of Michel Gondry

ReFocus: The International Directors Series

Series Editors: Robert Singer, Stefanie Van de Peer, and Gary D. Rhodes

Editorial Board: Lizelle Bisschoff, Stephanie Hemelryck Donald, Anna Misiak, and Des O'Rawe

ReFocus is a series of contemporary methodological and theoretical approaches to the interdisciplinary analyses and interpretations of international film directors, from the celebrated to the ignored, in direct relationship to their respective culture—its myths, values, and historical precepts—and the broader parameters of international film history and theory. The series provides a forum for introducing a broad spectrum of directors, working in and establishing movements, trends, cycles, and genres including those historical, currently popular, or emergent, and in need of critical assessment or reassessment. It ignores no director who created a historical space—either in or outside of the studio system—beginning with the origins of cinema and up to the present. *ReFocus* brings these film directors to a new audience of scholars and general readers of Film Studies.

Titles in the series include:

ReFocus: The Films of Susanne Bier
Edited by Missy Molloy, Mimi Nielsen, and Meryl Shriver-Rice

ReFocus: The Films of Francis Veber
Keith Corson

ReFocus: The Films of Jia Zhangke
Maureen Turim and Ying Xiao

ReFocus: The Films of Xavier Dolan
Edited by Andrée Lafontaine

ReFocus: The Films of Pedro Costa: Producing and Consuming Contemporary Art Cinema
Nuno Barradas Jorge

ReFocus: The Films of Sohrab Shahid Saless: Exile, Displacement and the Stateless Moving Image
Edited by Azadeh Fatehrad

ReFocus: The Films of Pablo Larraín
Edited by Laura Hatry

ReFocus: The Films of Michel Gondry
Edited by Marcelline Block and Jennifer Kirby

edinburghuniversitypress.com/series/refocint

ReFocus:
The Films of Michel Gondry

Edited by Marcelline Block and Jennifer Kirby

EDINBURGH
University Press

Edinburgh University Press is one of the leading university presses in the UK. We publish academic books and journals in our selected subject areas across the humanities and social sciences, combining cutting-edge scholarship with high editorial and production values to produce academic works of lasting importance. For more information visit our website: edinburghuniversitypress.com

© editorial matter and organisation Marcelline Block and Jennifer Kirby, 2022
© the chapters their several authors, 2022

Edinburgh University Press Ltd
The Tun—Holyrood Road
12 (2f) Jackson's Entry
Edinburgh EH8 8PJ

First published in hardback by Edinburgh University Press 2020

Typeset in 11/13 Ehrhardt MT by
IDSUK (DataConnection) Ltd

A CIP record for this book is available from the British Library

ISBN 978 1 4744 5601 2 (hardback)
ISBN 978 1 4744 5602 9 (paperback)
ISBN 978 1 4744 5603 6 (webready PDF)
ISBN 978 1 4744 5604 3 (epub)

The right of the contributors to be identified as authors of this work has been asserted in accordance with the Copyright, Designs and Patents Act 1988 and the Copyright and Related Rights Regulations 2003 (SI No. 2498).

Contents

List of Figures vii
Notes on Contributors viii
Acknowledgments xii

    Introduction: Michel Gondry as Transcultural Auteur 1
    Marcelline Block and Jennifer Kirby

Part I Dreams, Play, and Whimsy

1 "We Can Change the Whole Narrative": Crafting Play and Nostalgia in Michel Gondry's *The Science of Sleep* and *Mood Indigo* 17
   Danica van de Velde
2 In Dreams and in Love There are No Impossibilities: Michel Gondry's Cinema and the Aesthetics of the Oneiric 33
   Bruno Surace
3 I Am Collecting Beautiful Objects: Michel Gondry's Taxidermy of Emotions 49
   Jenny Pyke
4 The Cost of Whimsy in *Mood Indigo* and *The Grand Budapest Hotel* 66
   Mica Hilson

Part II French Cinema and Identity

5 *L'Amour fou* Revisited: The Surrealist Poetics of Michel Gondry 89
   Sian Mitchell
6 On the Road to Adulthood: *Microbe & Gasoline* and the French Road Movie 102
   Marcelline Block and Jennifer Kirby

Part III Narrative and *Eternal Sunshine of the Spotless Mind*

7 Rethinking Romantic Comedy through the Art Film: Michel Gondry's *Eternal Sunshine of the Spotless Mind* 117
Raffaele Ariano

8 Apocalypse Ever After: Lifted Veils and Transcendent Time in *Eternal Sunshine of the Spotless Mind* 132
Sheheryar B. Sheikh

Part IV Gondry in/on America

9 The Reel and Surreal of Race in America: Michel Gondry and the African–American Identity Crisis of Dave Chappelle 153
Monique Taylor

10 Memory *à la* Americana: From *Eternal Sunshine of the Spotless Mind* to *Be Kind Rewind* 167
Yu-Yun Hsieh

11 Playing with Superheroes: Genre, Aesthetics, and Deconstruction in *The Green Hornet* 184
Jennifer Kirby

Part V Multi-Media: Music Video and Television

12 "It Would Not Be Just Visual, It Could Have Words and a Story": Performance and Narrative in the Music Video Oeuvre of Michel Gondry 197
Daniel Klug

13 Death and Pickles: Thinking through Gondry's Neighborhood 213
Lisa DeTora

Index 221

Figures

1.1	Chloé's organs depicted as made of wool and thread in *Mood Indigo*	20
1.2	Stéphane uses cellophane and cotton wool to construct a scene in *The Science of Sleep*	24
2.1	Stéphane cooks a dream in *The Science of Sleep*	42
4.1	Manic whimsy as Chick and Alise race to the altar in *Mood Indigo*	75
4.2	Zero and Agatha, Wes Anderson's picturesque lower-class workers in *The Grand Budapest Hotel*	79
10.1	Joel and Clementine watch stars on the frozen surface of the Charles River in *Eternal Sunshine of the Spotless Mind*	174
10.2	Miss Falewicz encourages Mr. Fletcher to create his memories of Fats Waller in Passaic, New Jersey, in *Be Kind Rewind*	181

Notes on Contributors

Raffaele Ariano is research fellow at Vita-Salute San Raffaele University in Milan, where he obtained his Ph.D. and teaches Contemporary philosophy. He is a graduate of the University of Oxford. He has published a book on Michel Foucault and one on Lionel Trilling. His research interests are continental and post-analytic philosophy (Heidegger, Wittgenstein, Foucault, Rorty, Cavell); film-philosophy; philosophy of literature.

Marcelline Block is a graduate of Harvard and Princeton universities. Her publications include *Le Grain de la voix dans le monde anglophone et francophone* (2019); *An Anthology of French Singers from A to Z: Singin' in French* (2018); the first English translation of *Propaganda Documentaries in France, 1940–1944* by Jean-Pierre Bertin-Maghit (2016); *French Cinema and the Great War: Remembrance and Representation* (2016); *French Cinema in Close-up: La vie d'un acteur pour moi* (2015; named a Best Reference Book of 2015 by *Library Journal*); *Fan Phenomena: Marilyn Monroe* (2014); *Filmer Marseille* (2013); *World Film Locations: Marseilles* (2013); *World Film Locations: Paris* (2011; translated into Korean, 2014), and *Situating the Feminist Gaze and Spectatorship in Postwar Cinema* (2009). Her writing appears in *Afterall*, *Art Decades*, *Big Picture Magazine*, *Cahiers Tristan Corbière*, *Cineaste*, *The Guardian*, *Harvard French Review*, *Hook Literary Magazine*, *Periodical*, *Soledad*, *Vingtième siècle: revue d'histoire*, *Wages of Film*, and *Women in French Studies*, and is translated into Chinese, French, German, Italian, Korean, and Russian.

Lisa DeTora is Associate Professor of Writing Studies and Rhetoric at Hofstra University, where she is Director of STEM Writing. Her publications include *Heroes of Film, Comics and American Culture* (2009), *Regulatory Writing: An Overview* (2017), and *Bodies in Transition in the Health Humanities:*

Representations of Corporeality (2019), which presents essays on bodies, materiality, and embodiment from Montaigne to the present. She is co-editing a volume of essays presented at the Graphic Narrative Research Group of the International Comparative Literature Association. Recent and forthcoming publications discuss regulatory documentation in forming public opinion, US Right to Try legislation, quantum physics as a model for reading graphic narratives, and biomedical authorship ethics.

Mica Hilson is Assistant Professor of English and Communications at the American University of Armenia. His research on modern and contemporary literature, film, television, and critical theory has appeared in a variety of scholarly journals, including *Pacific Coast Philology*, *The Comparatist*, *Doris Lessing Studies*, and *The Harold Pinter Review*, as well as numerous essay collections, ranging from *Security and Hospitality in Literature and Culture* to *The Ethics and Rhetoric of Invasion Ecology*.

Yu-Yun Hsieh is an award-winning writer from Taiwan. She holds a Ph.D. in Comparative Literature from the Graduate Center, CUNY, where she completed her dissertation on adaptation and transculturation. She currently teaches at Cooper Union, Baruch College and Hunter College. Her work has appeared in *The Times Literary Supplement*, *The New York Times Book Review*, *World Literature Today*, and *Fa Film Appreciation Journal*. Her Chinese translation of Thomas Pynchon's *The Crying of Lot 49* was published in 2014. She was a fiction fellow of the Writers' Institute at the CUNY Graduate Center.

Jennifer Kirby received her Ph.D. in Media, Film and Television from the University of Auckland in 2018. She is currently a Senior Tutor in Media Studies at Massey University. Her research interests lie primarily in contemporary film and television, with a focus on the representation and organization of virtual and augmented spaces on screen, genre studies, and gender. Her work has been published in journals such as *Literature/Film Quarterly* and *Senses of Cinema*.

Daniel Klug is a Systems Scientist at the Institute for Software Research at Carnegie Mellon University. His main areas of research are Open Source communities, Societal Computing and Computer-based analysis of audio-visual media artifacts. From 2012 to 2018, he was an Assistant Researcher at the Seminar for Media Studies at the University of Basel, where he researched and published on reality TV, music videos, popular culture, and educational tools for analyzing audio-visual media artifacts. Homepage: http://daniel.klug.am.

Sian Mitchell is a Lecturer in Screen and Design at Deakin University, Melbourne, and Festival Director of the Melbourne Women in Film Festival. Her work has appeared in *Historic Environment*, *Peephole Journal*, *The London Film* *and Media Reader*, the National Film and Sound Archive (Canberra), and AFI Research Collection.

Jenny Pyke's research is concerned with artistic representations of feeling, particularly texts that present feeling and sympathy as overwhelming and ineffable. Her work includes articles about Charles Dickens's relationship to taxidermy; contemporary art and roadkill taxidermy; and cartography and map metaphors in modern Scottish novels. She has also written about Victorian crime and television adaptation for the *Journal of Victorian Culture Online*. Her current book project focuses on women in twentieth- and twenty-first-century rock music who are called "muses" but who are all creators and collaborators themselves. She is an associate teaching professor at Wake Forest University.

Sheheryar B. Sheikh is a Ph.D. candidate (ABD) in English at the University of Saskatchewan, where he is a Lecturer and TSDF Fellow researching apocalypse theory, post-9/11 American novels, and the marginalization of Muslims in USA. Sheheryar received his MFA from the University of Notre Dame, where he won Professor Steve Tomasula's La Vie de Bohème Award for Literary Excellence and a Nicholas Sparks Scholarship. His debut novel, *The Still Point of the Turning World* (2017), was nominated for the all-Pakistan Getz Pharma Prize, while his second novel, *Call Me Al: The Hero's Ha-Ha Journey* (2019), was a finalist for the same prize.

Bruno Surace received a Ph.D. in Semiotics and Media from the University of Turin. He is an Adjunct Professor in Semiotics, Cinema, and Audiovisual Communication and a research fellow in Psychology. His book *Il destino impresso: Per una teoria della destinalità nel cinema* was published in 2019. He edited *I discorsi della fine: Catastrofi, disastri, apocalissi* (2018) with Vincenzo Idone Cassone and Mattia Thibault, and is editing a book about the Japanese imaginary in Western society with Frank Jacob. In 2017 he was a Visiting Scholar at University College Cork, Ireland, in the Department of Film and Screen Media.

Monique Taylor, author of *Harlem Between Heaven and Hell* (2002) and other publications on gentrification, racial identities, and history in Harlem, also writes about food, film, and popular culture. She holds a Ph.D. and M.A. in Sociology from Harvard University and is a recipient of a Graves Award for Excellence in Teaching from the American Council of Learned Societies. She currently serves as Campus Dean and Executive Director at the Abu Dhabi campus of the New York Institute of Technology.

Danica van de Velde is a researcher at the University of Western Australia, where she completed her doctoral thesis on the cinema of Wong Kar-wai. Her work has recently been published in *ReFocus: The Films of Susanne Bier* (2018) and a special issue of *Frontiers of Literary Studies in China* (2017), focusing on women, writing, and visuality in contemporary China. She was the recipient of the *Senses of Cinema*—Monash Essay Prize in 2019 for her essay on the cinematic self-adaptations of Marguerite Duras.

Acknowledgments

We wish to most gratefully acknowledge the wonderful colleagues, scholars, and associates, including our families and friends, who have made the publication of this anthology possible. Our deepest gratitude goes to Robert Singer, Gary D. Rhodes, and Stefanie Van de Peer, series editors of *ReFocus: The International Director*, for their invaluable and insightful advice, guidance, leadership, and mentorship. Without their unwavering support at every step of the publication process, this collection would not have come to fruition. We extend all our thanks to the authors who contributed to this volume, whose dedication to the oeuvre of Michel Gondry and hard work on their chapters are most inspiring, and with whom we greatly enjoyed working. We are truly grateful to the contributors for sharing their impressive knowledge and insight about Michel Gondry in their texts published herewith. Our thanks go to Jo Penning for creating the index for the book. Research expenses associated with this volume were generously supported by a Professional Development Grant from the Modern Language Association which was awarded to Marcelline Block. We extend our sincere appreciation and profound gratefulness to the MLA for this grant. Marcelline wishes to dedicate this book to her mother, Jenny. We are most thankful to everyone at Edinburgh University Press, in particular Gillian Leslie and Richard Strachan, for their enduring devotion to seeing this book published.

Marcelline Block and Jennifer Kirby

INTRODUCTION

Michel Gondry as Transcultural Auteur

Marcelline Block and Jennifer Kirby

The oeuvre of French auteur Michel Gondry is both immensely varied, spanning multiple media and national contexts, and almost immediately recognizable due to "the variety of techniques through which Gondry repeatedly upsets comfortable philosophical assumptions by utilizing highly creative manipulations of the images that appear within a movie frame."[1] Born in Versailles in 1963, Gondry first rose to prominence as a director of consistently innovative music videos and advertisements, before directing his first feature film, *Human Nature*, in 2001. Gondry is the director of eight feature films, three documentaries, numerous short form works and eight episodes of the first two seasons of the Showtime television series *Kidding* (2018–), for which he is also an executive producer. His works frequently combine materials and media in unusual or unpredictable ways, including blending analogue and digital technologies, and emphasize collisions between different mental states as well as aesthetic innovation. For example, Gondry's 2002 music video for The White Stripes' "Fell in Love with a Girl" uses figures that appear to be made out of Legos, but which are in fact animated. Gondry has worked in his native French language, producing critically lauded films such as *The Science of Sleep* (*La Science des rêves*, 2006), *Mood Indigo* (*L'Écume des jours*, 2013) and *Microbe & Gasoline* (*Microbe et Gasoil*, 2015), alongside successful English language films, such as the mind-bending drama of memory removal and recovery *Eternal Sunshine of the Spotless Mind* (2004). For *Eternal Sunshine*, Gondry won the Academy Award for Best Original Screenplay for the screenplay which he co-wrote with Charlie Kaufman (b. 1958). According to Derek Hill, "*Eternal Sunshine of the Spotless Mind* could well be the epitome of the American New Wave" as it is "a complex yet commercial film that demands a commitment from the audience but also wants to satisfy, spark an emotional response, and entertain without pandering."[2] Indeed, in Christopher Grau's estimation:

> Arguably one of the best films of the past decade, *Eternal Sunshine* combines the highly original visual creativity of director Michel Gondry and the sharp intelligence of screenwriter Charlie Kaufman, both united and inspired by a simple but compelling idea about memory erasure first put forward by Gondry's friend, the French conceptual artist Pierre Bismuth. Utilizing Bismuth's conceit, the film manages to tread familiar territory in a novel way: the classic trope of a couple "divorcing" only to eventually, after some adventure, come together again is given a new twist thanks to a peculiar and powerful memory-removal technology.[3]

Gondry's works also vary greatly in scale, budget, and length, ranging from high-concept features to short films such as the surreal "Interior Design" in the omnibus movie *Tokyo!* (2008) to the personal project *The Thorn in the Heart* (*L'Épine dans le coeur*, 2009), a documentary focusing on his schoolteacher aunt Suzette. Another such personal project is Gondry's foray into animation with *Is the Man Who is Tall Happy?: An Animated Conversation with Noam Chomsky* (2013), an animated documentary of Gondry's discussions with Chomsky (b. 1928), a renowned American scholar of philosophy and linguistics as well as a major public intellectual, theorist, political activist, and Professor Emeritus at the Massachusetts Institute of Technology (MIT).

Despite their differences, these two films by Gondry focus upon the contributions of extraordinarily creative individuals. Similarly, Gondry's forays into American cinema include both the big-budget superhero film *The Green Hornet* (2011), in which an oafish immature playboy fashions himself as the titular masked vigilante, and *The We and the I* (2012), which takes place during a bus journey and stars a group of non-actors playing teenagers from a public school, based closely on their own lives and experiences. In both cases, however, Gondry confounds expectations. In *The Green Hornet*, he extensively uses analogue effects to create the impression of a child playing at being a superhero rather than relying solely upon sophisticated computer-generated imagery, reminding us that Gondry "has an uncanny ability to capture many of his most dazzling images via low-tech methods."[4] Writing in 2008, before the release of *The Green Hornet*, Hill observed that:

> Gondry so far has managed to keep his abundant visual ideas ramshackle and hence low budget, much of the time relying on in-camera solutions instead of CGI and other post-production techniques that would ultimately tarnish the funky low-tech. This mix of lo-fi applications with high-tech concepts, something that he routinely applied for his music

video work and advertisements, has helped give his films a look and feel unlike anyone else's.[5]

In *The We and the I*, Gondry adopts elements of social realism, such as the use of non-professionals and overlapping dialogue, but punctuates this film with stories told by the young people, accompanied by sequences resembling mobile phone footage, which often combine flashbacks with fantasies, rumors, and misunderstandings of events. This works to withhold information from and/or mislead the audience and highlights the students' public performances of themselves.

Even Gondry's non-fiction works incorporate unusual aesthetics that manage to convey the essence of their subjects impressionistically without adopting a typical documentary tone. For example, in the above-mentioned documentary *Is the Man Who is Tall Happy?: An Animated Conversation with Noam Chomsky*, Gondry's filmed interviews with Chomsky—named "the world's top public intellectual"[6]—are illustrated through hand-drawn animations made by Gondry that serve to explain the abstract or philosophical concepts covered in their conversations. Gondry's earlier concert film/documentary *Dave Chappelle's Block Party* (2005), plays with time and perspective to map the production and construction both of the personas of the performers featured and of the community spaces in which the film is set.

The overall argument of this collection is that Gondry is emblematic of transnational auteur filmmaking—with French funding involved even in some of his English-language and arguably most accessible work, such as his 2008 nostalgic comedy *Be Kind Rewind*—crossing aesthetic and cultural borders between national film industries as well as between art and popular cinema and between media. This collection avoids the kind of auteur criticism that Galt and Schoonover suggest "either personalizes style and mode of production out of all locational context or reifies style in terms of national cultural specificity."[7] Instead, we acknowledge that Gondry's work exemplifies the way "cinema's transnational flows might intersect with trajectories of film form."[8] The essays in this volume therefore identify connections and continuities between Gondry's films, such as the themes of fantasy, memory, and love. Yet they also place Gondry's oeuvre in dialogue with both French and American cinematic traditions and socio-cultural contexts, analyzing the insights that his often surrealist approach brings to topics such as history, race, and popular culture in his English-language films. Furthermore, they analyze his films through the framework of the genres in which Gondry has worked, including documentary, romantic comedy, the superhero film, and the road movie. This approach does not disavow Gondry's status as an auteur, but rather examines how his stylistic and thematic interests intersect with the various contexts in which he makes films.

Gondry's body of work defies classification according to traditional conceptions of European art cinema. Mark Betz explains that the European art film, especially since the modernist cinema of the late 1950s and 1960s, has traditionally been defined by four paradigms: "the variable spatial and temporal organizations of its design (form), the aesthetic heritage that serves as its animus and to which it frequently refers (cinema), the space and experience of viewing (spectatorship)," and, most importantly, "the signature of its director/creator (authorship)," which gives cohesion and meaning to the other elements.[9] These "formal-aesthetic" definitions of art cinema are often linked to a more "national-institutional" categorization, which views art cinema as fundamentally opposed to Hollywood filmmaking.[10] While Gondry displays many of these marks of European art filmmaking, such as the self-referential relationship to cinema and the creative approach to temporal and spatial organization, these marks unite both his French- and his English-language films. For example, *Microbe & Gasoline* heavily references the American road movie while *Be Kind Rewind* features amateur recreations of iconic American films in a love letter to cinema blended with the broad stylings of American comedian Jack Black. Similarly, both *The Science of Sleep* and *Eternal Sunshine of the Spotless Mind* explore complexly layered dream spaces. Thus, this collection echoes Harrod, Liz, and Timoshkina's assertion that increasing transnational production and globalization is challenging the traditional concept of European cinema as Hollywood's binary opposite, characterized by art filmmaking rather than entertainment, and complicating the identity of European cinema."[11] Gondry represents a contemporary globalized auteur whose films and other works display both numerous continuities and an eclecticism worth exploring further. This volume is organized into five sections that contextualize Gondry in relation to formal, thematic and narrative elements, aspects of transnational identity and multi-media experimentation.

DREAMS, PLAY, AND WHIMSY

Gondry has been lauded as a visual innovator due to his creative *mise-en-scène*, which often features analogue objects, outlandish inventions, and stop-motion, visually sumptuous invocations of dreams and fantasy, as well as a post-modern pop cultural sensibility. The first section of this collection, entitled "Dreams, Play, and Whimsy," offers several chapters that frame Gondry-as-director in terms of an overall surrealist tendency in his work, while also featuring articles about more specific elements of his visual aesthetic, such as the focus on handmade objects and collecting or oneiric aesthetics. Michael Richardson notes that while surrealism is often popularly applied to films that produce fantastical worlds, this application obscures the more precise concern of surrealism with "exploring the conjunctions, the points of contact, between different realms of existence."[12] This section of the volume features chapters that address the visual and narrative representation(s) of this collision between different realms in Gondry's films, particularly those of reality and fantasy as well as dreams and waking.

Danica van de Velde and Bruno Surace both directly address the creation of dream worlds or worlds inspired by dreams in Gondry's cinema. In this volume's first chapter, "'We Can Change the Whole Narrative': Crafting Play and Nostalgia in Michel Gondry's *The Science of Sleep* and *Mood Indigo*," van de Velde focuses on a specific element of Gondry's surrealist visual aesthetic: namely, the use of a "craft aesthetic" that often features handmade objects as a tool to construct a space of magical realism that complicates boundaries between dreams, nostalgia, fantasy, and real life in *The Science of Sleep* and *Mood Indigo*. *Science* is about the romance between dreamer Stéphane (Gael García Bernal) and his neighbor Stéphanie (Charlotte Gainsbourg), while *Mood Indigo*, a surreal romantic tragedy in which a man tries to save his beloved from dying of a flower growing in her lung, is Gondry's cinematic adaptation of French author Boris Vian's novel *L'Écume des jours* (1947). Van de Velde argues that although craft is often considered lowly within fine arts frameworks, in these two films, craft and handmade objects take on new value as vehicles of nostalgia and romance.

Next, Surace's chapter, "In Dreams and in Love There are No Impossibilities: Michel Gondry's Cinema and the Aesthetics of the Oneiric," offers an overarching framework for mapping an oneiric aesthetic across Gondry's films, beginning with his first feature, *Human Nature*. Surace argues that in all of Gondry's films, dreams embody three distinct but interrelated dimensions: part of the film's diegesis, part of a broader symbolic or political system which is not purely narrative, or as a frame for innovative modules of formal film construction, connecting content to a precise aesthetics of the oneiric.

Continuing both the examination of the materiality of objects and the employment of frameworks from contemporary art, Jenny Pyke's chapter, "I Am Collecting Beautiful Objects: Michel Gondry's Taxidermy of Emotions," uses a comparison with taxidermy as an art form to explore the way that Gondry creates objects infused with affect, not because of what they represent but because of how they are constructed. Like examples of taxidermy, these objects both contain a material history and generate sensation through their feeling of hapticity. Pyke explains how objects in *The Science of Sleep* function not only as containers of emotion but also as points of connection between the lovers Stéphane and Stéphanie, who communicate and share their way of seeing and imagining the world through objects and build relationships in tandem with their construction.

In the fourth and final chapter in this section of this volume, "The Cost of Whimsy in *Mood Indigo* and *The Grand Budapest Hotel*," Mica Hilson employs a new formalist framework to compare the elements of "twee" and "whimsy" in Gondry's *Mood Indigo* and contemporary auteur Wes Anderson's *The Grand Budapest Hotel* (2014). Hilson argues that Gondry's use of whimsical excess to self-reflexively address themes of over-consumption stands in opposition to Anderson's *The Grand Budapest Hotel*. Hilson furthermore notes that the fetishization of luxury items in Anderson's film contrasts with the do-it-yourself, craft aesthetic of Gondry's work. Hilson's comparative chapter illuminates both the aesthetic tendencies that Gondry shares with some of his more eccentric contemporaries and the qualities that set Gondry's work apart. Hilson's analysis asks the reader to consider whimsical aesthetics in their socio-economic context, rather than assuming that style negates substance.

FRENCH CINEMA AND IDENTITY

Despite the widespread acclaim and recognition that Gondry has received internationally, it is nevertheless valuable to contextualize his work within the history and traditions of French film. Michael Gott and Thibaut Schilt suggest that in today's global filmmaking environment, in which international co-productions dominate, the notion of "French-language" film is too restrictive, and instead advocate for the use of "*cinéma-monde*." "*Cinéma-monde*" is a term that describes how films engage with the francophone world through "some combination of linguistic or cultural affinities, geographic contacts, production connections or reception frameworks."[13] The two chapters in this volume's section on "French Cinema and Identity" address Gondry's interactions with France and its cinema not only through the production of French-language films, but also through an awareness of both the artistic legacy and contemporary climate of France.

Complementing Hilson's work comparing Gondry to Anderson, Sian Mitchell's chapter, "*L'Amour fou* Revisited: The Surrealist Poetics of Michel Gondry," traces the legacy of poetic realist director Jean Vigo (1905–34) in Gondry's work. Drawing on the theories of André Breton, Mitchell argues that early surrealism has influenced not only Gondry's visual style, but also his thematic interests. Mitchell notes how Gondry aesthetically explores the surrealist concept of *l'amour fou* (mad love), which appears in the way he depicts the intimate relationships of his protagonists as transforming the ontological and temporal qualities of their environments. Mitchell's chapter examines Gondry's films *Eternal Sunshine of the Spotless Mind* and *Mood Indigo* for traces of this influence and draws connections to Vigo's iconic *L'Atalante* (1934), positioning these works in the lineage of cinematic depictions of mad love. Mitchell argues that in both Gondry's and Vigo's films, *l'amour fou* is embodied through a love that also challenges normative conceptions of space and time.

Marcelline Block and Jennifer Kirby also consider the aspect of cinematic lineage and influence. In their chapter in this volume entitled "On the Road to Adulthood: *Microbe & Gasoline* and the French Road Movie," Block and Kirby argue that Gondry's most recent feature film, a picaresque narrative, draws from the conventions of the road movie through its focus on social outsiders, light-hearted depiction of run-ins with the police, and emphasis on male bonding. The film also provides a commentary on the notion and definition of "home" in France. *Microbe & Gasoline*, which follows two teenage boys taking a 250-mile-long journey through France in a makeshift house on wheels, links a coming-of-age narrative to a growing awareness of the complexities and divisions within France. In this film, Gondry depicts his trademark childhood play and whimsy alongside a sobering adult realization of the injustices that exist in the world. Representing yet another form of border-crossing, the film blends conventions from the American road movie with the French road movie's potential for "elaborating flexible, transnational and multicultural alternatives to a monolithic version of France."[14] It thus serves to reinforce Gondry's status as an auteur whose work is frequently transnational in character, recalling Hill's claim that Gondry is the spiritual heir not only to Jean Cocteau and Georges Méliès, but also to Walt Disney and Steven Spielberg.[15]

NARRATIVE AND *ETERNAL SUNSHINE OF THE SPOTLESS MIND*

Eternal Sunshine of the Spotless Mind is undoubtedly Gondry's best-known film. Writing in 2008, Hill stated that, through "displaying both Gondry's technical wizardry and his ability to keep the performances or emotional weight of the film from being bullied into subservience," *Eternal Sunshine* is considered "a real masterpiece" of the American New Wave.[16] *Eternal Sunshine* follows Joel, played by Jim Carrey, who has employed Lacuna Inc. to remove his memories of his ex-lover, Clementine (Kate Winslet). During the procedure, Joel realizes that he does not want to lose his memories and begins to try to hide Clementine within memories where she did not originally feature. Although essentially a love story, *Eternal Sunshine of the Spotless Mind* narrates its romance in reverse order, while also oscillating between a narrative in the present involving the technicians of Lacuna and a depiction of Joel's attempts to hide Clementine in the memory realm. *Eternal Sunshine* thus "offers an invitation to consider the multiple ways in which 'the past is given to us in its traces in the present.'"[17] The film's complex chronology and ontology has generated a body of scholarship on its ethical dilemmas, visual techniques, and cinematic approximation of memory. In the volume of essays devoted to the philosophical aspects of *Eternal Sunshine of the Spotless Mind*, editor Christopher Grau states that "*Eternal Sunshine* is a film that is not just worth seeing but worth dwelling on, puzzling over, and living with through repeated examination" due to its "complexity, nuance, and depth" and "richness, both philosophic and aesthetic."[18] In this volume, Raffaele Ariano and Sheheryar B. Sheikh offer new perspectives on the film's narrative invention.

In Chapter 7 of this volume, entitled "Rethinking Romantic Comedy through the Art Film: Michel Gondry's *Eternal Sunshine of the Spotless Mind*," Ariano examines *Eternal Sunshine of the Spotless Mind* as a hybrid of the art film and the romantic comedy. In this chapter, Ariano conceptualizes the "art romantic comedy" as a sub-genre that targets audiences that would typically reject the romantic comedy based upon conventions of taste and cultural hierarchy. Ariano places Gondry in a class of contemporary auteurs, including Paul Thomas Anderson, Noah Baumbach, Sofia Coppola, Greta Gerwig, and Alexander Payne, whose romantic comedies are characterized by qualities drawn from art and indie cinema. These characteristics include the expressive use of film style and implementation of metafictional devices, complex "sensitive" protagonists, and endings that are ambiguous and thus only partially "happy." Ariano applies this genre framework to an analysis of *Eternal Sunshine of the Spotless Mind*, but also places the film within wider trends in the genre of romantic comedy. Indeed, Grau states that "surely part of the appeal of *Eternal Sunshine* for many viewers is that it provides its own spin on the traditional Hollywood tactic of playing on the deep-seated wish lovers often have for second chances."[19]

Also concerned with the happy/unhappy ending, in "Apocalypse Ever After: Lifted Veils and Transcendent Time in *Eternal Sunshine of the Spotless Mind*," the eighth chapter, Sheikh interprets the narrative organization of *Eternal Sunshine*'s love story through the lens of apocalyptic literary theory. Drawing from the writing of Frank Kermode, Sheikh argues that the film's primary narrative problem, the disappearance of Clementine from Joel's memories, constitutes an eschatological occurrence on a personal scale. However, the film is "apocalyptic" in another sense: while Joel is trying to prevent this cataclysmic event, he revisits his memories and uncovers greater meaning in them, simultaneously revealing these details to the audience, and thus the film "lifts veils from" Joel's memories, which is the etymological meaning of the apocalypse. Sheikh argues that Gondry advocates strongly for the need to revisit and re-assess memory, rather than rejecting memories, even if they are painful. In Gondry's own words, "so far, technology has only succeeded in making us forget everything . . . except the things we don't want to remember."[20] This concern with both preserving—and, paradoxically, re-inventing—memory similarly features strongly in Gondry's other English-language films, as explored in the next section of this volume.

GONDRY IN/ON AMERICA

It is a well-known cliché that an outsider is often better positioned to draw insightful observations about a place than those who inhabit that place and thus do not necessarily notice its features and structural organization, which they regard as natural and not noteworthy. Gondry's films about and/or set in the United States use similar techniques and explore a number of common themes (memory, love, identity) that overlap with those set in France, but additionally provide a layer of commentary on American society and popular culture. In a trio of films set in America—*Dave Chappelle's Block Party*, *Be Kind Rewind*, and *The We and the I*—Gondry significantly explores the intersections between popular culture, community, and memory. In Chapter 9 of this volume, entitled "The Reel and Surreal of Race in America: Michel Gondry and the African–American Identity Crisis of Dave Chappelle," Monique Taylor addresses *Dave Chappelle's Block Party*. Taylor writes that

> in many of Michel Gondry's transnational/transatlantic cinematic collaborations, including with screenwriter Charlie Kaufman, public intellectual and scholar Noam Chomsky, and—most importantly for the purposes of this discussion—actor and comedian Dave Chappelle, Gondry plays the role of outsider-looking-in as both a participant in as well as an observer of aspects of American cultural conversations on memory, identity and language.

Ostensibly, *Dave Chappelle's Block Party* is a concert documentary which depicts the organization and performances of a "block party" hosted by African–American comedian Dave Chappelle in Brooklyn, New York. Chappelle's Brooklyn Block Party concert, the subject of Gondry's *Dave Chappelle's Block Party*, was a concert that featured performances by some of the biggest names in hip hop, rap, and R & B music, including ?uestlove, Erykah Badu, Mos Def, the Fugees reunited with Lauryn Hill, and Kanye West. Drawing upon Mark Anthony Neal's concept of the "post-soul aesthetic," which is a "meditation on contemporary issues such as deindustrialization, desegregation, the corporate annexation of black popular expression ... and the general commodification of black life and black culture,"[21] Taylor's chapter reads the documentary as a "post-soul" construction, bringing together Chappelle's post-soul sensibility and Gondry's surreal aesthetic in order to channel Chappelle's highly public personal and professional quest to "keep it real." Taylor finds that, as a film, Gondry's *Block Party*, rather than simply filming the concert, bridges the gap between the real and the surreal via a singular visual style and vocabulary. Taylor's chapter thus draws attention to *Block Party*'s construction of a hybrid and hyper-real community through the use of strategies such as movements back and forth in time between the entertainers' performances and the preparations leading up to the concert which highlight the production of the event, surreal visual embellishments, and prominent allusion to symbols of African–American identity. Taylor's discussion of Gondry's *Dave Chappelle's Block Party* is of particular resonance and relevance to our current historical moment in light of Chappelle's recent Block Party in Dayton, Ohio, on August 25, 2019, a benefit concert that Chappelle organized in the wake of the mass shooting that occurred in Dayton on August 4, 2019 and which claimed the lives of nine people, as well as Chappelle's return to stand-up comedy with his controversial new Netflix special, entitled *Dave Chappelle: Sticks and Stones,* which was released on August 26, 2019. Furthermore, on October 27, 2019, Chappelle was the recipient of the prestigious annual Mark Twain Prize for American Humor. This award is "considered the highest accolade in comedy and recognizes individuals who have had an impact on American society in the vein of 19th-century novelist and essayist Samuel Clemens, better known by his pseudonym, Mark Twain."[22] Chappelle had previously won an Emmy in 2017 for Best Guest Actor in a Comedy Series, honoring his monologue on comedy sketch show *SNL*, in which he controversially criticized the newly elected President of the United States, Donald J. Trump.

The notion of constructing community through visual images and performance is also central to Yu-Yun Hsieh's chapter, "Memory à la Americana: From *Eternal Sunshine of the Spotless Mind* to *Be Kind Rewind*," which presents a reading of both of these films. In the latter, two bumbling video-store clerks in the real-life setting of the town of Passaic, New Jersey, produce homemade versions of popular films after the VHS tapes of these films are accidentally erased through the process of demagnetization. When the clerks are forced to stop their cinematic productions due to copyright infringement, they decide instead to enlist the whole town in the making of a film about the legendary jazz musician Fats Waller (1904–43), who in the film is erroneously believed to have been from Passaic, when in reality Waller was born in New York City. Hsieh compares the exploration of personal memory in *Eternal Sunshine* with the production of collective memory in *Be Kind*, noting that in both cases "fictional" or "inauthentic" memories are created in order to preserve a relationship, whether between Joel and Clementine in the former or between the inhabitants of Passaic in the latter. Both films, Hseih explains, are about memories that are open to revision but preserve a kind of essence of truth.

Although less well known than *Eternal Sunshine* and *Be Kind*, Gondry's *The We and the I* shares many key ideas with his other films shot in the United States. *The We and the I* follows a group of mainly African–American or Latino inner-city students riding the bus home on the last day of school. In the film, the students are continually gossiping about one another and telling stories, which Gondry often presents as videos, such as those found on social media, or as messages spreading via text around the bus. The power relationships in the community of the schoolkids are sustained by these stories, along with often unreliable or second-hand memories. However, the film suggests that real connections are built only in the one-on-one exchanges in which the teenagers reveal their feelings and true experiences. The film emphasizes the construction of the narratives that determine how the youth within this community see one another and themselves.

Gondry's most recent English-language film, the superhero movie *The Green Hornet*, is also his least well-received. The film generally provoked a negative critical response due to its seemingly insignificant subject matter. However, in this volume, Jennifer Kirby's chapter, "Playing with Superheroes: Genre, Aesthetics, and Deconstruction in *The Green Hornet*," argues that the vitriolic criticism fails to acknowledge the extent to which this film can be read as a deconstruction of the generic codes and aesthetics of the predominantly American superhero genre from an outsider's perspective. Kirby demonstrates how, just as *The Green Hornet*'s incompetent playboy, Britt Reid (Seth Rogen), plays at his childhood ambition of being a superhero in the film, Gondry plays with the conventions of the superhero movie through both humorous revisionism and, more successfully, the use of analogue effects. In this respect, Gondry's trademark personal style blends with a broader emphasis in the contemporary superhero genre "on mutable modes of perception," but explores this enhanced perception through analogue rather than exclusively digital effects.[23] In this film, Gondry self-reflexively highlights the construction of American popular culture and mythology just as he explores the construction of myths that sustain communities in his earlier American films.

MULTI-MEDIA: MUSIC VIDEO AND TELEVISION

Gondry's body of work is characterized by a multi-media sensibility in two ways: individual works often combine multiple types of audio-visual material, such as analogue objects and digital effects in *The Green Hornet* or animation and recorded interview in *Is the Man Who is Tall Happy?*, while his oeuvre as a whole spans different genres including narrative film, documentary, music video, commercials, and the Showtime television series *Kidding*.

The final section of this collection acknowledges and explores this multimedia sensibility in Gondry's work in music videos and television. Indeed, "Gondry's innovative [music] videos have used groundbreaking techniques that have become pervasive in the film industry, such as the morphing of images, and the bullet time effect later made famous by *The Matrix*."[24]

In Hill's estimation:

Like the best music video directors, including Spike Jonze, Gondry does not merely shill product or offer up slapdash visuals to lull the viewer into a lotus sleep of pleasing though vapid entertainment. Delicious eye candy it may be, but many of Gondry's best videos—for acts the White Stripes, Björk, Cibo Mato (the video for 'Sugar Water' contains some of the finest use of split-screen cinematography ever), the Chemical Brothers, the Foo Fighters, Beck, his own early pop group Oui Oui (he played drums), and others—display the same sense of melancholy and hyper-realist fantasy that would later be visually explicated in the feature films.[25]

In Chapter 12, "'It Would Not Be Just Visual, It Could Have Words and a Story': Performance and Narrative in the Music Video Oeuvre of Michel Gondry," Daniel Klug emphasizes how Gondry crosses boundaries even within the sub-forms of the music video. Klug examines how Gondry's performance-based videos incorporate heterogeneous narrative elements and examples of audio-visual surplus, such as morphing and multiplication. As Grau observes:

> In his music videos, Gondry forces viewers to become aware of their implicit assumptions about both cinematic and ordinary perception by offering surprising reversals: optical effects manifest literal "traces" in space and time; doublings and repetitions that could be easily accomplished through optical or digital effects are achieved manually; typical patterns of causation are turned around; and spatial norms are persistently violated.[26]

In these respects, Gondry utilizes different types of performance in his music videos. Klug mentions several of Gondry's most well-known videos, including those for Daft Punk's song "All Around the World" as well as for Kylie Minogue and The White Stripes, before offering an extended analysis of Gondry's narrative music video for the Foo Fighters' track "Everlong."

In 2018, Gondry made his first extended foray into the world of television. He serves as executive producer and director of eight episodes of the first two seasons of Dave Holstein's half-hour Showtime comedy series *Kidding*, starring Jim Carrey, who previously appeared in Gondry's film *Eternal Sunshine of the Spotless Mind*. In *Kidding*, Carrey plays Jeff, aka Mr. Pickles, the host of a successful children's puppet television show, which he has developed with his father, who produces the show, and his sister, who designs and makes the puppets. Not only does the show reunite Gondry with his star of *Eternal Sunshine of the Spotless Mind*, but, as Lisa DeTora's chapter, "Death and Pickles: Thinking through Gondry's Neighborhood," explains, it returns Gondry to his perennial themes of the instability of identity and the difficulty of separating real life from imagination. Jeff articulates his thoughts and processes his emotions through the gleefully surreal puppet show and even imagines people in his life as puppets. His world is thrown into disarray when his father threatens to replace him with animation because he is consistently trying to smuggle adult themes into the show, thus causing Jeff to question the relationship between his own identity and that of Mr. Pickles. DeTora analyzes the first season of the show and its exploration of identity crisis, acknowledging its links with Gondry's wider body of work. *Kidding* Season Two premiered on Showtime on February 9, 2020, with two episodes in this second season directed by Gondry.

It is fitting that DeTora's piece is the final contribution to this volume, not only because *Kidding* is Gondry's most recent work, but also because the show is a culmination of so many of Gondry's main preoccupations. These include the way in which the puppets in *Kidding*—handcrafted objects that Jeff uses to process emotions—are not unlike the creations of Stéphane in *The Science of Sleep* and the exploration of recurring themes throughout Gondry's oeuvre, such as the inability/impossibility of distinguishing between reality and fantasy, the terror of being erased or altered, and the co-existence of extreme despair and hope. All of these ideas recur across the Gondrian universe and find expression in the diverse range of works that bear his stamp.

NOTES

1. Christopher Grau, "Introduction," in *Eternal Sunshine of the Spotless Mind (Philosophers on Film)*, ed. Christopher Grau (London and New York: Routledge, 2009), Kindle Edition, 10.
2. Derek Hill, *Charlie Kaufman and Hollywood's Merry Band of Pranksters, Fabulists and Dreamers: An Excursion into the American New Wave* (Harpenden: Kamera, 2008), Kindle Edition, Kindle location 2218 of 2840.
3. Grau, "Introduction," 1–2.
4. Hill, *Charlie Kaufman and Hollywood's Merry Band of Pranksters, Fabulists and Dreamers*, Kindle locations 2105–10 of 2840.
5. Hill, *Charlie Kaufman and Hollywood's Merry Band of Pranksters, Fabulists and Dreamers*, Kindle locations 2115–20 of 2840.
6. Duncan Campbell, "Chomsky Is Voted World's Top Public Intellectual," *The Guardian* (Guardian News and Media, October 18, 2005). Available at <https://www.theguardian.com/world/2005/oct/18/books.highereducation> (last accessed February 26, 2020).
7. Rosalind Galt and Karl Schoonover, "Introduction: The Impurity of Art Cinema," in *Global Art Cinema: New Theories and Histories*, eds Rosalind Galt and Karl Schoonover (Oxford: Oxford University Press, 2010), 9.
8. Galt and Schoonover, "Introduction," 3.
9. Mark Betz, *Beyond the Subtitle: Remapping European Art Cinema* (Minneapolis and London: University of Minnesota Press, 2009), 4.
10. Betz, *Beyond the Subtitle*, 10.
11. Mary Harrod, Mariana Liz, and Alissa Timoshkina, "The Europeanness of European Cinema: An Overview," in *The Europeanness of European Cinema: Identity, Meaning,*

      Globalization, eds Mary Harrod, Mariana Liz, and Alissa Timoshkina (London and New York: I. B. Tauris, 2015), 7.
12. Michael Richardson, *Surrealism and Cinema* (Oxford: Berg, 2006), 2.
13. Michael Gott and Thibaut Schilt, "Introduction: The Kaleidoscope of Cinéma-monde," in *Cinéma-monde: Decentred Perspectives on Global Filmmaking in French,* eds Michael Gott and Thibaut Schilt (Edinburgh: Edinburgh University Press, 2018), 2.
14. Michael Gott, *French-Language Road Cinema: Borders, Diaspora, Migration and 'New Europe'* (Edinburgh: Edinburgh University Press, 2016), 4.
15. Hill, *Charlie Kaufman and Hollywood's Merry Band of Pranksters, Fabulists and Dreamers,* Kindle location 2085 and 2108 of 2840.
16. Hill, *Charlie Kaufman and Hollywood's Merry Band of Pranksters, Fabulists and Dreamers,* Kindle location 2083 of 2840.
17. Grau, "Introduction," 11.
18. Grau, "Introduction," 2–3.
19. Grau, "Introduction," 4.
20. Michel Gondry, "My Memory Hurts," in *Eternal Sunshine of the Spotless Mind (Philosophers on Film),* ed. Christopher Grau (London and New York: Routledge, 2009), Kindle Edition, Kindle location 169 of 3097.
21. Mark Anthony Neal, *Soul Babies: Black Popular Culture and the Post-Soul Aesthetic* (New York: Routledge, 2002), Kindle Edition, 2.
22. Amir Vera, "Dave Chappelle Says Comedy 'Saved My Life' as He Accepts the Mark Twain Prize for American Humor," CNN (Cable News Network, October 28, 2019). Available at <https://www.cnn.com/2019/10/28/entertainment/dave-chappelle-mark-twain-award-humor/index.html> (last accessed February 26, 2020).
23. Lisa Gotto, "Fantastic Views: Superheroes, Visual Perception, and Digital Perspective," in *Superhero Synergies: Comic Book Characters Go Digital,* eds James N. Gilmore and Matthias Stork (Lanham, MD: Rowman & Littlefield, 2014), 47.
24. Grau, *Eternal Sunshine of the Spotless Mind (Philosophers on Film),* Kindle Edition, Kindle location 110 of 3097.
25. Hill, *Charlie Kaufman and Hollywood's Merry Band of Pranksters, Fabulists and Dreamers,* Kindle locations 2104–8 of 2804.
26. Grau, "Introduction," 10.

PART I

Dreams, Play, and Whimsy

CHAPTER 1

"We Can Change the Whole Narrative": Crafting Play and Nostalgia in Michel Gondry's *The Science of Sleep* and *Mood Indigo*

Danica van de Velde

The 2003 release of Palm Pictures' Directors Label DVD *The Work of Director Michel Gondry* introduced viewers not only to the origins of Gondry's distinct aesthetic sensibility through his music videos and short films, but also to an intimate view into his inspirations, obsessions, and approach to collaboration. In particular, the DVD's feature documentary, *I've Been 12 Forever*, unfolds as a sequence of fragments that create links between Gondry's personal history—his family, his failed relationships, and his dreams—and the trajectory of his oeuvre. The hint in the documentary's title of a perpetual state of adolescence is supported by Gondry's inventive approach to his films that continually gestures towards the memories and preoccupations of his youth. In one poignant moment, Gondry shares the journey from his school to his family home in Versailles:

> Somehow this route must be engraved in my brain. I mean physically engraved. Each corner of the street, the tree, root, garden, brick wall must be imprinted in my cells. Maybe if I dissolve my brain in acid we could see the shape of the streets as well as my house map.[1]

The compulsive return to the childhood home and its emotional geography runs throughout the documentary and is reinforced by a remark from Gondry's older brother, François:

> He mixed a lot of his world today with the world of his youth. Half of his videos are dreams that he had, his memories of a precise moment in his childhood [. . .] I think that it's there, in that world, that he's going to spend all his energy.[2]

Gondry's music videos and short features reveal the genesis of the self-referential dreamscape that continues to shape his oeuvre.

Tinged with nostalgia and childlike impulses, the imprint of Gondry's infatuation with the memories and dreams of his past finds unique expression in two of his feature films, *The Science of Sleep* (*La Science des rêves*, 2006) and *Mood Indigo* (*L'Écume des jours*, 2013). Although the origin of the script for each film arose from a different source, both films feature shy, socially awkward male protagonists who possess a spark for invention and are drawn unexpectedly into romantic relationships. *The Science of Sleep* was developed from Gondry's own script and has an obvious personal resonance in its portrayal of the imaginative dreamer, Stéphane (Gael García Bernal), who returns to his childhood home following the death of his father. As he attempts to resettle in France from Mexico and balance the uncreative job at a calendar factory that his mother has secured for him with his vivid dream world, he becomes slowly attracted to his next-door neighbor, Stéphanie (Charlotte Gainsbourg). The similarity of their names is not the only thing they have in common when they realize that they share a common language of make-believe through crafting and inventing objects. However, as Stéphane's feelings grow more intense, his ability to differentiate between reality and dreams proves unreliable and it is unclear whether Stéphanie's reciprocation of his feelings is taking place in his waking or dreaming life.

Mood Indigo, on the other hand, was adapted by Gondry and Luc Bossi from Boris Vian's 1947 novel *L'Écume des jours/Froth on the Daydream*. In both Vian's text and Gondry's film, the bachelor lifestyle of the wealthy central protagonist, Colin (Romain Duris), is transformed when he meets and falls in love with Chloé (Audrey Tautou). However, their whirlwind romance and betrothal are devastatingly interrupted when Chloé's lungs are infected with a fatal water lily. Colin, who was previously able to live comfortably from his inheritance, is soon forced to start working and sell his inventions to pay for bizarre treatments that only hold the mere promise of a cure. As Chloé becomes more ill and Colin falls into despair, their lives and those of the characters surrounding them unravel until Chloé's battle ends. The significance of *The Science of Sleep* and *Mood Indigo* within Gondry's broader cinematic universe converges not only on their parallel narratives of romantic disappointment, but also on the employment of handmade visual details that subvert conventional expectations of film form and the division between fantasy and reality.

The play between the realm of dreams and the everyday in both films invites the viewer into a space of magic realism that is inflected with a distinct craft aesthetic. The theorization of the genre of magic realism as making "visible the magic behind everyday objects" is noteworthy in the context of the literal crafting of the physical environments in Gondry's cinema.[3] In one of the dream sequences in *The Science of Sleep*, for example, Stéphane draws attention to the presence of handmade objects in the film narrative: "I am collecting beautiful objects. A pair of shoes. Some glasses. Telephone. Typewriter. They are made from wood and felt with apparent stitches. Their delicate, unfinished appearance is friendly and they are quiet." Regarded collectively, Gondry's broad oeuvre displays a keen interest in materiality via *mise- en-scène* that possesses a handmade or do-it-yourself (DIY) tactility. Functioning beyond mere decoration or place setting, the quirkily crafted objects play a key role in furthering the films' narratives, character development, and thematic resonance.

In considering the process of filmmaking that takes place within the diegesis of Gondry's *Be Kind Rewind* (2008), Pat Brereton argues that:

> The creativity found in sweding is how they choose to use found objects or cardboard props to simulate special effects instead of duplicating them technologically. Swedes exemplify an extreme do-it-yourself (DIY) form of smart indie filmmaking, embracing innovation through manipulating their inherent constraints.[4]

Although Brereton is speaking directly to the amateur filmmaking in *Be Kind Rewind* and the method of "sweding" developed by the film's characters—which involves remaking popular films on a non-existent budget with available resources—these comments are equally pertinent when looking at the crafted settings in *The Science of Sleep* and *Mood Indigo*. What requires critical attention is the fact that the handmade visuals in both films are not a result of budget constraints, but an aesthetic choice. In considering the fantastical handmade aesthetic of the films and taking the role of craft seriously, I argue that the film imagery is not merely a fun and evocative allegory of childhood naivety and wonder, but bespeaks a highly intellectual and visually complex approach to film production that refigures fantasy within the context of the everyday. In attending to the visual textures and the thematic conceits of the films, I will examine the intersection of cinematic style with the motifs of dreams, play, and memory to delineate Gondry's position as an auteur engaged in a poetics of nostalgic longing.

DELICATE, UNFINISHED, FRIENDLY AND QUIET: REPOSITIONING CRAFT IN THE FILM MEDIUM

The moment that marks the emotional shift in *Mood Indigo* portrays the first night of Colin and Chloé's honeymoon. As they sleep in their hotel room, a water lily floats through the window before being gently inhaled by Chloé. The camera then cuts to the interior of her body where the water lily rests among her internal organs, which are composed of felt, lace, and thread. The handcrafted scene is at once reminiscent of childhood craft projects that attempt to fashion the world from everyday materials. However, the employment of textile organs, as opposed to a realistic simulacrum, also underlines the construction of the fantasy that is highlighted from the beginning of the film, in which the viewer observes the highly referential crafting of the narrative. As the sound of clacking typewriter keys, heard over the opening credits, transitions to a scene of factory workers taking turns to type fragments of the text on rotating typewriters, the typed pages are then collected and threaded together on a sewing machine before revealing the title and author, *L'Écume des jours* and Boris Vian. In this instance, Gondry's turn to craft is not only an auteurist technique that imbues his films with childlike wonder, but also part of a self-reflexive methodology that draws the viewer's attention to the nature of the construction of the film.

While the intersection of craft with fine art, industrial design, and fashion has been the subject of critical attention, the live-action film medium has yet to be examined in an interdisciplinary analysis of craft practices. This is unsurprising, given the ever-improving technical advances in simulating reality on screen via the employment of computer-generated imagery (CGI) and digital effects. In many respects, the "craft" of film no longer resides in the hands of the filmmaker, but in the realm of the computer. In a landscape of pristine, hyper-real cinematic imagery, Gondry's films therefore represent a distinct vision that does not re-create reality, but creates it. The distinction between re-creation and creation cuts through the spirit of invention that permeates both *The Science of Sleep* and *Mood Indigo*, and is emphasized by Gondry's preference for using raw materials to imbue the *mise-en-scène* with a handcrafted sensibility. For example,

Figure 1.1 Chloé's organs depicted as made of wool and thread in *Mood Indigo* (Studio Canal, 2013)

the mouse that lives in Colin and Chloé's apartment in *Mood Indigo* could easily have been fabricated digitally in the likeness of a real mouse. In Gondry's hands, however, actor Sacha Bourdo is dressed in a textile mouse costume evocative of a child's fancy dress clothing. Notably, Gondry has commented on the creative decision to use a handmade aesthetic in *Mood Indigo*:

> There is a poetic effect that cannot be created [. . .] with computer[s], although they can become very handy in [*sic*] some occasion[s]. But I think to make it handcrafted corresponds to the tone of the story; what touched me when I was an adolescent, and I wanted to transcribe this feeling.[5]

Accordingly, Gondry's preference for a handcrafted approach is equally concerned with the exploration of a nostalgic, emotional geography, a theme to which I will return later in this chapter.

The limited or selective use of digital manipulation in Gondry's oeuvre is not confined to *Mood Indigo*, but is present through the handcrafted quirks of the majority of his work, from music videos and commercial shorts to feature films. This is particularly evident in his music videos, which include the lo-fi trickery employed in Beck's "Deadweight" (1997); the painted cardboard cityscape in Metronomy's "Love Letters" (2014); the use of projector visuals to create haunting, spectral images in The White Stripes' "Dead Leaves and the Dirty Ground" (2002); and the transformation of the body of Emma de Caunes into a life-sized plastic replica of the retro board game Operation in Radiohead's "Knives Out" (2001). All four music videos create fantastical spaces not through digital effects, but through inventive set design, costuming, and tricks of perception. Gondry's visual style then provides a useful frame through which to unpack the concept and process of craft, which, as Paul Greenhalgh notes, has historically possessed a fluid identity that has made it difficult to define.[6]

Forging a connection between human touch and the process of creating, craft has principally been theorized in relation to the materials and techniques employed in the production of the crafted object. Leading craft scholar Glenn Adamson, however, attempts to liberate craft from its simple associations with methodology and materials, contending that craft is "an approach, an attitude, or a habit of action. Craft only exists in motion. It is a way of doing things."[7] Adamson's reference to the existence of craft in motion is inextricably bound up with the capacity of a handmade object to inscribe narrative in the imperfections of its construction. In other words, crafted objects often reveal more about the journey of creation than the end result. Moreover, they are often tied to sentimental and nostalgic lineages, which evoke a craftsmanship handed down over generations.[8] This emphasis on the process of making, as well as the tactile and sensuous nature of the finished product, has resulted in craft's uneasy relationship with fine art. Indeed, handicrafts have generally been stripped of any aesthetic considerations and, in the words of Howard Risatti, are unfortunately "still so deeply embedded in the life-world of ordinary experience as strictly functional objects that [. . .] they are simply incapable of generating aesthetic experience."[9] This view is compounded by the unshakeable gender and domestic connotations that have been attributed to craft activities, particularly those involving needlework and textiles, which position craft within the private (feminine) space and fine art in public (masculine) space.

Despite the lowly positioning of craft within a fine arts framework, the intimacy and authenticity that are part of the crafting process have crucially allowed room for dissent and subversion. Louise Mazanti, in direct contrast to traditional readings of craft, argues that handmade objects collapse the "art/life dichotomy," existing in both spheres and simultaneously gesturing towards aesthetics and the quotidian experience.[10] Valerie Cassel Oliver expands on this opening up of the possibilities of craft, highlighting its historical and contemporary engagement with "philosophical and social concerns [. . .] such as existentialism, aesthetic hierarchies, and the commercialization of art, identity, and culture."[11] What both Mazanti and Oliver's respective readings achieve is shifting critical attention away from the documented limitations of craft to the aesthetic and cultural work that can be achieved within the liminal space that it inhabits. Significantly, Gondry's cinematic appropriation of handmade processes is equally concerned with liminality and the transgression of boundaries, whereby the craft aesthetics in both *The Science of Sleep* and *Mood Indigo* draw the attention of the viewer to the notion of the film image as a crafted product. In exposing the mechanics of visual construction by eschewing digital methods of film manipulation, Gondry's use of crafted objects and scenography works to both reinforce and disrupt the boundaries of reality and dream/fantasy within both films' diegeses. In so doing, Gondry recoups the aesthetic considerations that have been divorced from craft and refigures them within the visual and thematic contexts of his films, linking the handmade with the motifs of play and nostalgia. For the purposes of this chapter, I will employ the term craft to principally delineate Gondry's approach to aesthetics by focusing on the manner in which the physical construction of handmade objects contributes to furthering both the ideological work of Gondry's childlike approach to perception and the visual textures of the films as crafted products in their own right.

The importance of materiality in *The Science of Sleep* is intriguingly emphasized in a song that accompanies the final credits, entitled "Golden the Pony Boy." Sung by Charlotte Gainsbourg, who plays Stéphanie, these lyrics reconstruct the film's narrative through reference to materials and objects of play:

Cotton and cardboard, cellophane and paper, thread, needle to employ
All felt and fabric, birds fly and cats play
Golden the Pony Boy.
Made out of cloth and standing so still, just like a simple toy
Grey as the sky on a day without sun
Golden the Pony Boy.
Screwdrivers, rubber bands, glue guns and pliers, tools to create or destroy
Patiently waiting, un-calculating
Golden the Pony Boy.
Flying wheels and colored reels spin into motion
Bringing him lots of joy
Trot, canter, gallop
Over land and sea
Golden the Pony Boy.

When Golden the Pony Boy—a fabric horse that Stéphanie names after her first impression of Stéphane—is initially introduced in the film, Stéphane mistakes him for an object that Stéphanie has made; however, she reveals that he has been adopted: "When I found him he was so sad that I had to buy him for a lot. He is never going to leave me now." Stéphane's subsequent decision to break into Stéphanie's apartment to take the horse in order to alter its construction with mechanized parts that allow it to gallop independently draws Stéphanie into his crafted dream space. This is particularly underlined in the scene in which Stéphane, who has fallen asleep while speaking to Stéphanie on the telephone, is able to sustain a direct line of communication to her via the telephone to describe his dream as it unfolds. Gondry explores this confusion between waking reality and dreaming through the privileging of handmade objects that magically transcend both spaces in Stéphane and Stéphanie's fraught romance. Indeed, Stéphane confesses his love for Stéphanie specifically through a craft lens: "I love her because she makes things. You know? She makes things with her hands. It's as if her synapse was married directly to her fingers."

Although Stéphane is initially attracted to Stéphanie's friend, Zoé (Emma de Caunes), the transition of his feelings from Zoé to Stéphanie is born out of their mutual language for playfully fabricating and embellishing their reality. When Stéphanie shares her creation of a white felt boat that is looking for its mother and the sea (in a play on the French words *mère* [mother] and *mer* [sea]), Stéphane helps her construct the imagined scene by using blue and white cellophane to create the sea and cotton wool to produce clouds. The fantasy is highlighted when Stéphane is able to magically suspend the cotton wool clouds in Stéphanie's apartment by playing a specific note on her piano: "Each structure has its own region and frequency. You just have to hit the right chord at the right time." In such scenes, literal acts of crafting provide access into a realm of fantasy, such as when Stéphane's cobbled invention of a "one second time machine," which allows the user to travel one second into either the past or the future, is played out by Stéphane and Stéphanie, despite the temporal impossibility. As they begin to co-habit Stéphane's dreams, even when their connection is fading in reality, the process of making by hand becomes their lovers' discourse, or at least the one that Stéphane wishes would break into their reality. The role of craft in the film is not merely used as a visual backdrop; rather the film actively engages with the ability to create and make objects as a way to re-invent the world as one would like it to be. As Peter Dormer writes, "Making things is a way of anchoring one's obsession in one's imagination. (Making by craft is not the only way of gaining the understanding of and possessing the objects of one's desire, but it is a powerful one.)"[12] For Stéphane, the invention and creation bound up with craft become the means through which to both understand and shape his world.

This overt use of a craft aesthetic as part of the narrative in *The Science of Sleep* can be contrasted to the manner in which it is employed in *Mood Indigo*. Although both films embed craft aesthetics as a visual diversion from the harsh realities that occur within their respective narratives—namely, Chloé's terminal illness and the emotional pain Stéphane experiences through his unrequited romantic feelings—*Mood Indigo* features fewer scenes of hand-making activity, but still bears the traces of Gondry's craft ethos. For example, following Chloé's death and the appalling "pauper's funeral" that Colin can barely

Figure 1.2 Stéphane uses cellophane and cotton wool to construct a scene in *The Science of Sleep* (Gaumont, 2006)

afford for her, the film returns to the decayed ruins of their apartment, where their house mouse gathers up the drawings that Chloé completed during her bedrest and takes them to the factory featured at the start of the film. The paper upon which Chloé has completed her illustrations serves as the backdrop to the workers' text, and, when it is sewn together, the illustrations form a flip book. With the flick of each page, the film that the viewer has just witnessed is re-imagined in the stop-motion animation of Chloé's collected drawings; however, Chloé's narrative ends when she and Colin share their first kiss in the underground forest. Chloé's ending abruptly departs from the denouement of Vian's novel, which concludes with the mouse's final act of suicide, by retreating into a safe, dream space. In a similar vein, the ending of *The Science of Sleep* diverts the focus away from Stéphane and Stéphanie's final altercation to feature them riding Golden the Pony Boy through the forest before boarding the white felt boat and drifting off on a cellophane sea. In this respect, both films use methods of craft to create endings that shift attention away from the harshness of reality to recapture the innocence that has been lost as the narratives unfold. In much the same way that a child will use craft methods to create the elements of their play space, craft is used—to quote Chloé's friend, Alise (Aïssa Maiga), in *Mood Indigo*—to "change the whole narrative."

DREAMS OF PLAY AND SPATIAL FANTASIES

In *The Science of Sleep*, the crafting of narrative and the symbolism of DIY are also key to forwarding the film's romantic dream logic. During the opening scene, the viewer watches an episode of "Stéphane TV," in which Stéphane breaks down the construction of dreams in the style of a cooking program: "Hi! Welcome back to another episode of *Télévision Éducative*. Tonight, I'll show you how dreams are prepared." Set in a mock television studio replete with walls made from egg cartons and cameras composed of cardboard, Stéphane, self-reflexively mimicking Gondry's employment of found objects in his films, mixes a selection of everyday objects in a large pot as though he is preparing a culinary dish. His recipe for reverie employs "a delicate combination of complex ingredients," including black paint to represent "random thoughts," spaghetti to symbolize "memories from the past," cologne to evoke "love, relationships, friendships and all those 'ships'," and vinyl records to elicit "songs you heard from the day." As a haze of red-tinted smoke emerges from the pot, the screen on the back wall of the makeshift studio projects the unfolding dream that Stéphane enters by parting the plastic shower curtain that separates the studio from his dream space. In his dream Stéphane speaks with his father, who has recently passed away, and the conversation is imagined as spin art, a visual style in which paint is poured onto a spinning canvas resulting in a psychedelic splattering of color. The motion of the paint mimics the trajectory of a dream in the sense that the finished product of the spin art technique is unknown until the spinning has been completed, in much the same way that the action of a dream is not controllable. Here, Gondry attempts to visually articulate the unstable trajectory of dreaming, exposing the viewer to Stéphane's oneiric geography.

Interestingly, Gondry regards "Stéphane TV" as an:

> antechamber or a purgatory [. . .] I wanted people to know when they are in a dream and when they are in reality. What was important for me was capturing the notion of Stephane and Stephanie [sic] sharing the same vision, or, as we say, sharing the same dream. To me it's a sign of love and its [sic] very romantic. [13]

Although it was Gondry's intention to create two separate realms within his film, it is up for debate whether this has been achieved. Scenes such as the launch of Stéphane's "Disasterology" calendar at his local bar and his awakening from a ski holiday nightmare with his feet in a freezer at the foot of his bed make a clear demarcation between reality and dream within the film's diegesis seemingly inconceivable. Indeed, as Stéphane's dreaming life seeps into his waking life, the film knowingly signals to the viewer that they are entering a surreal realm when Stéphane's boss, Monsieur Pouchet (Pierre Vaneck), comments at his calendar launch that "We've leaped forward into absurdity." Rather than realizing his intended goal of separating reality and dream in the film, I contend that Gondry instead employs the film medium to visualize how dreams impinge on waking life to activate the magic of the everyday.

The close relationship between film aesthetics and dreams has been explored by scholars who have highlighted the visual connections between the processes of film editing and the non-linear, fragmented images arising from the dreaming subject. Thorsten Botz-Bornstein observes that "To discuss dream theory in the context of film studies means moving from the original, clinical context within which dream theory was initially developed, to an environment established by primarily aesthetic concerns."[14] Botz-Bornstein frames his analysis through the term "dreamtense," which is used to delineate the specific spatio-temporal unfolding of dreams within the space of film: "Dreams take place 'elsewhere' [. . .]. The task of film dream is to create 'places' which have not been constructed by an architect given to daydreams but which exist through certain aesthetic presuppositions."[15] This construction of an alternative or parallel space into which fantasies and latent desires are projected is a common theme in Gondry's cinema. For example, in Matthew Campora's examination of the layers of memory in *Eternal Sunshine of the Spotless Mind* (2004), he argues that the film is "a multi-stranded narrative with multiple ontologies."[16] In Campora's reading, the layering of different realities, specifically what he terms the "waking" and "internal-subjective" threads of the film, lends a process of "hypermediacy" that defamiliarizes the action "to increase the perceptual awareness of the viewer."[17] This making-strange of the familiar is therefore not only a technique to move between different diegetic realms within the film narrative, but also a means to further engage the viewer's awareness of the act of watching. In this sense, the multi-nodal structure of Gondry's films both complements and intensifies the high level of self-awareness that he achieves through the use of handmade objects. This paradox at the heart of Gondry's cinema is therefore the desire to draw the viewer into the fantasy, while also making its status as a constructed narrative evident.

The blurring of the boundaries between seemingly distinct ontological spaces in *The Science of Sleep* and *Mood Indigo* is achieved by rendering the divide between the real and the oneiric as slippery and mutable. Indeed, as both films progress, it becomes increasingly difficult to navigate waking and reverie, and to ascertain whether the action is the reality of the characters' lived experiences or the projection of the interiorized spaces of their consciousness. This can be seen in the manner in which Stéphane's waking life in *The Science of Sleep* is progressively intruded upon and interrupted by his fantasies, to the point where his mother confides, "Since he was 6, he's inverted dream and reality." Similarly, *Mood Indigo* is replete with bizarre moments that deny verisimilitude, such as the post-wedding picnic scene where Colin and Chloé share the same physical space, but she is sitting in the sunshine while he is in the pouring rain. This destabilization of an accepted reality is again linked to both films' appropriation of a handmade aesthetic, while also forwarding a childlike point of view that is present in much of Gondry's work. However, where his foray into the Hollywood action hero genre with *The Green Hornet* (2011), for example, starts from the perspective of a child who is playing with a superhero toy, the structure of reality and play in *The Science of Sleep* and *Mood Indigo* is far more complex.

By engaging in acts of play that are evocative of childhood, the characters are attempting to re-imagine their realities. Indeed, Marina Warner writes that films that position the world through the eyes of a child are trying "to slough off our own fallen nature and return to some dream possibility."[18] For both Stéphane and Colin, the desire to return is linked to regaining the period of time before their respective hearts were broken. In this sense, the films' shared moods of romantic disenchantment and a failure to disentangle reality and fantasy converge on the fault lines of nostalgic longing. In looking at the insertion of fantasy in both films, I propose to consider the characters not merely as dreamers, but as nostalgic playmates attempting to recoup a lost innocence. In appropriating play, I am reducing it to its most simple meaning to refer to being engaged in an instance of "spontaneous, self-initiated and self-regulated activity [. . .] which is relatively risk free and not necessarily goal-oriented."[19]

In other words, I am examining how the characters in the films react to the exigencies of reality by infusing their lives with a playful sense of wonderment through game-playing and make-believe.

In Myke Bartlett's reading of *Be Kind Rewind* and the process of "sweding," he argues that:

> Children essentially find a voice through mimicry, imitating their parents before moving on to television or film, which mimics the known world in more exciting shades. Sweding seems to mirror this process, suggesting that even as adults we never tire of play.[20]

While in *Be Kind Rewind* the characters playfully insert themselves into the narratives of well-known films such as *Ghostbusters* (Ivan Reitman, 1984) and *Driving Miss Daisy* (Bruce Beresford, 1989), the notion of play in *The Science of Sleep* and *Mood Indigo* is embedded principally within the iconography of the films. Where Stéphane and Stéphanie spend much of their time playing games of pretense and imagination enacted through handmade inventions, Colin and Chloé's Paris is filled with magical objects, such as coin-operated clouds that float over the city and parties catered with snacks served from miniature toy ovens. The idea of play in Gondry's films is supported by the presence of these objects, which, in their ability to provide amusement without serving a specific function, can be seen as toys that further the illusion of their games.

In much the same way that dreams are theorized as inhabiting an alternative space, play also unfolds in a unique time–space setting. Patricia Anne Masters argues that "play occupies a distinct locality and occurs within a limited time. It is bracketed, and as another-worldly experience, play allows individuals to create alternative worlds and identities far removed from their everyday lives."[21] Similar to the temporality of a dream, play allows for the revision of time in an echo of Stéphane's above-mentioned "one second time machine" in *The Science of Sleep* (see also below). Just as Stéphane attempts to alter his unsatisfactory romantic interactions with Stéphanie in the present moment by skipping forward and backward one second in time, the act of play is tied to a melancholy that the characters wish to escape. Although both films largely take place in the domestic realm, aligning with the gendered codification of the home as a space of crafting, the dreams contained within the walls of the home spill onto the public spaces of the city, which is imagined as a playground. The fact that both films make marked references to architectural construction—in the form of Stéphane's imagined cardboard cityscape in *The Science of Sleep* and the construction site of Les Halles in *Mood Indigo*—foregrounds the characters' roles in re-creating the environment that surrounds them as a site of play that also sees them attempting to change the very course of the developing narrative.

IMPRINTING HOME

The capacity of the "one second time machine" featured in *The Science of Sleep* to return the characters to the past, if only for one second, provides a temporary break from the dullness of real time, which ties into the nostalgia that saturates the *mise-en-scène* in the choice of old-fashioned items. The importance of objects is also a feature of *Mood Indigo*, where Colin's toylike gadgetry stands in for technological advances, such as his creation of the "pianocktail," a hybrid piano and bar where each "note triggers a spirit, liqueur or flavor" to create a signature drink. While the pianocktail is lifted directly from Vian's book, Gondry also repurposes vintage technology in the film, including a Rubik's Cube date planner and a coffee machine made from a brass gramophone. Gondry's approach, however, is distinct from the trend of nostalgia films that employ methods of pastiche to recall the past in the sense that the objects in his films are not being used to evoke a specific point in time, but rather a yearning for childhood.[22] These objects of play are invariably evocative of the past; however, their symbolism as retro objects is crucially not apparent to the characters. Rather, the sense of the past attributed to the objects and the emphasis on make-believe and play in the narratives speak directly to a sub-text of nostalgia and an obsession with recapturing the happiness of the past, whether it is Colin's desire to return to his first kiss with Chloé or Stéphane's claim that he wishes he could go back to before he liked Stéphanie.

In contextualizing nostalgia, Svetlana Boym connects it to its original Greek etymology:

> Nostalgia (from *nostos*—return to home, and *algia*—longing) is a longing for a home that no longer exists or has never existed. Nostalgia is a sentiment of loss and displacement, but it is also a romance with one's own fantasy.[23]

Boym further breaks down the term to give two examples of nostalgia: reflective and restorative. Whereas reflective nostalgia resides within the pain of longing associated with nostalgia's loss, restorative nostalgia focuses on the act of returning and "proposes to rebuild the lost home and patch up the memory gaps."[24] In presenting denouements that privilege the cohesion of the happy ending, Gondry is engaged in an attempt to rebuild the nostalgic past in an ideal image of romantic unity. The implausibility of the final moments in *The Science of Sleep* and Gondry's rejection of Vian's ending in *Mood Indigo* presents his films as tabulae rasae in which he can indulge his characters' desire to rewrite the narrative.

The presence of nostalgia in *The Science of Sleep* and *Mood Indigo* exists both within and outside the cinematic frame. The oneiric landscape in *The

Science of Sleep is informed by Gondry's own memories and dreams from his youth to the extent that he filmed in the apartment complex where he grew up.[25] This iconography of childhood is particularly encapsulated in the apartment in which the teenage paraphernalia of punk rock posters and cartoon drawings plastered on the walls of Stéphane's childhood bedroom evince a suspended state of adolescence. The film also shares a particular genealogy with the music video that Gondry directed for the Foo Fighters' song "Everlong" (1997), because Gondry's recurring nightmare from his childhood of his hands growing out of proportion to his body, which features in the music video, is also replicated in one of Stéphane's dream sequences.[26] Similarly, while Gondry and Bossi's adaptation of *Mood Indigo* is faithful to Vian's text, the film is inflected by Gondry's thematic concern with the state of childhood, whereby Vian's melancholically surrealist narrative of terminal illness is given the further sub-text of the loss of innocence. Significantly, Gondry has framed the film in interviews through his experience of reading Vian's novel as an adolescent and has gone so far as to refer to its creation as a "coming home movie."[27] Although this may have merely been a passing comment made by Gondry, the merging of the narrative on the site of the home speaks not only of the homesickness evoked by nostalgia, but also of the relevance of the domestic space to the narrative.

In Vian's novel, Chloé's illness is manifest through the deterioration of Colin's apartment:

> Through the panes on each side you could just pick out a wan, tarnished sun. The centre of each was covered with black spots. A few skimpy handfuls of rays had got through into the corridor, but, as soon as they touched the ceramic tiles that were once so brilliant, they turned to liquid and trickled away into long damp stains. The walls exuded a smell like locked cellars.[28]

Gondry reproduces the decaying home in *Mood Indigo*; however, it is not merely portrayed as an embodiment of the fatal flower that has become lodged in Chloé's lungs, but is a metaphor for Colin's disconnection from his previous naive self. When he is forced to work in a series of unfulfilling and demoralizing jobs to pay for the flowers that are required as Chloé's treatment, he stops inventing and the previous magic in his home dissipates. Madame Davis, Colin's downstairs neighbor, attempts to comfort Colin with the statement that the apartment has changed due to the passage of time: "My place is doing the same thing. But I think it's an illusion. As you go through life, spaces seem smaller." The underlying sentiment of Madame Davis's remark is that the passage from adolescence to adulthood marks a change in perception—a transition that Gondry is all too aware of and that, in circumventing the denouement of Vian's text, he positively refutes.

This chapter has argued that one of the central threads tying together Gondry's work as an auteur is a nostalgic preoccupation with childhood that is manifest both thematically and within the handmade textures of his films. Arguably tracing the contours of Gondry's personal narrative, when Stéphane returns to his childhood home in *The Science of Sleep* he uncovers boxes of colored cellophane, toilet rolls, plastic bottle tops, pine cones, bonbon wrappers, and old family photographs. In this one scene, Gondry captures the major concerns of both his broader cinema and this chapter: namely, handmade play and the return home. The imprint of the route from his school to his home that he refers to in *I've Been 12 Forever* is engraved in the self-reflexive nuances of *The Science of Sleep* and *Mood Indigo*, whereby the memories and dreams from Gondry's own youth feed directly into the rewriting of the films' narratives. Using the tactile materials of childhood craft projects, Gondry, as the restorative nostalgic, attempts to piece together the shattered ruins of his films' romances, blending dream and nostalgia in their everyday reality.

NOTES

1. Michel Gondry, "I've Been 12 Forever (Part 1 Age 12–12)," in *The Work of Director Michel Gondry: A Collection of Music Videos, Short Films, Documentaries and Stories* (New York: Palm Pictures, 2003).
2. Gondry, "I've Been 12 Forever."
3. Ursula Kluwick, *Exploring Magic Realism in Salman Rushdie's Fiction* (Florence: Taylor and Francis, 2013), 7.
4. Pat Brereton, *Smart Cinema: DVD Add-Ons and New Audience Pleasures* (Basingstoke: Palgrave Macmillan, 2012), 60.
5. Andrew Pulver and Henry Barnes, "Michel Gondry on *Mood Indigo*: 'It has a special connection with adolescence'—video interview," *The Guardian* (July 31, 2014). Available at <https://www.theguardian.com/film/video/2014/jul/31/michel-gondry-mood-indigo-video-interview> (last accessed July 13, 2017).
6. Paul Greenhalgh, "The History of Craft," in *The Culture of Craft: Status and Future*, ed. Peter Dormer (Manchester and New York: Manchester University Press, 1997), 20–1.
7. Glenn Adamson, *Thinking Through Craft* (Oxford and New York: Berg, 2007), 4.
8. Shu Hung and Joesph Magliaro, *By Hand: The Use of Craft in Contemporary Art* (New York: Princeton Architectural Press, 2007), 12.
9. Howard Risatti, *A Theory of Craft: Function and Aesthetic Expression* (Chapel Hill: University of North Carolina Press, 2007), 304.
10. Louise Mazanti, "Super-Objects: Craft as an Aesthetic Position," in *Extra/Ordinary: Craft and Contemporary Art*, ed. Maria Elena Buszek (Durham, NC, and London: Duke University Press, 2011), 60.
11. Valerie Cassel Oliver, ed., "Craft Out of Action," in *Hand+Made: The Performative Impulse in Art and Craft* (Houston: Contemporary Arts Museum Houston, 2010), 12.
12. Peter Dormer, ed., "Craft and the Turing Test for Practical Thinking," in *The Culture of Craft: Status and Future* (Manchester and New York: Manchester University Press, 1997), 152.

13. Jason Wood, *Last Words: Considering Contemporary Cinema* (New York: Columbia University Press, 2014), 38.
14. Thorsten Botz-Bornstein, *Films and Dreams: Tarkovsky, Bergman, Sokurov, Kubrick, and Wong Kar-wai* (Lanham, MD: Lexington Books, 2007), ix.
15. Botz-Bornstein, *Films and Dreams*, 119.
16. Matthew Campora, "Art Cinema and New Hollywood: Multiform Narrative and Sonic Metalepsis in *Eternal Sunshine of the Spotless Mind*," *New Review of Film and Television Studies*, 7, no. 2 (June 2009): 120.
17. Campora, "Art Cinema," 123.
18. Marina Warner, "Through a Child's Eyes," in *Cinema and the Realms of Enchantment: Lectures, Seminars and Essays by Marina Warner and Others*, ed. Duncan Petrie (London: BFI, 1993), 42.
19. Irina Verenikina, Pauline Harris and Pauline Lysaught, "Child's Play: Computer Games, Theories of Play and Children's Development," Paper presented at IFIP Working Group 3.5 Conference: Young Children and Learning Technologies, Western Sydney University at Parramatta, July 2003.
20. Myke Bartlett, "Imitation as Inspiration: DIY Filmmaking in *Son of Rambow* and *Be Kind Rewind*," *Screen Education*, 51 (2008): 38.
21. Patricia Anne Masters, "Play Theory, Playing, and Culture," *Sociology Compass*, 2, no. 3 (2008): 857.
22. Vera Dika, *Recycled Culture in Contemporary Art and Film: The Uses of Nostalgia* (Cambridge: Cambridge University Press, 2003), 3.
23. Svetlana Boym, *The Future of Nostalgia* (New York: Basic Books, 2001), xiii.
24. Boym, *The Future of Nostalgia*, 41.
25. Wood, *Last Words*, 37.
26. Gondry, "I've Been 12 Forever."
27. Pulver and Barnes, "Michel Gondry on *Mood Indigo*."
28. Boris Vian, *Froth on the Daydream*, trans. Stanley Chapman (London: Rapp & Carroll, 1967), 151.

CHAPTER 2

In Dreams and in Love There are No Impossibilities: Michel Gondry's Cinema and the Aesthetics of the Oneiric

Bruno Surace

I recommend that you read this chapter while listening to Duke Ellington.

THE DIRECTOR OF DREAMS

Michel Gondry's cinema contains a dominant red thread, a key isotopy which seems to emerge obsessively: the theme of the dream and its offshoots. It does not always involve dream *strictu sensu*, which foresees a dreamer and that which is dreamt. At times the dream becomes an atmospheric component that permeates certain moments of the film, at others it is the absolute protagonist. In any case, it is the oneiric dimension that strongly substantivizes Gondry's aesthetics and stylistic "monogram," from his first feature film, *Human Nature* in 2001, to his latest, *Microbe & Gasoline* (*Microbe et Gasoil*) in 2015.

Dream in Gondry's cinema is always a struggle against reality, an attempt to dispossess the latter of its ontological superiority and conquer for itself a place of honor in the condition of being. It is not reality which becomes dream but, on the contrary, dream which declares itself *real*. One might venture that it is a matter, oxymoronically, of "oneiric realism," which is a bit like artistic or literary magic realism where fantastic elements merge harmoniously in a realistic landscape. Oneirism spreads as a legitimate mode of existence in the world of Gondry's characters, the reification of their poetic and painful *otherness*, the appropriation of a space. Take, for instance, Nathan Bronfman (Tim Robbins), who narrates the whole of *Human Nature* from the netherworld in a splendid *prosopopoeia*, which has all the appearance of a dream "from the dead"; the sad struggle of Joel Barish (Jim Carrey) with his own memories, which in *Eternal*

Sunshine of the Spotless Mind (2004) occurs completely within a dream; or the life of Stéphane Miroux (Gael García Bernal) in *The Science of Sleep* (*La Science des rêves*, 2006), which is entirely a dream.

In all of Gondry's films, dreams embody three distinct but interrelated dimensions:

1. They are part of the diegesis—that is, of the universe of the narrated story—in a more-or-less pervasive, but extremely significant, manner (in other words, they are not episodic or lateral dreams);
2. They form part of a broader symbolic or political system which is not purely narrative, constituting some kind of manifestation of thought tied to the theme of otherness;
3. They function as a counterpart to innovative modules of formal film construction, indissolubly linking the plane of expression with that of content, thanks to a precise aesthetics of the oneiric.

The emergence of these three dimensions implies the need to treat Gondry's filmography as though it were marked by a fundamental unity, a poetic project which certainly associates it with contemporary cinematographers of otherness, from Tim Burton to David Lynch, and which deserves to be investigated autonomously. This chapter discusses a consideration of the three dimensions of dream in the cinema of the visionary from Versailles.

THE DREAM STORIES

As stated previously, dream performs a leading role in essentially all of Michel Gondry's films. Certainly, *The Science of Sleep* is at the top of the list, "a tender, bizarre, and melancholic film where reality and dream constantly blend."[1] Here the protagonist is the eccentric Stéphane, who, upon returning to Paris from Mexico after his father's death, falls in love with Stéphanie (Charlotte Gainsbourg). Since childhood, Stéphane has suffered from a possibly pathological condition which induces him to continuously mix dream with reality. His is a half-world, where oneirism compensates for the inability to accept the greyness of the way things are. Dream is thus a material agent, which hides behind everyday objects and gives shape to their ineffability (inadvertently evoking Eugenio Montale's poetics of objects),[2] exploding in the charm of colors and whimsicalities which Gondry renders with an array of stratagems that goes beyond the post-modern special effect. Computer graphics are banished from a realm where craftwork, made of cellophane and papier-mâché, perfectly traces the way in which Stéphane's mind manipulates reality. Stéphanie, for her part, constitutes the element that threatens the stability of this house of cards, allowing herself at first blush to be drawn into Stéphane's kaleidoscope and its joyous explosion of fantasy, but then dragging the protagonist back into the vortex of responsibility of an ordinary life and all that follows in its wake.

Thus Stéphane and Stéphanie, a predestined couple right from their homonymity, merge in fascination and disenchantment, representing the unstable equilibrium on which the world's being is based, a codified world where there is no place for the chaos of pure dream, which perhaps is a good thing, so as to avoid the outcome of a nihilistic, solipsistic humanity, doubled over its own personal traumas. Since childhood, furthermore, Stéphane has been accumulating traumas, from his parents' divorce to his father's death from cancer, which he does not work out by means of externalization, but indeed—perhaps—nurtures, creating an agreeable world or comfort zone for them. Dream is an art which one has to know how to channel or harness according to a method, and such a hermeneutics demonstrates how Gondry's is not one of those only too widespread lackluster oneiric ideologies that extols unreality and flight as the only ways to existential realization.

Dreams and their antidotes therefore move on parallel tracks, and there is no way to flee from pain for eternity. This is illustrated in *Eternal Sunshine of the Spotless Mind*, where Stéphane's playful oneirism makes way for Joel's nightmare journey. Here, protagonist Joel (Jim Carrey), after falling in love with the flamboyant Clementine (Kate Winslet), rediscovers a reason for living an otherwise depressing life. An extraordinary love story unfolds with this eccentric woman, but with time the relationship frays, perhaps because of irreconcilable character differences. Thus Clementine, in a rush of impetuosity, decides to turn to a futuristic agency which specializes in the removal of memories and literally has Joel eliminated from her mind, so that in desperation he decides to undergo the same operation. From this moment on, oneirism erupts into the narration and the focus moves onto Joel's dreams. The operation carried out by this company, Lacuna Inc., in fact occurs at a moment in which the mind is particularly open and malleable—that is, during sleep—after a careful mapping built up during wakefulness, thanks to the association between the sight of objects with the memory that must be cancelled and the individuation of areas of the brain involved in the sudden emotion experienced thereafter. Indeed, the link between objects and people is extremely strong for Gondry, to the extent that in his 2009 *Tokyo!*[3] the protagonist is literally transfigured into a chair in order to be with her inattentive lover.

In *Eternal Sunshine*, Joel's journey in his own dreams therefore assumes the valence of a lucid dream, a bit like in Alejandro Amenábar's *Open Your Eyes* (*Abre los ojos*, 1997), remade by Cameron Crowe as *Vanilla Sky* (2001): it is a conscious journey in the lee of the two worlds, where the dreamer knows he is in the dream and can continue to live the dream and exercise his own agency.[4] Joel's intra-oneiric struggle is that of a man who does not accept the cancellation of an important memory from his life, even though it is painful, but who unfortunately must reckon with the programmatic elimination from his mind of Clementine, who literally disappears in front of his eyes and whom he cannot but continue to talk to, even while aware of her ghostliness: he is talking not to her, but to a representation of her. Here the dream is therefore the ominous vehicle for the fulfilment of a ruinous choice, dictated by anguish. In the end, however, as with Stéphane and Stéphanie, despite their reciprocal cancellation Joel and Clementine are also permitted a bittersweet parting and the hope of reunion.

The transliteration from joyous to painful dream is therefore perceived as a fundamental step in the experience of self-awareness. The sweetened folds of the dream conceal reality with all its injustices. Love is the centripetal force of this oneiric teleology, and Gondry's cinema seems never to abandon this thesis. Gondry's *Mood Indigo (L'Écume des jours)* of 2013—based on Boris Vian's novel—describes the love story between Colin (Romain Duris) and Chloé (Audrey Tautou). Here the dream is no longer a single character's emanation which contaminates the entire world, as with Stéphane in *The Science of Sleep*, but it is the world itself that takes on the semblance of a dream. Colin is a dandy in a fanciful Paris, scattered with machines and experiences that appear to have been extracted from *The Science of Sleep*; Chloé is light-hearted and blithesome, a sort of incarnation of the atmospheres evoked by Duke Ellington, a musician beloved of the male protagonist. Their love is predestined and culminates in a marriage which, however, rapidly disintegrates, this time not on account of the unraveling of the relationship between the two protagonists but because the woman falls prey to an illness which causes a water lily to grow in her lung. The fairy-tale atmosphere thus assumes ever darker tones, and the candy-floss photography becomes tinged with sepia hues and veers towards black and white. Chloé is going to die, and the perfect dream life of the lovers collides violently with the unexpected burdens of harsh reality: Colin's money begins to diminish, he is obliged to work (that is, to devote time to exertion and subtract it from dreaming), his fabulous apartment (a bus suspended between two buildings) gets smaller, his group of friends begins to fade away, and, above all, Chloé's condition does not improve. The days melt away like the foam of the French title. The dream has turned into a nightmare: that is, it has disclosed what has always been its true nature—imponderable and uncontrollable.

In their own way, all of Gondry's protagonists have to reckon with a progressive loss of control over their oneiric content, passing from the enthusiasm of being able effortlessly to manipulate it to the agonizing awareness of being enslaved by it, as if it were an autonomous entity or a perverse subconsciousness, as if—in a Freudian way—the latent content were incontrovertibly irrupting into the manifest content. Obviously, each of the stories narrated up to now lends itself to one or more metaphorical interpretations: they are all stories about traumas that are difficult to accept and have been converted into a toylike, childlike dimension, the definitive instance of disempowerment or a return to the Oedipal cradle where the mother's protection cannot be attacked by the incrustations of adult existence.

In this sense, paradoxically, the most extreme case is the director's first feature film, which conceals his poetic manifesto. *Human Nature* is, in fact, a highly entertaining film, marked by the abstruseness typical of films written by Charlie Kaufman, who also wrote *Eternal Sunshine of the Spotless Mind*. In addition to working with Gondry, Kaufman collaborated multiple times with Spike Jonze, a director interested in many of the ideas I present here. The protagonist of *Human Nature*, Nathan, is a scientist who consecrates his life to a single purpose: educating mice in high-society manners. This mission not only is scientific, but also fulfils the profoundly obsessive disposition of this character, scarred by the trauma of having an overly oppressive mother, verging on the sadistic, and a manic father fixated with evolution and with the superiority of human beings in relation to monkeys, a superiority which culminates precisely in the development of good manners.

For Nathan, these precepts become a "twitch" in a compulsive existence, which is turned upside down by his meeting with the beautiful Lily (Patricia Arquette), who nurses a secret: she suffers from a hormonal anomaly which condemns her to persistent hirsutism that requires her to depilate her entire body daily in order to hide this condition. When Nathan discovers her illness, the phantoms of the past manifest themselves, making it difficult for him to live with a woman who displays monkeylike characteristics, especially after a further relationship with his sensual French colleague, Gabrielle (Miranda Otto). The entire sequence of events is narrated by Nathan himself, who speaks from the afterworld, in a warm ambience—an aseptic white room—which substantivizes his confused *prosopopoeia*. It is therefore not precisely a dream, but a kind of otherworldly manifestation that frames the whole narrative in oneiric terms: neither here nor there, but elsewhere.

The director's other films are less unmistakably oneiric; however, they turn out to be based on dreamers capable of bending reality with the strength of their fantasy. In *Be Kind Rewind* (2008), Jerry (Jack Black) and Mike (Mos Def) undertake the touching mission of reversing the destiny of an old video store, which is experiencing a crisis as a result of the advent of the DVD, and whose VHS tapes have all been demagnetized. The two protagonists thus commit themselves to reshooting these films in homespun versions that are very close to parody. In this case, too, Gondry's array of visual tools is masterfully displayed and, true to pattern, a point is reached where the reality again forcefully takes control of the dream of the protagonists, in the form of the major cinematographic companies which adjure them to cease their work as it is a flagrant violation of copyright laws. The ending, once again bittersweet, shows the meeting between dream and reality in the projection of one of the films that has been "sweded" by Jerry and Mike, which constitutes an important shared moment for their community, and perhaps is the first step towards a turning point, inevitably made up of compromises: "*Be Kind Rewind* offered a sweetly nostalgic and amusingly postmodern ode to cinema's glorious tactile qualities, its function as a community rallying point and its magical potential as an ad-hoc creative outlet."[5]

The protagonist of *The Green Hornet* in 2011 (inspired by the character of the same name created by George W. Trendle and Fran Striker in 1936) similarly becomes a dreamer. Britt Reid (Seth Rogen), the slothful son of a millionaire, decides, after a life of idleness and vice, to impersonate the figure of a rather singular superhero, pretending to be a criminal in order to approach evil people and defeat them, as well as challenging the dangerous mafioso Benjamin Chudnosfsky (Christoph Waltz). Here, paper and artisanal special effects give way to the persistent use of digital technology (similar in some ways to that in *Eternal Sunshine of the Spotless Mind*), but Gondry retains his customary attention to the visual register and to innovative solutions. Britt Reid, like all Gondrian "heroes," is a character built in such a way that his self-awareness develops hand in hand with the unfolding of the story. Nevertheless, he follows an inverse route in regard to his relationship with dream. The characters in the other films start out as dreamers and subsequently have to come to terms with reality and seek a balance between "pipe dreams" and having one's "feet on the ground," whereas Britt moves in an opposite direction—a bit like Joel in *Eternal Sunshine*—from a state of spiritual emptiness to the gradual filling of this void with an increasingly powerful dream (that of being a sort of superhero who vanquishes Evil and in so doing gives meaning to his life). Britt is not compelled to abandon this new oneiric dimension but may indeed nurture it.

In *Microbe & Gasoline*, Daniel (Ange Dargent) finally returns to being a kind of Stéphane, a figure of otherness. This shy, introverted young boy, short in stature (hence the nickname "Microbe"), best manages to express himself through his drawings (like Stéphane, who works as a creative artist for an advertising agency). He makes friends with Théo (Théophile Baquet), with whom he builds a surreal automobile that embodies the entire Gondrian visual imaginary, and the two set out on a fantastic journey through France, dreaming of finding something new with which to elude the boredom of everyday existence. Whereas in all his feature films Gondry presents men and women who in some way revert to childhood, here for the first time he effects the antithetical process: two children—others, outcasts, authentic dreamers—embark on a road movie of French hues which takes on all the traits of a *Bildungsroman*. As always, the euphoria of the fulfilment of the dream is followed by the onset of awareness and by a bittersweet finale, as occurs in life, which oscillates between the present and a nostalgic past, between happiness and pain.

THE POWER OF DREAMS

The isotopy of the dream in Gondry's cinema is thus not to be understood as purely narrative, but assumes the contours of an ideological device which goes beyond mere diegesis. The protagonists of the above-mentioned films, in fact, share worldviews and proprioception that render them completely singular individuals. Theirs is a mutual search for identity which comes into constant conflict with sensations of otherness, of inadequacy, and of discomfort. The director effectuates a continual reflection on what it means to fulfil one's pre-established role in modern society, and on the difficulty of finding oneself when personal sensitivity clashes with the circumstances of daily life.

Gondry's films may or may not contemplate the presence of antagonists, as in the cases of *The Green Hornet* and *The Science of Sleep* respectively; the protagonists' worst enemy, however, always resides inside their own selves. The characters live in a dual dimension: on the one hand, they are privileged in that they have a different outlook on life, which enables them concretely to "put a patch" on the world's ugliness, starting from bursts of subjectivity which transform dreams into reality, and yet, on the other, at some point in the storyline their heightened sensibility reveals a cutting edge. Trauma, even if it is concealed in Technicolor dreams, remains the driving force behind forms of change which the protagonists, all of them men (the director's alter egos), are unwilling to bring about. The trauma of change and loss may take the form of a premise (as in *Human Nature*, *The Green Hornet*, *The Science of Sleep*, *Be Kind Rewind*, and *Microbe & Gasoline*), a present reality (as in *Eternal Sunshine of the Spotless Mind*), or a final consequence (as in *Mood Indigo*). In every case it is ineluctable, and the dreams revolve around it, try to cloak it, but in the end are obliged to face the fact that its symbolic and emotional power is always there, that the ritual grief or mourning for which they are a surrogate must be worked through in reality as well, outside of the metaphor, in all its crudity.

Nevertheless, Gondry's dreams are not only phantoms or simulacra. In them can be traced, as was previously alluded to, a residual positivity which points to the politicity which spans his entire filmography. Superficially, in fact, they constitute a bridge between the solitary protagonists and the other characters, as the former establish strong ties with the latter in a frantic society which typically fosters weak ties. These connections are initially consolidated; subsequently, on encountering a trauma (loss, growth, death) they become frayed; but in any case, they graft onto their "heroes" a kind of *raison d'être* that overcomes their existential solipsism. The characters fall desperately in love, or they form great friendships. Love and friendship, complex and in a sense perhaps ineffable sentiments, are the result of the dream as a search for a match in diversity, for someone who gives credence to the vision, conceding a break from the strain of the monotony of the real.

In this way Stéphane and Stéphanie are united, as his material dreams, reified in abstruse machines, are shared with her. Similarly, Joel and Clementine come together, her fascinating spontaneity enabling her to revitalize him with new dreamlike material, which he will then try desperately to hold on to in his mind during the extirpation performed by Lacuna Inc. It is also how the friendship between Britt and the faithful Kato (Jay Chou) is cemented, as a function of shared personal self-realization even before the comic-book battle against the bad guys. Likewise, the friendships between Daniel and Théo, two youngsters who need to grow up, and between Jerry and Mike, two men who need to return to childhood, are forged. In this way, finally, the sad irony of existence places its trauma on Colin and Chloé, and even more on Nathan, who, in fact, in Gondry's most dramatic film (and paradoxically the funniest), turns out to be a pathetic figure incapable of surviving his obsessions, a victim of his own self, confined to a limbo of perfect candor—that perfection which he has always sought in life—to recount his tale of defeat *in aeternum*.

Love and friendship are therefore inserted into a common oneiric perspective, and put to the test in the process of their descent into reality. The dream is a fortification against solitude: sharing it means sharing a different semiotic system to that imposed by society, and surviving means finding a situation of compromise. Whoever fails, perishes.

This idea is almost Foucauldian and deals with two typologies of power relationship. The first is the power relationship that exists between society and the individual (or rather between society and the imaginary of the individual); the second concerns individuals and dreams. Regarding the first, the issue is general and refers to Gondry's entire filmography. The reiterated representation of otherness and of its capacity to construct oneiric ontologies is a clear declaration of non-acceptance of the forms of imaginary imposed by the other, maybe a Lacanian *Big Other*. After all, for Michel Foucault power and knowledge are closely interrelated, since "there is no power relation without the correlative constitution of a field of knowledge, nor any knowledge that does not presuppose and constitute at the same time power relations."[6] Gondry's films display a marked subjectivity and impossible stories which deliberately overstep the standards of what is commonly termed "normality."

The director's work, however, never becomes fairy tale or fable. In these types of narrative, in fact, the impossible (talking animals, absurd plots) is brought back into the norm and soaked in moralistic intent, for the purpose of perpetrating ideological forms that are dear to one or other society. In Gondry's films, the dreamlike atmospheres and all their bizarre offshoots have no basic moral objective; they are as they are because this is the way they are. This does not constitute a tautology, but signifies that the mechanisms of the mind must not necessarily be subject to the mechanisms of the world. That Nathan's job consists of teaching good manners to mice, or that his pupil Puff (Rhys Ifans) is a human who has spent his life in the jungle like Rudyard Kipling's Mowgli, is perfectly accepted in the narrative world of the film; that Chloé's illness is caused by a water lily growing in her lung or that Colin's personal chef is a little mouse (again) is absolutely legitimate. And not because the stories are set on faraway planets or crazy worlds. In the world of *Human Nature* there are courts, there is science which adopts the same methods as real science (for example, the process of trial and error), and in *Mood Indigo*, the events take place in Paris, where there is a "real-like" philosophy (Jean-Sol Partre, for instance). What occurs is simply an inversion in power relationships. It is no longer society, with its work, its rhythms, and its rituals, which bends dreams but, on the contrary, dreams that bend society—the very society inhabited by the film spectators.

This, however, leads to the second point, and that is the power relationship between dreamer and that which is dreamt. If, in fact, dream in Gondry's cinema has the power not only to interpolate with reality, but indeed also to dictate the rules of social functioning in reality, the problem arises when the dream abandons its subordinate position in relation to the dreamer and starts to rule the dreamer as well. This always happens, and is why Gondry's films should not be seen as forms of "oneiric utopias." The dream is not a utopia. It may carry out allegorical functions, provide useful non-standard interpretations, and serve as a brief escape route, but in the end, one has to reckon with reality and its traumas. In this sense, Gondry's cinema is anything but a simplistic ideological acclamation of subjectivity, or a commendation of folly *à la* Erasmus of Rotterdam.

It would be a mistake to interpret the director's films in this manner: a world inhabited by billions of people able to modify reality with their dreams would be not merely confused, but unlivable or infernal. Reality is not necessarily dictatorial; existence here rather than in the realm of elsewhere is to be understood in the director's films as common ground for shared growth. For this reason the films' protagonists are never truly alone. Theirs is an existential solitude which can be resolved precisely thanks to the help of the other, who is able to accompany them and to share the dream and its hidden trauma. This is the dream as psychotherapeutic support: "dreams have sometimes been introduced in films as part of a depiction of psychotherapeutic process."[7] If the dream overcomes the dreamer and takes possession of him/her, then it becomes obsession and compulsion: in other words, a protective ritual cage which momentarily distances pain but amplifies its reach, as happens to Nathan in *Human Nature*, a tragic mask, or to Joel and Clementine, who in order to avoid pain even mercilessly cancel—and subsequently regret doing so—a part of their own existence.

THE SHAPE OF DREAMS

Michel Gondry's feature films contain three formal dream typologies, which confirm the idea of a close relationship between expression and content. The first, which I have discussed at length, is the artisanal dream, constructed with the aid of cardboard and papier-mâché, models, wood, and all playing on live recording without the intervention of post-digital production. The second is the digital dream, where instead the special effect is created with the help of computer graphics. The third is the mixed dream, where there is no prevalence of one or the other typology, but an organic integration of the dream in the formal registers used for the non-dream parts of the film.

The first typology can be identified in *The Science of Sleep* and *Mood Indigo*, doubtless the director's most francophile works. The very first scene of *The Science of Sleep* begins, in fact, in a dream, or rather in a metadream, a kind of oneiric antechamber which anticipates the opening credits. Here Stéphane presents his personal mental television, from a studio made entirely of egg cartons and other paper materials. He speaks to a non-existent audience (yet still receives applause) and manages all the phases of the broadcast. He plays the drums and the organ to create the soundtrack and then hurries to the centre of the studio and in a presenter-like way explains the "dream recipe."

Figure 2.1 Stéphane cooks a dream in *The Science of Sleep* (Gaumont, 2006)

Placing a large pot on the stove, he recites the ingredients as he throws them in: a few random thoughts (dark paint ostentatiously squeezed from a tube), a pinch of the day's reminiscences (a yellowish powder), a few memories from the past (a good handful of spaghetti), followed by love, relations, emotions, and "all the other things that end in -tion" (a generous dash of cologne), the songs listened to during the day (some vinyl records). Each ingredient undergoes a transformation from mental to physical, and produces a very loud noise when it is cast into the pot. Once all the ingredients have been added, a dense pink smoke emerges, indicating the success of the recipe, and the dream is about to start. Stéphane agitatedly opens a shower curtain on the back wall of the studio and enters to enjoy his dream. At this point, the opening credits begin, completely abstract: splotches of paint or watercolor follow one upon the other and Stéphane has an impromptu dialogue with his father, who had died of cancer. He knows he is in a dream: earlier he says that he is speaking softly in order not to wake himself up. The opening credits are superimposed on the spots of paint—a rare moment of pure abstractionism on the part of the filmmaker—and Stéphane associates them with a concert featuring Duke Ellington, the same artist who will be fundamental to the symbolic sequel, *Mood Indigo*.

In *Mood Indigo*, the first contact between Colin and Chloé is set in a marvelous club in the Belle Époque style where the dancers are surreally engaged in the "biglemoi" dance. Here, to the notes of Duke Ellington broadcast in polyvision on three different screens, the dance is portrayed as follows: while the torso and head are real, the dancers' legs appear conspicuously oblong and made of some substance such as foam rubber. The dancers' lopsided posture seems at times to challenge the laws of physics. The result is nevertheless a charming group dance, where dream and reality touch, until it is time to sit at the table and eat and the dancing is abruptly interrupted, although in the meanwhile love has blossomed between Colin and Chloé. *The Science of Sleep* and *Mood Indigo* therefore utilize the typology of the artisanal dream, as does *Be Kind Rewind*, for example. The actors are required to face the oneiric material directly and, above all, to link it to real environments. The resulting interaction is firmly anchored, in that each scene is built in settings constructed *ad hoc*, instead of the fantastic effect being added on subsequently with green screen or other such means. From a hermeneutic point of view, the proximity of dream to reality has a strengthening effect, as well as articulating a further challenge on Gondry's part to a certain standardization of the dream in postmodern cinema, often entrusted to the potentiality of the computer. What is yielded is a plastic reality: "the oeuvre of Michel Gondry has made much out of staging purposefully 'inept' or what might be called 'naïve' special effects."[8]

The second typology of the dream is adopted in *Eternal Sunshine of the Spotless Mind* and *The Green Hornet*. In the first case, however, the utilization of computer graphics, albeit still present, is controlled through the excellent employment of numerous stratagems of editing and cinematographic post-production. The sequences inside Joel's dreams pass from dream to nightmare with increasingly skillful use of visual solutions, be they artisanal (linked to the first typology)[9] or digital. In Gondry's cinema there is always a basis of artisanality. A splendid sequence sees Joel in a car, chasing after the remembrance of Clementine by night. Clementine runs away, while a car crashes down onto the earth from the sky to signify the protagonist's mnemonic disintegration. Again we have oneiric material which becomes physical material. In the instant when Clementine is framed, the viewer experiences a sensation of discomfort, both on account of her detached behavior and because of a visual given that is not immediately intelligible: she is walking on only one leg. The other leg has been digitally deleted, but the frame is so rapid that this fact remains in one's mind only at a subconscious level, and is only fully realized the second time around. Clementine, out of focus, crosses the road, and Joel frantically parks his car in order to follow her on foot along a deserted avenue lined with shops. After a few steps in the direction of the now distant Clementine, Joel finds himself in front of the very car he has just left, while behind him there is an empty street—he has returned to where he started.

How is it possible that the vehicle should be there? It is possible because we are inside a dream, where the space–time continuum is modified, more so if it is a dream which is being manipulated from the outside, where memories are erased and remodeled little by little. Meanwhile, the posters in the shop windows have become blank: here, too, digital cancellation has occurred. The digital, however, even though it operates on the sidelines, does not intervene in the sequence's climax in which Joel, entrapped in his dream, simply runs blindly. This is conveyed by means of a skillful filmmaking ploy: during the race from his car towards Clementine, Joel passes behind a light-pole for an instant (one or two frames at most). This is all Gondry needs to develop a fake sequence plan. The director in fact mounts the rest of the scene with another shot in which Joel is running in the opposite direction (that is, towards the car), and then captures this second shot in a mirror, thus making Joel seem to be running always in the same direction and yet returning to the same place, whereas the scene has actually been filmed by interrupting the shot in the middle and editing it with one of the two mirrored parts. It would have been much easier to achieve with digital technology, but the technical expedient adopted is directly connected with Gondry's aesthetic idea of the artisanal in cinema, which should always be linked with a reflection on the technical characteristics of medium and language: "In an era when every other Hollywood blockbuster is awash with digital effects, Gondry's old-school effects (*Eternal Sunshine of the Spotless Mind*) have a peculiar visual immediacy that makes them immediately distinguishable."[10]

It could therefore be argued that, in fact, *Eternal Sunshine of the Spotless Mind* is a film based more on the third typology, that of the mixed dream, than on the second, which is that of the purely digital dream. In *The Green Hornet*, instead, the implementation of the digital is more insistent (even though there is no lack of gimmicks tied to the film camera), and the green screen is used. Nevertheless, Gondry confirms the distance that separates him from certain standards by always placing the emphasis on the contemplation of the cinematographic image. In one of the first scenes where Kato and Britt meet, the latter is under attack by a dangerous band of street thugs. Kato, who sees everything from his car, rushes to his aid, engaging in a fight with the gang. The scene is rendered by means of an innovative technique:

- Kato sizes up the members of the gang and their weapons. This is shown first with a camera movement towards Kato's eye, and then with a reverse shot in subjective camera view in which the criminals' arms are digitally highlighted in red.
- Kato leaps onto the hood of the vehicle in order to get a running start and attack his rivals. However, the hood would not be long enough for an adequate run-up, and so it is telescopically multiplied, allowing our hero sufficient length to gather speed. How this is possible in diegetic terms remains a mystery, yet it is clear that it should be interpreted as Kato's ability to bend space and time in subjective terms, thus making oneirism prevail over realism, thanks to his being skilled in martial arts, but also because of his goodness of heart.
- Kato attacks the band. A long shot presents the scene in its entirety. Kato's movements are in slow motion, those of the gang at normal speed, all in the same frame. The result in terms of perception is that of a character able to control space and time energetically, with total control over the narration, which is projected extra-diegetically onto a metalinguistic register.

The introduction in the same field of two different shooting speeds is truly symptomatic of a continuous stretching towards cinematic experimentation, even when Gondry employs what today are considered the more "traditional" digital special effects. For the director, the film is not only a place where stories of love and friendship unfold, but also a canvas where an array of languages are enunciated in constant tension, always in search of the new.

This is evident, in fact, from his very first film. In *Human Nature*, indeed, Nathan's narration from his white room becomes gradually jumpier, as the protagonist realizes that he is entrapped in this limbo. When he decides to go, he tries to move out of the frame—in other words, to leave the room—but the moment he exits from one side he reappears on the other.[11] He is not locked in by key, but is locked forever inside the shot. Gondry always executes a fundamental metafilmic meditation: the film declares itself to be such, it reflects its limits, explores its potentiality, and proudly declares itself to be first and foremost an expressive form.

THE DIALOGUE OF DREAMS

The relationship between cinema and dreams is as long as the history of cinema itself. In films like *Waiting for the Midnight Express* (*Aspettando il diretto di mezzanotte*, Anonymous, 1911) or even *Cabiria* (Giovanni Pastrone, 1914), dream plays a fundamental role, presented in a manner which is formally dissimilar to the current cinematographic dream. In this type of dream, dreamer and that which is dreamt—the two axes which reify dream—are, in fact, collocated in the same shot, which is known as the autarkic shot. This, in fact, makes the early conception of dream not all that different from Michel Gondry's. In his films, too, the representational ontology is the result of interpolation between dream and dreamer in a shared scopic space. From a hermeneutic point of view, neither Pastrone nor Gondry offers an interpretative strategy suggested by the montage.

In a very famous oneiric scene in *The Conversation* (Francis Ford Coppola, 1974), the story of a spy who gets sucked into a vortex of paranoia in which he believes he is being spied upon, it is the editing and a series of scenic effects that convey the separation between reality and fantasy in the dream or nightmare. The film contains two particularly significant oneiric sequences:

> The first is that of Harry's dream, a sequence lasting a full four minutes which constitutes a text book case. The moment in which Harry falls asleep, and passes from a physical to a mental space, is introduced by extensive camera movement, zooming out. Immediately after that, we are in the dream allospace. It is easy for the spectator to tell dream and reality apart, both because editing alternates the dream with frames of Harry tossing and turning in his sleep, and because the formal configurations that regulate the dream space are very different from those which regulate the rest of the film. From the beginning we are exposed to close-ups disturbed by a kind of *shaky cam*, and by surreal, unnerving sounds. The rift from the point of view of image and sound cannot but suggest the passage to the allospace. The places in the dream are then surreally isolated, and the whole scene is pervaded by smoke which, together with pallid photography, is a typical way of suggesting a dream without intervening in the filming procedures. It is, in fact, a visual metaphor: smoke in the scene suggests the fuzzy mind of the person who is dreaming. The digressive tendency of the protagonist in this

sequence is also indicative: he tries to explain himself to the woman with whom he is obsessed, recalling important phases in his life.[12]

The way in which the oneiric dimension is constructed here is therefore substantially different from Gondry's cinema. Here dream and reality, even though they may be associated by the director, remain formally distinct on the filmic plane, whereas in Gondry's work they are perfectly fused.

In fact, and in conclusion, Gondry's work is simultaneously a form of poetics of image, a political battle, an aesthetic manifestation, and a metafilmic reflection that overarches a precise declaration of love towards the cinema, as the favorite vehicle of dreams. As Colin McGinn says:

> There are a number of respects in which the experience of dreams matches the film experience, which I will merely list: sensory-affective fusion, in which the image is shaped to fit the emotion; spatial and temporal discontinuity, as the viewer or dreamer is taken abruptly from one place and time to another, without traveling continuously through the intermediate space and time; montage, whereby thematic unity is maintained without obedience to the laws of nature; the intricate mixing of reality and fantasy in both dream and film; the way people's minds are put into the foreground in both types of experience; the prevalence of pronounced or extreme bodily movement in dreams and films, often movement not found in ordinary life; the way dreams and films engage with some of our baser fears and desires; the high degree of mental absorption characteristic of dreaming and film viewing. The general point here is that the mental apparatus that is operative during dreams is also operative during the film experience: the apparatus of dreaming—its vocabulary and modus operandi—is brought to bear in the interpretation of the movie image. It is *as if* we were dreaming.[13]

All these considerations, which for McGinn are an implicit given of cinematographic experience, become for Michel Gondry an explicit fact. His personal dreams dialogue with his cinematographic alter egos and these, in turn, dialogue with us. We watch the films, and it is, to cite McGinn above, "as if we were dreaming."

NOTES

1. Giuseppe Civitarese, *The Necessary Dream: New Theories and Techniques of Interpretation in Psychoanalysis* (London: Karnac, 2014), 105.
2. Alfredo Giuliani, writer and poet belonging to the Italian neo-avant-garde collective known as Group 63, writes of Montale that "Having transcended the crepuscular

confession and wary sentimental expressionism deriving from Pascoli, here is the object-metaphor which becomes the expressive sign that words attempt to draw, here the syntax suggested by the logical rhythm which works as a joining-point between objects and words, thus seeking the movement of breathing. [. . .] In this way the *identity* of objects, *evocation and gnomic discourse* are intertwined in memory until they compose the ghost's momentary truths. In the end it is they, the objects, which speak for him" (Alfredo Giuliani, "Recensione a Eugenio Montale: La bufera e altro" (*Il verri*, I, 1956), 93, my translation). These considerations are applicable to Gondry's cinema in a transliterated way, in an environment where poetic word becomes filmic image.

3. A 2009 anthology film with episodes directed by Leos Carax and Bong Joon-ho (recalling Martin Scorsese, Francis Ford Coppola, and Woody Allen's 1989 experiment in *New York Stories*).
4. Michel Gondry himself declares that he at times experiences *waking dreams*, as recorded in Dylan Tuccillo, Jared Zeizel, and Thomas Peisel, *A Field Guide to Lucid Dreaming: Mastering the Art of Oneironautics* (New York: Workman, 2013), 11.
5. Little White Lies, *What I Love About Movies* (London: Faber and Faber, 2014), 82.
6. Michel Foucault, *Discipline and Punish: The Birth of the Prison* (New York: Vintage Books, 1977), 27.
7. Philip King, Kelly Bulkeley, and Bernard Walt, *Dreaming in the Classroom: Practices, Methods, and Resources in Dream Education* (Albany: SUNY, 2011), 123.
8. Julie A. Tumock, *Plastic Reality: Special Effects, Technology, and the Emergence of 1970s Blockbuster Aesthetics* (New York: Columbia University Press, 2015), 271.
9. See also Steven Rawle, "Reconstructing Memory: Visual Virtuality in *Eternal Sunshine of the Spotless Mind*," in *Millennial Cinema: Memory in Global Film*, eds Amresh Sinha and Terence McSweeney (London and New York: Wallflower, 2011), pp. 17–36.
10. Curt Cloninger, *Hot-Wiring Your Creative Process: Strategies for Print and New Media Designers* (Berkeley: New Riders, 2007), 146.
11. Something similar happens to Neo (Keanu Reeves) in *The Matrix Revolutions* (Andy and Larry Wachowski, 2003), when he is in the subway—a topic place in the saga—and tries to get out by running from one side of it toward the tunnel, only to find himself on the other side again.
12. Bruno Surace, "Cinema, Allospaces, and the Unfilmable," in *New Approaches to Cinematic Space*, eds Filipa Rosário and Iván Villarmea Álvarez (New York and London: Routledge, 2019), 216–27.
13. Colin McGinn, "A Multimodal Theory of Film Experience," in *Thinking Reality and Time Through Film*, eds Christine Reeh and José Manuel Martins (Newcastle upon Tyne: Cambridge Scholars, 2017), 153.

CHAPTER 3

I Am Collecting Beautiful Objects: Michel Gondry's Taxidermy of Emotions

Jenny Pyke

One of the very first uses of photography in mid-nineteenth-century England was post-mortem memorialization, especially photographs of dead children and infants. Infants were often photographed as if sleeping peacefully in a cradle, or were held by living siblings in a family tableau. Children and adults might even be propped up as if alive for a final (and in most cases, first) photograph. The practice was soon popular in North America, as well.

Many photographers seemed to find the practice distasteful, but they still provided the service because of the strong demand for it: Audrey Linkman notes that many British photographers, especially, chose to be unnamed on such work, resulting in an archive of unattributed photographs obviously taken by professionals, as well as fewer technical articles attributed to British photographers.[1] George Bradforde, one such disapproving photographer, wrote, however: "If the departed were truly beloved, nothing . . . can ever efface the dear features from the mind's eye: it needs not a cold, crude photograph representing the last dreary stage of humanity to recall those lineaments."[2] But he misses the point. Mothers held these physical representations, these objects, and cradled them, rocked them. Sang to them.[3] The printed photograph is a visual form of memory, but it is also tangible materiality in the face of the unreachable. The child cannot be *touched*, but the child is *felt*.

I offer this affectual history as a framework for mapping a relationship between the sensation of touch, the "feeling" of emotion, and the capacity of visual mediums to create embodied sensation. Drawing on such a framework, this chapter seeks to offer a new affectual reading of Michel Gondry's world of objects in his films and videos, by viewing the objects through the lens of contemporary art taxidermy. In the case of the grieving mothers above, the photograph, as material object, becomes a form of taxidermy, not because it tries to replicate the body of a child, which the photographers saw as morbid, but because it serves as a material body for the emotions themselves.

In his films and music videos, Gondry calls attention to objects that are set apart and announced as made. I suggest that this enacts a taxidermy of emotions, largely through sensory association and what Laura U. Marks defines as "haptic visuality," the embodied sensation that one knows how something feels by looking at it.[4] The handmade objects in Gondry's work act as discrete sites of feeling that seem to be touchable even in the two-dimensional medium of film. This phenomenon is the same haptic visuality held by the viewer of a taxidermized animal that is in a glass case, on a display pedestal, or in a museum diorama. The viewer "recognizes" what an "animal" is and what it would feel like, and the animal object is perceived as touch*able*, even if the actual touch would betray the associations. In Gondry's films and videos, the viewer recognizes accessible basic materials and beginner DIY modes of making—yarn, glue, tape, cardboard, and felt—and engages with a sense history of the materials themselves, and by extension, with the intense and unregulated feelings of childhood.

Formulating these art objects as a form of rogue taxidermy and considering recent thinking on contemporary taxidermy art offer a new understanding of how Gondry's objects carry the emotional narratives of his films and videos. Gondry has said that he is criticized as being good at visual aspects of his medium but not strong with narrative or story.[5] I argue that these objects hold the emotional narratives. Gondry's objects become a narrative form themselves, through sensation.

The taxidermy most useful for developing such a reading of Gondry's work is the contemporary art movement that includes "rogue taxidermy" and roadkill "repair art." Repair art is a form of hybridization that, by its very nature, presents tensions. Animals found dead by the side of the road, casualties of human expansion and modern life, are repositioned in domestic scenes for juxtaposition between the animal and the human, as in Kimberly Witham's photograph, "Luxe" (2007). Others are lovingly and literally repaired with steampunk mechanics, as in Lisa Black's piece, "Fixed Fawn" (2007). There is a tenderness to these pieces, and a strangeness, and the surprising instinct to touch something that has already been dead, as if the hand can imagine its softness, as if it would feel warm and alive, repaired. To touch a taxidermized animal, however, betrays the promised sensation. It will feel hard, cold, artificial, strange. The visual understanding of the sensation, founded on memory and nostalgia, and even fantasy (of animals, pets, wildness), is what delivers the idea of the object as touch*able*. In other words, touch*able* can deliver feeling as much as, or even more than, "touched." In some branches of rogue taxidermy, animals are completely fabricated and made with no animal components at all. They are staged in dioramas or mounted to replicate taxidermy, becoming a commentary on the history of taxidermy and animals, a punk critique of the pretense and absurdity of taxidermy. All of these animal objects, however, are also affective. They hold associations and evoke sensation on the part of observers. Although standing and looking at a dead animal could easily be conceived as a form of distanced spectatorship, the sense associations construct this form of vision as a form of participation and engagement. In these respects, taxidermy is in a very similar relationship to its viewers, as are Gondry's handmade objects to their audiences: a familiar object that exists in life and has intense sense associations but that is out of physical reach because of display parameters.

Focusing on Gondry's 2006 film *The Science of Sleep* (*La Science des rêves*), I argue that handmade objects carry the affectual narrative in a way that is felt rather than spoken, the objects existing in the lacunae within what is actually a familiar and recognizable thwarted love story set in a film that borrows from traditions of surrealism and magic realism. Although the main characters, Stéphane (Gael García Bernal) and Stéphanie (Charlotte Gainsbourg), are both presented as deep *feelers*, they are also presented as thwarted *speakers*. This disjuncture causes intense frustration for both, as well as for the audience. Psychologically, each finds it hard to believe that the other really loves them, which leads to the tragedy of romantic errors. However, this psychological obstacle is emblematized and made legible in the film as a linguistic puzzle: Stéphane, a Spanish speaker, is constantly trying to share the ideas in process in his head, but neither English nor French is his first language, so language is not readily available to him. Stéphane stumbles and uses phrases that sound simplistic and naive.[6] Stéphanie does not speak Spanish, but is comfortable in both French and English. However, Stéphanie's fluency does not help her say what she is feeling. She is self-conscious and cynical, often retreating into preternatural calm as a form of distance. In these ways, the film presents the many difficulties of *saying*. While these obstacles lead to frustration for characters and audience, the collisions also throw into relief how hard it can be to say what one feels.

Despite the suppression of communication, feelings—love, doubt, desire, terror, ambition, dread, anger, grief, jealousy, romance, and joy—scream and bang and float and fly and gallop throughout the film, in the form of handmade creations and inventions. Objects serve to challenge preconceived notions in the film and to introduce important concepts: for instance, special glasses that allow one to see differently. Objects also play a practical part in the plot to bridge the two characters. Stéphane and Stéphanie share special objects with each other and create objects together. The objects are catalysts for conversation.

But the objects also carry emotions and feelings, not because of what they represent concretely—not because they are a horse, a phone, clouds, a boat, a portable time machine—but because of how they are constructed. Like the post-mortem photographs of children, like a taxidermized arctic fox, with soft and luminous, lifelike fur that is now perfectly still for the human gaze, the film objects carry feelings because of a sense history associated with them. They are made of felt, fat yarn, crunchy cellophane, old buttons, a cassette player, an old metal box with switches and colored wires wrapped around it. The materials hold our sense of touch and childhood imagination, both: imagination made touchable.

We can understand the affectual function of these objects in the film if we draw connections to the way that taxidermy evokes sensation. Taxidermy's associations are also a personal history of affect and sensation: soft, fur, stuffed animals, pets, thinking one knows how an animal would feel if touched. The concrete animal object is a portal to abstraction, to feelings and ideas and fantasies: "nature," "wildness," "quiet," and even "animal." Handmade objects in Gondry's work combine familiar objects of daily life with the sensation of soft, childlike materials. The objects are doubly familiar (by name and in their materials) and yet also brought out of their normal mode and thereby noticeable in a new way: at once known and newly noticeable. This is related to arguments that the habitual inhibits perception, that objects in unnatural or uncustomary use are perceived again.[7]

THE SCIENCE OF SLEEP

Gondry has said that the main criticism of his work is that it is childlike, and that he is not good at narrative, as he explains in an interview with *The New York Times* in 2006:

> 'Other than being called childlike, the criticism that I most often receive is that I can't really tell a story. That while I have a strong sense of the visual, my narrative skills are weak.' He looked pained. 'I would like to think, instead, that my movies are more like real life. In a relationship, so much goes unsaid, but that doesn't mean the emotion is not felt. In my films, I want to show all the abstract ways that people can affect us when we are in love.[8]

This invocation of mimesis seems like a funny assertion for someone often associated with surrealism and even with excessive or precious whimsy. Gondry suggests here that people do not or cannot say everything to each other when they are in love, and that they feel much more than they say. Even more crucially, he argues that his films actively represent that chasm, and are more "like real life" for it. The absence of an easily accessed narrative is itself a narrative about relationships and love. I argue that not only does he actively represent that chasm, but also he fills it back in with an emotional narrative composed of affectual objects. Through them, Gondry makes visible the invisible spirits of affect: as cited above, "I want to show all the abstract ways that people can affect us when we are in love," he says. The objects are the narrative that cannot be held in language.

In other words, when Gondry says this about the effects of being in love in the interview with *The New York Times*, he is defending negative space: the arching, expansive lacunae that might to others be a missing story or narrative. It is important that he is not rejecting the desire for story as a way of defending his form; he is laying claim to the other story in relationships, the un-notated part of the map, where the sea monster would be.

In *The Science of Sleep*, the story of what is not said by Stéphane and Stéphanie is told in a visual narrative through handmade objects. These objects are referential "things" and also are not; they are objects liberated from functionality that still represent the original functional objects. The stuffed fabric telephone and cardboard glasses without lenses in the cave of beautiful objects are "a telephone" and "some glasses," but they do not pretend to have those uses. In this way, these objects hold sensation and feeling in ways similar to taxidermy. The taxidermized animal signifies animal but is also severed from that living subject. The stuffed animal is still and captive for our inspection, as we stand in front of it in its unnatural and uncustomary use and have time to think about how it makes us feel.

A. O. Scott described the simultaneous plot/no plot experience of *The Science of Sleep* this way:

> 'The Science of Sleep' . . . is so profoundly idiosyncratic, and so confident in its oddity, that any attempt to describe it is bound to be misleading. Plot summary, therefore, is both irrelevant and impossible. Which is not to say that the movie lacks a story, only that, like a dream, the narrative moves sideways as well as forward, revising and contradicting itself as it goes along. Mr. Gondry . . . makes a plausible case that a love story (which is what 'The Science of Sleep' is) cannot really be told any other way. Love is too bound up with memories, fantasies, projections and misperceptions to conform to a conventional, linear structure.[9]

It is crucial to acknowledge that this film is a love story. Stéphane meets Stéphanie, and the two fall in love, make things together, and claw their way through the impossible mire of other people's interpretation of their relationship and through the maze of their own fragile egos. Like the plot of a Shakespearean play or an episode of the television sitcom *Three's Company*, *The Science of Sleep* exploits confusion, complication, and misdirection. Paradoxically, what most often leads to misunderstanding is the way in which both characters are so certain that they already know what the other thinks and feels. Literary critic Rae Greiner has explained the paradoxical way in which omniscience works against expanded understanding, in terms of omniscient narrators but also characters.[10] Characters who think they are omniscient, who believe they already know their own and others' stories, never fully engage in wondering, or therefore in the process of imagination required for sympathetic encounter. Every character in *The Science of Sleep* is so certain of their reading of others that they do not open themselves to wonder or to ask. When Stéphane and Stéphanie finally reveal their hurt in an argument and decide to meet for an actual date, the audience watches Stéphane storm to Stéphanie's apartment instead, because he is so sure she stood him up. The film cuts to Stéphanie waiting at the café, an expressionless face of self-fulfilled prophetic defeat, staring ahead, smoking her cigarette, her own omniscience confirmed.

Their scene that follows this disaster will be their final scene of dialogue, face to face in Stéphanie's apartment, trying to say goodbye before Stéphane moves back to Mexico. They are exhausted by themselves and each other: caustic, angry, hurt, and stunned that words can be so powerful and so useless, both. And in that moment, when words have turned on them completely, Stéphane looks up and sees that Stéphanie finished a fabric boat they imagined and designed together. He had assumed she would not see it through.

The boat, an object, is their origin. Over it, they found each other in imagination. The boat carries them, first into openness and play, in the early scene, and then literally, away from the film that tries to hold them, by its nature, in a story. The fact that Stéphanie has finished it, and finished it by including his ideas, is a jarring counter-narrative to Stéphane's own childish narrative that no one will do what they promise or, by extension, love him. Here is material evidence that he was wrong. The finished boat, among other things, disrupts his petulant omniscience, so that he can imagine the possibility of other narratives.

And from this revelation that has as its catalyst an object, their narrative turns away from words completely to the affectual objects they made together. There are no more words. The objects carry them. Golden the Pony Boy, a stuffed horse still made of rough fabric and yarn, carries them to the waiting boat surrounded by "le mer." They hold on, to Golden and to each other, smiling and relaxed, escaping the bounds of narrative and language.

It would be easy to see the ending as avoiding resolution. But I will now step back to look closely at the objects doing this affectual work, that make what I read as an object-narrated ending possible: the 3-D glasses, the boat, the one-second time machine, the cave, and Golden the Pony Boy. The 3-D glasses and the time machine appear early in the film, and both of those objects disrupt and expand ideas about perception and feeling, setting the rules of play for audience and characters. The cave is dreamy metacontemplation—documenting the objects as made things and as holding significance for the characters and their relationship. The boat and horse are the objects through which the characters work and build together, through which they trust each other, and it is those synthesizing objects that carry them away together. The narrative turns to an affectual narrative, however, not because the objects are symbolic, and not in the way of a stylized Wes Anderson aesthetic vignette. The objects carry the emotional story, the abstraction of all the feelings and gaps in saying.

THE AFFECTUAL OBJECTS

The 3-D glasses

When Stéphane first meets Stéphanie and her best friend Zoe, they ask what he does. He explains that while he is currently a calendar machinist, the profession he would most like is inventor. To show them what he means, he pulls out an invention he happens to have with him: 3-D glasses. The 3-D glasses, in this way, introduce Stéphane to the two women, and introduce the way objects will figure in this film. The glasses, therefore, are his answer to being asked who he really is. Stéphane says with excitement that his invention makes it possible to see real life in 3-D. He is so enthusiastic that it might inspire excitement in the audience, until Stéphanie smiles, and says, "Isn't life already in 3-D?" Stéphane is flummoxed for a moment, then answers, "No. Well. Yeah. But . . . do you wanna see?" To demonstrate, he picks up a framed painting from the apartment.

With the glasses, the normal painting indeed looks 3-D, as we see through Zoe's eyes. The figures seem to jump away from the painted scene like the picture wheel seen through a child's old View-Master. The painting is transformed, the specific definition of "real life" is expanded and challenged, as of course a painting is *in* real life, even if the scene on the canvas is not "real life." In this example, the film is laying out its challenges for the audience and the characters within, and the "invention"—glasses cut out of cardboard and not altered or painted in any way—establishes that a visual medium (the painting) can seem touchable in a different way, and can hold more dimensions than it seems to. This is a map, a scholarly lesson for viewing film.

The invention of glasses that can make anything 3-D is magic realism, but the glasses are also doubly familiar. First, they are in the rectangular shape of the 3-D glasses handed out at movies. This is critical because this first object is something that in real life makes films three-dimensional. Second, however, the glasses are cut out of simple, thin cardboard, not painted or covered or decorated. They could be made easily with materials found at home. In this unconventional use, the simple materials are even more recognizable and perceptible. The glasses are a material placeholder for suddenly thinking about the ways in which people allow themselves to see the world around them, and all the fear and discovery that involves. The cardboard and childlike construction holds sense memory and is therefore nostalgic and emotional.

Although Stéphane and Stéphanie do not yet know each other, their exchange around this object—simple, childlike, a plea—poses complex questions without losing joy: "Isn't real life already in 3-D?" "No. Well. Yeah. But . . . do you wanna see?" It is a choice, the exchange suggests, to try to see and to feel in different ways, to see in ways you have not before.

The horse

Stéphane's next visit to Stéphanie introduces another object, this time hers. Stéphane stands at Stéphanie's menagerie of handmade animals and picks up a small horse. He (we learn the horse is a he) is made of gray fabric with a slight texture, a jute or muslin, and visible white stitches with thick thread. Small white buttons are the eyes, and more of the off-white string is a mane. The black stitches attaching the button eyes function like irises, but are somewhat blank, the uncanny expression of a doll that may or may not be thinking and feeling.

Stéphane asks, "What's his name?" as if it is a given that this is a loved pet, a treasured object that has subjecthood. Stéphanie pauses, and we learn later in the film that she is making up a name on the spot, and that she is naming the horse after Stéphane. In this moment, however, she says only, ". . . Gol. . .den the Pony Boy." She gives the pony a name that says it is a boy who is like a pony, gathering Stéphane into Golden and Golden into Stéphane simultaneously. Through the horse, they seem to fall a little more in love. "When I found him," Stéphanie says, "he was so sad . . . that I had to buy him . . . He's never going to leave me now." This last claim is more playful than possessive, but Stéphanie's eyes hold more emotion than the joke. Stéphane smiles as he tells Stéphanie that although she is the mother, she also needs to think of Golden's interests.

There is play in their words from the start, but as Stéphanie's eyes fill with tears, their words move away from the actual topics of conversation they might share. Each is saying more, about attachment, about love, about sadness, about mothers, but each also cannot say the real things behind their playful allegory. In this way, there is still a gap between them linguistically. But "between them" literally, physically, and affectively, is Golden the Pony Boy. They both touch the horse, look down at it, express feelings and thoughts through the horse. The horse-object (made for Gondry by artist Laura Faggioni), in its pathos and its imagined or perceived sadness, its story of sadness, gives permission for more sadness or melancholy to be laid up on it; the weathered and stitched horse seems to sanction and absorb their feelings. They do not need to be scared of speaking the words "leaving" and "afraid" and "mother" and "love" while they are touching Golden. And in its handmade softness, the horse allows the two of them to touch *through* it and to feel that they are holding on to each other. Ultimately, this will be Golden the Pony Boy's role in the film; he will carry them away together. They will need no words at the end of the film as he carries them, and this scene prepares the viewer to understand that.

From the teetering precipice of their intimacy over the horse, Stéphanie suddenly retreats to a more official tone, remembering that she invited Stéphane in so that she could check his injured hand. But this only brings more intimacy, because hands are the most intimate extensions of themselves to which they could retreat. As Eve Kosofsky Sedgwick writes, reaching out to touch is itself a space of encounter, even before or without the touch.[11] Both of them are makers and artists, and they notice each other's hands immediately. They show each other tricks with their hands, creating optical illusions that invoke the film's earlier question, raised by the 3-D glasses, regarding what it takes to allow oneself to see. In this moment, self-conscious and restrained Stéphanie decides to show Stéphane something she has made. This is the first time Stéphanie has shared something she has made, the first time we know that she also loves to make things. In this way, she reveals herself to Stéphane in a moment of magic, play, and intimacy made possible through objects.

The boat and its "scene"

Stéphanie stands up after touching Stéphane's hand and says, "Look. I made this boat in fabric. I have to put it in a small forest, as a set-up. The boat is looking for its mer, which is—it sounds like both mother [*mère*] and sea [*mer*] in French." She holds a strong but soft structure in her hands, like fabric papier-mâché, a simple, white, shallow boat about a foot long.

Stéphane says, "So the forest inside the boat? That's genius. That's a vegetable Noah's Arc!" "No," she explains. She is putting the boat in a forest looking for the sea (/its mother). Stéphane loves his misunderstanding, and convinces her. She nods: "You'll make the sea, okay?" And in this moment of synthesis, with a project together, they come back to their hands, holding each parallel to the other's to mimic how the movement of the boat and sea will work. They have already shared the knowledge that their hands can make and hold illusions; through games they have already tricked their brains into not knowing whose hand was whose. Now their hands and eyes and brains will work together. They rush to the faucet to imagine water together. Out flows blue shiny cellophane. Because they both see the same thing, the viewer sees it, as they exclaim simultaneously: "Cellophane!!"

These moments of shared vision perhaps hold the most magic realism of the film. This magic, like their shared names, demonstrates how alike they actually are, and how unlike other people. Rushing back into the living room, they pull cotton batting from boxes to form clouds. Stéphane yells, "Wait!"—and goes to the piano. He tries a chord, then another, then the right chord creates the synesthetic energy tension to suspend the cotton clouds in mid-air. They are joyous. The cotton and cellophane and plans for the boat and its forest scene are a narrative of falling in love, a feeling that would be reduced and distorted if put into words. Even the strange idiom for falling in love indicates the impossibility of giving it language, as the metaphor resorts to an unexpected and uncontrolled action to describe the state of feeling. This scene, running around the apartment talking about DIY materials for projects, is their love scene. In the believe/mistrust/believe/mistrust rhythm of the film, this is a moment of believing, in play, in magic, in feelings, and that the other likes them—that they are both lik*able*.

The cave

Even without knowing that Gondry created an entire film out of conversations with Noam Chomsky, entitled *Is the Man Who is Tall Happy?* (2013), it would be hard not to read the cave as an allusion to Plato's allegory. How do we move from thinking we are naming the real things—those forms that stand on their own outside our opinion and our experience of them—and move to naming the concepts, our understanding? Or as some scholars have said, perhaps the more accessible question is how do we move from thinking that we are naming something specific and stable to knowing that we can only really describe our understanding or experience (shared or individual) of it? The allegory of the cave is often summarized and taught as a question or "problem" of linguistics: "The problem arises if we try to give a linguistic account of understanding."[12]

But the cave in *The Science of Sleep* is also, crucially, a gallery. In this scene, Stéphane discusses the objects themselves *as* objects. He has the organizing power of the curator. "I am collecting beautiful objects," he says, in voiceover narration.

> A pair of shoes, some glasses, telephone, typewriter. They are made from wood and felt, with apparent stitches. Their delicate and finished appearance is friendly. They are quiet. Stéphanie made them and I will expose them in an exhibition . . . There's this amazing blanket. It's thick red felt with big white stitches. Wild animals are running on it.

The stillness and comfort of this soft felt blanket holds life. Animals just in outline form, in their shapes, are brought to life. As Stéphanie sews, the camera comes closer to show that her sewing machine is a strange soft construction that allows the fingers to press more like typing. The entire affectual thematics of the film are brought together for observation in this scene. The voiceover narration is a like short lecture about how to understand the film from this point forward. This scene stops the interpersonal chaos to frame Stéphane and Stéphanie being brought together through objects. They speak to each other with easy affection in this scene, a loving couple. Stéphane explains the materials, and explains that the construction is all visible. The making is not hidden here. These are not special effects. These objects are available to you to understand and feel. These objects are not trying to trick you.

This scene also dramatizes the way that the two connect at this point still only through the objects. Stéphane reaches his hand out to try to touch Stéphanie, to be comforted by her physically. But he cannot reach her. She is high in a bed that replicates her real loft bed in her apartment. They are just barely able to touch fingers. But all around them are the soft objects she makes for him to share with the world. From this dream map, the film goes to the next scene of realism: Stéphane shows up at Stéphanie's apartment to make the boat they planned in the earlier love scene. She is happy to see him, and gives him a friendly kiss. The previous cave scene seems like a tangential dream, but actually was preparation for this scene. The cave monologue provides the audience with a way to understand both the significance of the objects and what is about to happen next.

The one-second time machine

When Stéphane comes over to work on the boat scene with Stéphanie, he brings from his mother's old teaching supplies a box of shiny, multicolored candy wrappers to use as the sea, and buried in the crunchy wrappers, a gift. Already acting as the water they are intended to represent, the wrappers spill out of the box as Stéphanie digs to find the object within, lifting out an old metal machine that looks like an invention a child might make in a workshop over a weekend. The creation combines two chunky retro objects: the steel contraption, and a large flash-cube attachment that would be pressed down into the top of a camera, making a satisfying noise every time it clicked into place—a smooth row of square bulbs that would leave no ambiguity about whether the flash is on, or about what is bringing light to the image. "What is it?" Stéphanie asks. "It's a one-second time machine." "One second? What are you going to do with one second?" "Well," Stéphane says, "It just adds up. Life is too precious." This exchange almost precisely echoes their earlier exchange about the 3-D glasses and expanding one's notion of what it means to see. Here, Stéphane—and by extension, the film—poses a similar question about time. Time is made up of seconds, and therefore every one of those seconds holds significance. Rather than a precious reminder to treasure every moment, however, Stéphane's time machine dissects time into a unit most people do not even think of as making space for a spoken sentence. The time machine does not allow for full engagement in a previous or future time. It does allow a sort of obsessive attention to thinking about what one did a second ago. This time machine avoids quantum physics' questions about paradoxes or changing history, because one cannot actually do anything differently when traveling through Stéphane's machine. One can only replay the previous second. Or one can experience the next second that is about to occur in the future, and then immediately experience it again, as it plays out in real time. In this way, in fact, the time machine is really more like a recording. The characters are viewing themselves, similarly to the scenes in the dream television studio. But this is an embodied experience: a recording that carries embodied, tactile sensation.

Like the 3-D glasses to see real life, then, the one-second time machine is less about questions of time travel and more about what it means to get to feel something again, or to notice it in a new way because it is out of place, in an unconventional or unnatural position. The machine would enable one to look at what exists in the edges and tiny spaces between words and "important" dialogue and events: for example, the feeling that is propelling what the viewer sees as the noticeable narratives and arcs.

Susan Stewart writes that time does change when one is in play with objects, in relation to their relative size and to their mechanics.[13] Toys, as non-literal representations of things, distort our sense of our place in relation to those things: specifically, our sense of our own relative size and our sense of how time passes. She compares the inanimate toy, the mechanical, the miniature, and the gigantic, and says precisely that playing with such objects initiates reverie, the powerful state of wakeful dreaming. We sever our socially regulated relationship to time.

This refiguring of time is specifically the function that the one-second time machine performs. It is a toylike object, a sensual object full of things to click, press, and turn. As the two focus on it together, play with it, they change their understanding of time.[14] And extrapolating, this relationship of *referential object* to *reverie* describes the affective catalyst function that all of the objects perform. This formulation also directly parallels how taxidermic objects hold an affectual experience for viewers.

TAXIDERMY AND GONDRY'S OBJECTS

As part of taxidermy's biggest revival since the nineteenth century, decorative collecting—and the skill of taxidermy itself—are now the territory of fashionable counter-cultures. Director Wes Anderson frequents Deyrolle, the combination natural history library and store in Paris. Beautifully laid-out shops in New York (The Evolution Store and Brooklyn Taxidermy) and London (including the new Still Life taxidermy art café and store) look more like museum gift shops than hunter's dens. The Evolution Store (Greenwich Village) allows shoppers to browse for a mounted chipmunk, rat, or peacock, with categories like "real skulls" right next to "home accessories," and as part of this resurgence, Juicy Couture stores began to decorate with mounts and antlers (significantly, with real animal taxidermy rather than simulated art pieces). A trend of taxidermy reality television shows like *Immortalized* (2013) and *American Stuffers* (2011) became part of the pervasive maker–reality-show genre, including sexy goth artisans and a small company specializing in pet memorial taxidermy, respectively. The self-described "equity punks," Brew Dogs, in Scotland created a limited-edition beer bottled in roadkill squirrels for £700 a bottle, and the limited number sold out immediately. They called this brew "The End of History." In Brooklyn, vegetarians are signing up for classes to learn how to stuff birds and squirrels and other small animals.[15] Taxidermy has moved out of the territory of the hunting trophy.

As part of this movement, rogue taxidermy creates taxidermy animals that are set in diorama scenes or mounted, but are made of no animal materials. Many of the pieces are humorous, purposely messy or like the furry abominable snow monster from an old children's Claymation special. The pieces are irreverent and deconstruct or challenge ideas of taxidermy as an esteemed tradition. And those that look more realistic perhaps pose a question of whether real dead animal bodies are needed at all for the art. Rogue taxidermy is like seeing charming toy stuffed animals made stiff and still, and placed in a "realistic" animal setting, that realistic setting only making them seem strange.

These contested borders of taxidermy provide a way of understanding the intense reaction to Gondry's Grammy-winning music video for Björk's song "Human Behavior" (1993). The "Human Behavior" video was the first popular introduction to Gondry's world of made animals and serves as a site for examining ideas he takes to film.[16] The animals and insects in the video are at an important conceptual intersection for my theoretical comparison: stuffed animals as comforting toys, "stuffed" animals as taxidermy, and a more expansive and inclusive understanding of Gondry's DIY objects.

In Gondry's video for "Human Behavior," a gigantic stuffed teddy bear moves slowly through a forest scene, and an oversized mechanical insect flies a little askew, as if from puppet strings. A cute fake hedgehog scuttles through brush. The creatures interact with cars, with a hunter, and with Björk, who is a kind of philosopher-Goldilocks, sitting at a table singing and eating porridge as the bear takes care of business outside the cottage. The house she sits in is a tableau of the domestic: table, chair, a light hanging from the ceiling. It is also, however, completely open to the wildness of the nighttime forest and shakes like a play fort. It seems to be her house, but uncertainty is the source of the uncanny tension and energy of the video and song. Is she supposed to be in this house? Is she the only human here? What are houses? Whose way of life makes sense? Is she in danger from the toy animals of the video? Or in comfort?

Like the touchable objects in *The Science of Sleep*, the animals are familiar and seem touchable, the soft stuffed animals from the comfort of childhood. But they are uncanny, the familiar made unfamiliar. They are stuffed animals in what is paradoxically an unnatural and unconventional setting in nature. Watching the ways in which the animals seem like animals, but also not, allows viewers to perceive them and study them and think about how they make us feel, which amplifies Björk's lyrics ("there is no logic to human behavior"). Our reaction to these creatures is based on a synthesis of our associations with animals, or with our association of the concept of "animal," alive and in their "natural" habitat, and our associations and sense memory of the materials: soft synthetic fur and buttons, safe to hold and pet and hug. And this is where they become so clearly not only "teddy bears" and "insects," but Gondry objects: their construction is apparent, their materials are recognizable; they look *made*. As human life and the too-bright headlights of cars come close to threatening the stuffed animals and insects in the video, all the questions taken up by both roadkill "repair art" taxidermy and rogue taxidermy are invoked, and the video plays directly with the same set of questions and sensations and associations. The "Human Behavior" video is a lush (and plush) sense experience, but it is also eerie and jarring enough to inspire a complex embodied reaction from viewers, watching creature objects that carry our own embodied stories of childhood (the materials) and adulthood (houses, cars, the violence of our fetishized commodities).

The contemporary taxidermy-art photograph "Luxe," by Kimberly Witham, evokes the same tensions as the Björk video, with actual taxidermy. Like Gondry, Witham layers art forms to create her pieces. The finished work is a photograph, but Witham also creates the taxidermy within the photographs. In "Luxe," a stag sits on a luxurious canopy bed as if alive, looking at the camera. A hunter's arm in camouflage jacket reaches out from behind the canopy to hold the stag's antlers up, demonstrating that the animal is dead. Once this is noticed, the subtle red on the animal's back legs becomes more apparent, as injury. This is the same discomfiting relationship of forest animal to domestic scene that creates the uncanny tension in the "Human Behavior" video. The juxtaposition is startling and draws attention to the wild animal as out of place in the world because we humans have taken over, and to the domestic scenes themselves as absurd and theatrical in their aspirational perfection and in their complete separation from the wild. But these photographs are powerful primarily because of the sense associations around the animals: the deer, silent, staring, soft fur, graceful limbs. All of this feels almost obvious, our modern collision with our fantasies about nature. However, from this example, which feels legible to us, we can see that the same relationships of memory, abstraction, sense association, and emotional objects are transposed to Gondry's affectual objects throughout his work.

CONCLUSION

The word taxidermy means arrangement of skin. In the most traditional or formal rule of taxidermy, it is the skin that makes a piece taxidermy. Everything else can be fabricated. It is also the skin that Gondry is so conscious of in his affectual objects: materials that are familiar to *our skin*. A taxidermy of affect is held in the craft-room skin of felt or velvet or cardboard; emotions are cradled, studied, held close. And, of course, it is the skin of film that mediates between viewer and the explorations that Gondry imagines and invents.

In *The Science of Sleep*, in the cave, Stéphane says, "I am collecting beautiful objects," and talks about how each object feels, what it is made of, how Stéphanie makes them. Michel Gondry, as well, has said in interviews that he makes and collects objects that remind him of an ex-girlfriend, a sad memory. This is both the power of objects and the power of curating. Gondry curates a museum of our own feelings and associations as objects speak in the spaces around the humans who are struggling. As those characters bump up against the limits of words, against their own self-doubt, against the impossibility of expressing the fear and intensity of love, Gondry's affectual objects become anchors for the emotions floating aimlessly in the rooms. In their materials and in the obvious, democratic nature of their construction, they push out with the sensation of touch. They are sites of feeling, in both meanings of the word.

Comparing Gondry's emotional objects to the sensation of taxidermy allows for a new understanding of his different kinds of artistic production: an archive often made coherent by words like "childlike." It is a reading that rejects a critique of his work as lacking narrative, but without collapsing into offering an alternative traditional narrative. It offers a new lens through which to understand the emotion and panic of the collapsing walls of houses around the characters of *Eternal Sunshine of the Spotless Mind*, the material culture of VHS tapes that can be held in the hand in *Be Kind Rewind* (as well as those reconstructed films themselves as a form of taxidermy). It brings a new way of understanding *Microbe & Gasoline* (*Microbe et Gasoil*, 2015) when the young characters make the objects themselves in their own idea of what home should feel like, and a new way of thinking about the particular way that a crafted flower activates feelings of loss and sadness, beyond words, in *Mood Indigo* (*L'Écume des jours*, 2015).

Touch is a form of intimacy, risk, and connection, even when stimulated by haptic visuality. Sedgwick suggests that "even more immediately than other perceptual systems [. . .] the sense of touch makes nonsense out of any dualistic understanding of agency and passivity; to touch is always already to reach out."[17] These touchable gestural objects that promise recognizable sensation—taxidermized, lifelike animals and Gondry's soft, childlike representations of daily life—collapse distinctions between public and private, rational and emotional, child self and adult self.

In desperately trying to describe his love for Stéphanie, Stéphane says to his friend, "I love her because she makes things, with her hands. It's as if her synapses were married directly to her fingers. Like this . . . in this way," and he holds his hands in front of him, moving his fingers slowly, studying them with amazement. What he describes is not Stéphanie's beauty or even the art that she creates, but the part of her that touches and reaches out. Hands get hurt and are bandaged and healed. Hands invent glasses to create a clearer vision of the world. Hands type screenplays that are themselves about making rather than saying. And hands build you a soft boat that will carry you away in water made of cellophane, away from the chaos of other people's—or even your own—faulty narratives.

NOTES

1. Audrey Linkman, "Taken from Life: Post-Mortem Portraiture in Britain, 1860–1910," *History of Photography*, 30, no. 4 (2006): 309–47. For a detailed discussion of post-mortem portraiture and photography, see also Audrey Linkman, *Photography and Death* (London: Reaktion, 2011).
2. Qtd in Nicola Bown, "Empty Hands," *Australasian Journal of Victorian Studies*, 14, no. 2 (2009): 8–24.
3. For more on this phenomenon, see Nicola Bown's article, above. For an explication of Victorians' very early (almost immediate) sophisticated interventions into the truth claims and uses of photography, see Jennifer Tucker, *Nature Exposed: Photography as Eyewitness in Victorian Science* (Baltimore: Johns Hopkins University Press, 2013).
4. Laura Marks presents her foundational theory of haptic visuality as she formulates the ways "a number of works of intercultural cinema use haptic images to engage the viewer tactilely and to define a kind of knowledge based in touch" in her argument regarding sensory forms of cultural knowledge in this body of films (*The Skin of the Film*, 22). I rely on Marks's formulation, but take haptic visuality away from film to the visual culture of taxidermy in order to extricate and examine the objects separate from the film before returning them to the film. On the subject of touch, specifically, Jennifer Barker's important book *The Tactile Eye: Touch and the Cinematic Experience* maps a theoretical understanding of the feeling of physical connection between viewer and film, discussing, for example, the way eye contact *is* contact and perception is connection. In this essay, I focus on Gondry's objects, which I argue are set out to be contemplated as already tactile objects, so I am focusing on that aspect of haptic visuality around handmade objects that one *could* theoretically touch: what I refer to as the sensation of the touch*able*. Laura U. Marks and Dana Polan, *The Skin of the Film: Intercultural Cinema, Embodiment, and the Senses* (Durham, NC: Duke University Press, 1999). Jennifer Barker, *The Tactile Eye: Touch and the Cinematic Experience* (Berkeley: University of California Press, 2009).
5. Lynn Hirschberg, "Le Romantique," *The New York Times* (September 17, 2006). Available at <https://www.nytimes.com/2006/09/17/magazine/le-romantique.html> (last accessed February 26, 2020).

6. Many reviews called *The Science of Sleep* autobiographical and compared Stéphane to Gondry, while Gondry has described his own experience as an artist who did not understand the language around him at the beginning of his career. He says, in the same 2006 *New York Times* interview, "When I first moved to America, in 1997 . . . I understood one word out of 10. So I would recreate whatever was said based on those few words . . . It was even worse with music. When I first started making videos, I didn't understand the English lyrics. So I looked at the rhythms, and I replicated an abstraction, which made my videos closer to what the musicians usually meant in the beginning. I could never be exact in my work, and that was a good thing." Without the distraction of thinking words *could* be reliable signifiers, he suggests, he was led to feeling and meaning in ways that were perhaps even more accurate.
7. Bill Brown brings this idea from William James and Theodor Adorno (Bill Brown, *A Sense of Things: The Object Matter of American Literature* (Chicago: Chicago University Press, 2003)) and Clare Pettit brings Brown's formulation to her excellent reading of object culture and the Charles Dickens museum (Clare Pettit, "On Stuff," *Interdisciplinary Studies in the Long Nineteenth Century*, 6 (2008). Available at <http://doi.org/10.16995/ntn.474> (last accessed February 26, 2020)).
8. Hirschberg, "Le Romantique."
9. A. O. Scott, "A Parisian Love Story in Forward, and Sideways, Motion," *The New York Times* (September 22, 2006). Available at <https://www.nytimes.com/2006/09/22/movies/22slee.html> (last accessed February 26, 2020).
10. Rae Greiner, *Sympathetic Realism in Nineteenth-Century British Fiction* (Baltimore: Johns Hopkins University Press, 2013).
11. Eve Kosofsky Sedgwick, *Touching Feeling: Affect, Pedagogy, Performativity* (Durham, NC: Duke University Press, 2003).
12. S. Marc Cohen, Theory of Forms, February 28, 2015. Available at <https://faculty.washington.edu/smcohen/320/thforms.htm> (last accessed February 26, 2020). While there are, of course, many more components in any understanding of the allegory and the subsequent problem as it is formulated, being aware of this first line of dissemination for popular understanding of the theory is helpful in thinking about how a popular film might play with the idea.
13. Susan Stewart, *On Longing: Narratives of the Miniature, the Gigantic, the Souvenir, the Collection* (Baltimore: Johns Hopkins University Press, 1984).
14. Stewart's analysis of how play with "toys" changes the person's awareness of their own body is directly relevant to an understanding of Stéphane's gigantic hands. In dreams about work, Stéphane's hands are so big that they do not function. Some reviewers have found this scene cartoonish, less subtle or effective as magic realism. But that is the work of the gigantic: although the miniature makes the body gigantic, the gigantic transforms the body into miniature, especially pointing to the body's suddenly perceived "toylike" and "insignificant" aspects (Stewart, *On Longing*, 70, 71). His hands are all that they want from him at work, but his hands are not the inventor's or artist's hands he wants them to be.
15. Melissa Milgrom, *Still Life: Adventures in Taxidermy* (Boston: Mariner Books, 2011). Milgrom writes that the new generation of vegan taxidermists learn the craft with the aim of becoming less disconnected from the earth, nature, environment, world.
16. Although Gondry's film *Human Nature* (2001) explores the borders between humans and other animals, the film is different enough that I will not address it in the space of this article, which is specifically discussing objects and visual culture.
17. Sedgwick, *Touching Feeling*.

CHAPTER 4

The Cost of Whimsy in *Mood Indigo* and *The Grand Budapest Hotel*

Mica Hilson

Wes Anderson and Michel Gondry are both critically acclaimed directors whose work has frequently been described as "whimsical" and "twee."[1] Yet Anderson's *The Grand Budapest Hotel* and Gondry's *Mood Indigo* (*L'Écume des jours*), which were both released in the United States in 2014, were received very differently by American film critics. Anderson's *The Grand Budapest Hotel* was feted as one of the best films of the year, with many critics noting approvingly how its "twee" elements were balanced with a consideration of more "serious" themes. This perhaps accounts for the fact that *The Grand Budapest Hotel* was the first of Anderson's films to receive an Academy Award nomination for Best Picture, one of nine total nominations it received at that year's Oscars. By contrast, Gondry's *Mood Indigo* was harshly criticized as a film that, in the words of A. A. Dowd, "suffers from whimsy overload."[2]

Drawing from the methods of so-called New Formalists such as Sianne Ngai, I use these two films to critically interrogate what we mean when we use the affective terms "whimsical" and "twee."[3] Although it is understandable that Anderson and Gondry's films are grouped together under these catch-all terms—in part, by marketers who are well aware of how the words "whimsical" and "quirky" can attract a certain set of filmgoers—the nebulous usage of these words can blind viewers to how Gondry's aesthetics and politics radically differ from Anderson's. Through a close analysis of the two films, I argue that *Mood Indigo* self-critically uses whimsy to highlight themes of economics and income inequality, topics that *The Grand Budapest Hotel* insistently disavows through its twee aesthetic.

WHIMSICAL VERSUS TWEE

Writers frequently use "whimsical" in relation to Wes Anderson's oeuvre.[4] Yet is "whimsical" really the right term for Anderson's aesthetic? The answer perhaps depends on which dictionary is consulted. The *Cambridge Dictionary* defines it as "unusual and strange in a way that might be funny or annoying."[5] Merriam-Webster, on the other hand, defines the word as "resulting from or characterized by whim or caprice . . . subject to erratic behavior or unpredictable change."[6] It is easy to see how Anderson's aesthetic might fit the first definition: his films are full of carefully curated quaint objects, and signature stylistic choices, including his centered, symmetrical framing and use of Futura font, indeed appear "unusual and strange in a way that might be funny or annoying."

However, if we follow Merriam-Webster's lead and define the whimsical primarily in terms of "whim or caprice," then it seems incorrect to characterize Anderson as a whimsical filmmaker. The word "whim" implies some degree of spontaneity and improvisation, two words that one would never use to describe Anderson's directorial technique. This is the director who spent tens of thousands of dollars in preproduction, making an animated version of *The Grand Budapest Hotel*, choreographing every shot before the actors ever arrived.[7] However, it must be noted that there are two ways to define *whims*: as speculations and as demands. Anderson's on-screen world is certainly one where his directorial whims and fetishes are indulged, which is perhaps one of the key reasons that they are described as "twee."

As Marc Spitz, who wrote the book on *Twee*, notes, this aesthetic is largely defined by the way it fetishizes "childhood and its attendant innocence," and he cites Anderson's films as a prime example.[8] Yet when critics describe Anderson's films in terms of a nostalgia for childhood, they tend to leave out an important qualifier: namely, that they are conjuring a particular kind of upper-middle-class childhood, one in which the child is coddled and his whims are indulged, where the child's finicky attitude might even be encouraged as a sign of discriminating taste. The precocious child protagonists in many of Anderson's films fit this paradigm, as their strict adherence to a narrow range of styles is depicted as a charming eccentricity. For instance, the flashback scene in *The Royal Tenenbaums* (2001) shows young Chas Tenenbaum dressing in a closet full of neatly filed identical black suit jackets, white oxford shirts, and black striped ties. Spitz's description of Anderson's *Moonrise Kingdom* (2012), in which "there's a literal storm coming to threaten the blissful, pure childhood of its two heroes,"[9] can be extended to many of Anderson's movies, which tend toward the pathologically twee—seeking to defer the subject's encounter with a world that does not operate according to his whims, where the borders of his hermetically sealed universe can no longer hold. The titular Grand Budapest Hotel, for instance, is represented as a veritable twee Eden, an idyllic world governed by strictly observed tastes and customs, unchanged until the Second World War and the Cold War finally intrude.

Are Gondry's films twee? Spitz certainly thought so, although he points out that Gondry depicts "haunted characters existing in a world in which the whimsy is not as neatly boxed in as it is in Anderson's creations. It feels homemade . . . and just on the verge of falling apart."[10] Indeed, we can see some hallmarks of twee sensibility in many of Gondry's works: an emphasis on sensitive outsiders (*The Science of Sleep*, 2006), a fascination with outmoded styles (*Be Kind Rewind*, 2008), a focus on protagonists who are either adolescents or childlike adults (*Human Nature*, 2001; *Eternal Sunshine of the Spotless Mind*, 2004). However, I would argue that Gondry's *tweeness* belongs to an entirely different strand of childlike thinking—not that of the child who is indulged in his finicky tastes, but rather, that of the child who is indulged in his imaginative play, who is given the time and materials he needs to keep generating a stream of new ideas as he listens to his passing whims. Whimsy becomes, when defined in these terms, a celebration of the ephemeral and the impulsive, a willingness to take sudden left turns and expend energy on potentially useless activities rather than keeping a straight head and investing in the future. Anderson's twee, precocious child protagonists, by contrast, are just the opposite of Gondry's: they are highly goal-oriented, regimented, and making investments for the future (literally so in the case of *The Royal Tenenbaums*' Chas).

Gondry's characteristic aesthetic, with its DIY inventiveness, often characterized by his use of objects and sets that appear handcrafted or homemade, and its dreamlike qualities, fits this definition of whimsy. He litters the screen with the products of a restless tinkerer, objects meant to display his ceaseless creative activity, but not really built to last (and, indeed, frequently built of visibly flimsy materials). In interviews, Gondry has discussed coming from a family of inventors—his grandfather invented the Clavioline synthesizer in the 1940s—and how this background influenced him to

> like to make experiments, to put things together and see what the results are. I'd mix stuff. Like, when I was a kid, my favorite two drinks were orange juice and milk, and one day I wanted to make my favorite, favorite drink. So I mixed them up, both of them, and it was disgusting! But at least I tried it![11]

This understanding of whimsy as imaginative invention has led Gondry to be sensitive to critiques of his work as excessively whimsical; he told *Esquire* interviewer Jason Guerrasio,

I read sometimes, "It's way too whimsical," and I think, what does it mean to be whimsical? Why do you use that as a negative word? This means I can't do something that's different from others? Or that's surprising or imaginative? They say, "It's too imaginative." So I think fuck that.[12]

However, there is a cost to such a display of whimsy. Both as a music video director and as a feature filmmaker, one of Gondry's hallmarks has been a surrealist dream logic. Such "dream logic" depends on an *over-abundance* of images, one that is actually costly to produce, as each change of scene and each different object represents a new expenditure. Thus, the glossiest surrealistic music videos, such as Mark Romanek's 1995 video for Madonna's "Bedtime Story," can cost millions of dollars to produce. Gondry's work, however, is slightly more economical, as he often employs a DIY aesthetic that emphasizes inexpensive-looking props and practical effects, with minimal use of CGI. The charm of low-budget effects work is even the explicit theme of an earlier Gondry film, *Be Kind Rewind*.

DIY work is not a luxury good in precisely the same way that high-end furnishings and apparel appear within an Anderson film. When Anderson's camera lovingly lingers over Louis Vuitton luggage, viewers are meant to see that it is high-quality and made by professionals working for a brand with a distinguished reputation. The comparatively amateurish-looking DIY creations of Gondry's films meet none of those criteria for determining luxury, and yet they are a luxury simply in the sense that they represent the expenditure of considerable time on work with no immediate use or exchange value. They prominently demonstrate that their maker has a wealth of time to waste on creating art for art's sake.

One might thus draw a lineage between Gondry's whimsical surrealism and the work produced by the well-to-do artists who comprised the *fin de siècle* decadent movement, who could afford to produce useless artistic trifles. One of the key tensions within the concept of whimsical DIY, I would suggest, is that it marks a resistance to the values of the marketplace, but paradoxically serves as a marker of cultural capital, signifying that the maker has leisure time, knowledge, and creative energies to waste. In that sense, both Anderson's meticulously twee monuments to professionalism and Gondry's rough-hewn, whimsical celebrations of amateurism could be considered as decadent luxury products. Indeed, the impeccable-looking *Grand Budapest Hotel* and the handmade-looking *Mood Indigo* actually carried the same reported production budget: approximately $25 million in the case of both the former[13] and the latter.[14]

That said, it is important to draw distinctions between the Collector sensibility represented by Anderson and the Maker sensibility espoused by both

Gondry and his films. Some critics seem disappointed that Gondry is not more of a collector. On the film site IndieWire, interviewer Alex Suskind asks Gondry if he has saved and collected the handmade props used in his films. The director explains that

> it would be too much cost to keep them . . . But it seems once it's in the film, it doesn't have to exist for real, which is a shame because if people like the film, they want to see the real object next to it. But very little has been saved. Its time is the film.[15]

Props from Anderson's *The Grand Budapest Hotel*, however, were carefully preserved and have already gone on display as part of exhibitions in several European cities, including the "A Brief Survey of Graphic Design from the Empire of Zubrowka (1932–1968)" show in Dublin.[16] In the same interview with Gondry, Suskind wanted to know how he conceived of *Mood Indigo*'s Pianocktail device (a piano-cum-bar in which each note triggers the release of a particular liqueur or spirit) "and, most importantly, where can I buy one."[17] This mode of spectatorship—viewing the film as a catalog of covetable consumer goods—would seem to go against Gondry's DIY ethos, but it is entirely in keeping with Anderson's approach. Indeed, by collaborating with brands such as Louis Vuitton, Anderson has even encouraged the perception of his films as assemblages of tastefully curated, finely crafted luxury goods. Working with Marc Jacobs, who was at that time Louis Vuitton's creative director, Anderson designed the iconic vintage luggage carried by the brothers in *The Darjeeling Limited* (2007). These pieces were preserved and later auctioned off for charity.[18] Several years later, an entrepreneurial Italian fan produced a similar luggage design as part of his boutique label, Very Troubled Child (this brand name itself is a reference from Anderson's *Moonrise Kingdom*).[19] Anderson fans apparently have a voracious consumer appetite for such products, as they have become a cottage industry. For instance, on the website for the Society of the Crossed Keys—a reference to a guild of concierges featured in *The Grand Budapest Hotel*—one can buy products that are inspired by or re-create props from a variety of Anderson films, including an authentic-looking "Lobby Boy" hat and a "Mendl's Patisserie Cake Box"[20] from *The Grand Budapest Hotel*. It is perhaps no surprise that the filmmaker's fans are fixated on collecting pieces of Andersonia, given that Anderson himself is an inveterate collector with a discriminating curatorial eye. To design props for *The Grand Budapest Hotel*, he worked with graphic designer Annie Atkins and production designers Adam Stockhausen and Anna Pinnock, and then "looked at hundreds of pieces of design from Eastern Europe at the beginning of the last century as reference."[21]

Gondry, however, eschews this sort of referential approach; he has noted that "in general, I try to pick from my own dreams and my own imagination... I don't try to get inspiration from existing forms of art that are completed, and forms of art too similar to filmmaking."[22] Rather than encouraging fans to share his same taste in cultural consumption, he has tried to empower them to become their own cultural producers. After the release of his *Be Kind Rewind*, a movie in which the protagonists create their own homemade remakes of big-budget Hollywood movies, Gondry released the short how-to book *You'll Like This Film Because You're In It: The* Be Kind Rewind *Protocol*, an "inspirational guide to independent film making [e]dited and art directed by Gondry himself."[23] At the New York art gallery Deitch Projects—and later at a series of museums around the world, from Moscow to Tokyo to São Paulo—he also constructed an interactive exhibition called "Michel Gondry's Home Movie Factory." As one museum website explains:

> Gondry's idea is to enable people to experience filmmaking first-hand and make it open and accessible to everyone, by giving them a chance to be creative. Participation in the Home Movie Factory is free and requires no special training or knowledge ... Participants will work in small groups independently, with complete creative control over all aspects of the project.[24]

Gondry's public statements about this project indicate that he viewed it as deeply political: "ultimately, I am hoping to create a network of creativity and communication that is guaranteed to be free and independent from any commercial institution."[25] Another interview tied the project to notions of fighting inequality: "when I do these Film Factories, I try to share my luck of being creative to [sic] people who don't have this privilege."[26] During the same period, when Gondry's traveling exhibition was empowering amateurs to try their hand at directing, his own official films frequently employed amateur actors, like the leads of *The We and the I* (2012) and *Microbe & Gasoline* (*Microbe et Gasoil*, 2015). Thus, Gondry not only depicts but also practices the notion that amateurs are sources of untapped creative potential who can become makers of films, not just consumers.

MANIC EXCESS AND DEPRESSIVE AUSTERITY IN *MOOD INDIGO*

Gondry began directing music videos when he was drummer for the new wave band Oui Oui. The DIY mentality was a large part of new wave culture and its forerunner, punk: in 1977, one punk fanzine famously published a diagram showing three guitar chords, then writing the boldfaced instruction: "NOW FORM A BAND."[27] Punk and new wave musicians were (in)famous for producing irreverent cover versions of classic rock and soul songs, often radically changing the tempo and the vocal affect. Think, for instance, of Devo's cover of the Rolling Stones' "Satisfaction" or the Flying Lizards' cover of Barrett Strong's "Money." In both cases, the original song's plaintive yearning is transmuted into a flat, mechanical series of repetitions; consequently, the emphasis of the lyrics shifts, from Barrett Strong's soulful "I *need* money" to the Flying Lizards' deliberately soulless "I need *money*." The technique is akin to the Brechtian alienation effect, as these defamiliarizing covers de-emphasize the individual singer's self-expression and call attention to the systemic problems being addressed in the lyrics (namely, consumer capitalism's never-ending cycle of unfulfilled desire).

Gondry's *Mood Indigo* is itself a kind of new wave cover version of a beloved classic, Boris Vian's 1947 novel *L'Écume des jours* (which has appeared in English under the titles *Froth on the Daydream*, *Foam of the Daze*, and *Mood Indigo*). Hailed by Raymond Queneau as "the most poignant love story of our time,"[28] Vian's novel has become "a book whose reading still serves as a rite of passage for French adolescents, as reading '*The Catcher in the Rye*' does for Americans."[29] Many critics, however, concluded that Gondry's adaptation lacked the original's romantic charm. In *The New Yorker*, Alexandra Schwartz complained that

> for about the first hour of '*Mood Indigo*,' the director has a very good time playing in Colin and Chloe's world . . . But at a certain point the heaped-on whimsy begins to grate, and then to suffocate. The film is superficial in the purest sense: it looks wonderful, but so much visual cleverness overpowers the imagination, blocking it from doing any deeper work.[30]

A. A. Dowd offered an even harsher judgment: "*Mood Indigo* plays like some extreme behavioral experiment, an attempt to determine just how much whimsy, exactly, an audience can endure . . . Whimsy for whimsy's sake is just too much to take."[31]

Schwartz bases her negative judgment of the film on an assumed dichotomy between "superficial . . . visual cleverness" and "deeper work," while Dowd contrasts Gondry's aestheticism ("whimsy for whimsy's sake") with the "genuine emotion" he feels is lacking in the film. Neither critic seems to allow for the possibility that aesthetic excess might be part of a "deep" philosophical and affective project, and neither appears to have considered that Gondry might be deliberately provoking the sense of discomfort they report feeling. Vian's novel, in fact, contains commentary about economic exploitation and deprivation, but these themes have been obscured as the book has gained a reputation as a classic romance. Like the new wave cover songs discussed above, Gondry's adaptation uses unnaturally jittery tempos and affects to rework Vian's classic and bring its less pleasant themes to the forefront.

When whimsy is used "appropriately," with some degree of tasteful discretion, as in Jean-Pierre Jeunet's *Amélie* (2001) or even Gondry's own *Eternal Sunshine of the Spotless Mind*, viewers rarely have to think about issues of labor, waste, or status; we can enjoy the parade of whimsical images as sources of aesthetic pleasure. But in the opening scenes of *Mood Indigo*, when the "parade" of whimsical images speeds by too quickly to enjoy—becoming a "whimsy overload," a veritable twelve-car pile-up of whimsy—then questions about waste and expenditure come to the forefront. As Dowd writes, "doorbells scuttle about like insects, bodies contort into strange shapes when dancing, and mice—or rather, tiny men dressed like mice—blow bubbles at the humans cavorting overhead. And that's just the first five minutes."[32]

In these opening scenes, Gondry gives viewers what they ostensibly want from a fantastically whimsical movie, but he gives it to them in excess, to the point where it no longer serves as a source of pleasure and where viewers might question why they wanted it in the first place. Even these first moments in Colin's toy-filled bachelor apartment, the film's most twee setting, depict it as an unstable and unsustainable space. Colin's bath leaks into the apartment below, plates of food rearrange themselves on the kitchen table, and live eels wriggle in and out of the faucets, all rendered in jittery stop-motion animation. Although the scenes are brightly lit and the characters are smiling, the stop-motion effects and quick cuts create more of a manic mood than a happy one. When, in the second half of the movie, Colin's apartment becomes dim and dilapidated, the depressive and austere atmosphere seems more like the logical extension of the opening's manic excess than its antithesis; the manic excess many critics found so exhausting also exhausts itself.

Anderson's *The Grand Budapest Hotel* provides an instructive contrast, since that titular space is represented as a perfectly ordered twee world, where a set of refined customs are sustained and seem perfectly capable of continuing indefinitely—like a perfectly engineered, tightly wound, ornately carved Swiss clock—until ultimately they are tragically swept away by a tsunami of outside historical forces. As multiple critics have noted, Anderson clearly wants us to mourn the loss of that twee world; the film's dominant tone is nostalgia, a word originally coined to describe pain over a missing or lost home. Yet it is less clear whether Gondry expects us to feel nostalgia for the site of manic excess we witness in *Mood Indigo*'s first few minutes.

This sense of ambivalence over whimsy and excess spills over into the movie's representation of its ostensible protagonist, Colin, played by Romain

Duris. There are moments when Colin appears as a stand-in for the director, as a prodigious inventor of whimsical devices. But Colin is also a profligate consumer, someone who is initially defined by his economic privilege. The opening narration informs us that "Colin had sufficient wealth to live comfortably without working," and the first scenes highlight the array of luxury goods in his apartment. He is also often very unlikable, especially in the opening act of the movie, which emphasizes the dark side of his tweeness: his solipsistic affectations, his extreme privilege, and his childish acquisitiveness. Indeed, the whole romance plot is sparked by Colin's angry discovery that his best friends both have girlfriends, but he does not; he bangs the table and shouts, "I demand to fall in love, too!"

Colin's friend Chick (Gad Elmaleh) is even more of a grotesque figure, who is obsessed with acquisition but cares little about creative work or human relationships. Fanatical about collecting everything produced by the philosopher Jean-Sol Partre, he is unable to resist the chance to buy Partre's books and memorabilia. Early in the movie, a generous Colin hands his friend a sizeable wad of cash, so that Chick can afford to marry his girlfriend Alise (Aïssa Maïga). Yet, in an agonizing series of scenes spread throughout the movie's second half, we see Chick squandering this money on Partre merchandise, driving Alise mad as he further defers their marriage.

The trope of over-consumption even extends to the film's cast, which is over-stuffed with actors from some of France's biggest box-office hits, playing variations on their most popular roles. Yet the very familiarity of these stars and their personas is used to discomfit the viewer. For instance, we first see Omar Sy, who played an African immigrant housekeeper in the blockbuster interracial buddy comedy *The Intouchables* (*Intouchables*, Olivier Nakache, 2011), in a similar role, making dinner for Colin. However, *Mood Indigo* deliberately complicates our understanding of their relationship; we are later told that Sy's character Nicolas is Colin's lawyer, as well as one of his closest friends, who is paid for performing legal services but only cleans and cooks for Colin as an unpaid hobby.

Similarly, the film's depiction of the romance between Colin and Chloé (Audrey Tautou) plays upon the audience's familiarity with the two stars and the quirky romantic comedies in which they have frequently appeared, such as in Cédric Klapisch's *Auberge espagnole* (*Pot Luck*) trilogy of films; the romance is represented in a kind of manic shorthand, jumping from the "meet cute" to the "first date" to the "proposal." Again, Gondry is giving the audience "what we want," the various courses of cinematic "comfort food" we expect from the genre, but he forces us to scarf down this "comfort food" as if we were contestants in a competitive eating contest. And indeed, the romance culminates in a literal race to the altar that is framed in terms of a contest between Colin and Chloé and supporting characters Chick and Alise.

Figure 4.1 Manic whimsy as Chick (Gad Elmaleh) and Alise (Aïssa Maïga) race to the altar in *Mood Indigo* (Studio Canal, 2013)

That sense of manic over-consumption effectively foreshadows the twist that occurs midway through the movie, when Chloé develops a condition not unlike consumption, though it might better be described as a terminal case of whimsy: a water lily growing in her lung. The pace of the movie—and the visually inventive spectacles it throws at us—noticeably begins to slow down at this point, as Colin gradually goes bankrupt paying for Chloé's medical bills. The contrast with the movie's frenetically edited opening act makes the long takes in these depressing later scenes seem even more excruciatingly drawn out. Even the color scheme of the movie changes. Many of the early scenes are brightly lit, with saturated colors, but once Chloé becomes sick, the film progressively grows dimmer and grayer; by the final ten minutes, it is effectively a black-and-white movie.

The slow-paced scenes in the film's second half are laborious in more ways than one. As Colin loses his fortune paying Chloé's medical bills, he is forced to take a series of increasingly demeaning menial jobs, and we observe his slow humiliation in painstaking detail. One job literally requires him only to be a warm body, lying naked over a mound seeded with "proton guns," which grow in response to his body heat; sadly, Colin lacks the professional skill to complete even this job, and he is fired after his proton guns come up limp. Gondry himself appears as the doctor who treats Chloé's case, then later offers Colin a partial refund when the treatment does not work, murmuring "I think I made a mistake." This cameo role is fitting, given Gondry's own experiences; in an interview with Marlow Stern, he reveals,

> with *Mood Indigo*, I had a girlfriend who got really sick in America and I had to pay for the hospital bills . . . Fortunately, I could contribute money to saving her by doing work that wasn't so horrible to do. I'd directed four commercials in a row, so I had a big amount of money and we could pay for all the best treatment.[33]

Here, Gondry acknowledges his dual status as a whimsical independent filmmaker driven by his own vision and as a creative professional for hire motivated by financial concerns. As he has noted, his more commercial projects help finance labors of love like *Mood Indigo*, and the film repeatedly reminds us of the expenditure that has gone into creating its spectacles. Colin receives an itemized medical bill, shown in close-up, after Chloé has surgery to remove the flower from her lung, in one of the most visually elaborate, expensive-looking scenes in the film's austere second half. Chloé's death, on the other hand, coincides with Colin's bankruptcy, and thus Gondry's staging of her funeral is equally sparse, as though he has run out of resources to provide her with a grand send-off. The priest who earlier married Colin and Chloé asks, "How much do you want to spend? You probably want a beautiful service. I can do you something very nice for 2,000." After Colin reveals that he is now a pauper, the disgusted priest proclaims, "It'll be an appalling funeral," which is followed by a smash cut to Chloé's coffin being unceremoniously tossed out a window and landing on a car below.

As Chloé's health declines along with Colin's finances, the central set—Colin's fantastically equipped apartment—gradually falls into dirt and disrepair. This is despite the best efforts of the most twee figures in the movie: the cheerful supporting characters who seemingly exist only to serve, including not only Sy's housekeeper/lawyer, but also a helpful mouse who lives in the apartment. Such loyal, unpaid helper figures appear frequently in the children's media that often serve as a source of inspiration for "twee" filmmakers (Anderson especially), but Gondry takes this trope in an unexpected, uncomfortably real direction by showing the helper-mouse increasingly overwhelmed by the labor of cleaning the ever-dirtier apartment, at one point even seriously injuring himself in the process of cleaning. Creating and maintaining a magically twee space like Colin's apartment is thus shown to be physically taxing and perhaps even futile work.

POVERTY AND PROFESSIONALISM IN *THE GRAND BUDAPEST HOTEL*

If Gondry was critiqued for not capturing the "storybook romance"[34] and "fairy tale"[35] of Vian's novel, Anderson's *The Grand Budapest Hotel* was critically hailed as a beautiful tribute to the work of a different modernist author, Stefan Zweig. Max Nelson writes that "Anderson hasn't so much adapted Zweig's writings as channeled their spirit, reconstructed their atmospheres and taken up their major obsessions."[36] Nelson further observes parallels between

> Anderson's style—his static, portrait-like framing of people and objects, or the way he packs the background and periphery of each frame with carefully-arranged details, garnishes and decorations—[which] is designed to fix the moment in place, to perfect it, commemorate it, and embalm it

and the aesthetic of "Zweig, a writer with a deep elegiac streak and a love for artful, precise, carefully adorned sentences."[37] Anderson himself has been keen to promote this similarity: for Pushkin Press, he put together an edited collection entitled *The Society of the Crossed Keys*. Although this guild of concierges appears nowhere in Zweig's own work, *The Society of the Crossed Keys*, along with an introduction by Anderson, "contains Wes Anderson's selections from the writings of the great Austrian author Stefan Zweig, whose life and work inspired *The Grand Budapest Hotel*."[38]

I would suggest, however, that the aesthetic similarities between Zweig's writing and Anderson's film are merely superficial, and that many of Zweig's ideas run directly counter to Anderson's, particularly economic themes. Perhaps best known to film buffs as the author behind *Letter to an Unknown Woman*, adapted into a classic melodrama by Max Ophüls in 1948, Zweig packed his fiction with rich descriptive detail, giving readers a vivid sense of the luxury within early twentieth-century *Mitteleuropa*. However, unlike Anderson, Zweig also emphasized the wide economic disparities and the sense of deprivation and despair experienced by many. Many of his works are set in opulent hotels, not unlike the Grand Budapest, but even as he encourages us to take pleasure in surveying every luxurious detail, Zweig insistently reminds us of their dark sides and human costs. For instance, in *The Post Office Girl*, an ironic take on the Cinderella story, Christine, the impoverished title character, has the chance to be a guest at an elegant Swiss hotel. As she looks around her room, she makes:

> Discovery upon discovery: the washbasin, white and shiny as a seashell with nickel-plated fixtures, the armchairs, soft and deep and so enveloping

that it takes an effort to get up again, the polished hardwood of the furniture, harmonizing with the spring-green wallpaper, and here on the table to welcome her a vibrant variegated carnation in a long-stem vase, like a colorful salute from a crystal trumpet.[39]

Then she catches sight of her own reflection in the mirror: the "sight of the bulky, garish yellow travel coat, the straw hat bent out of shape above the stricken face, is like a blow," and she contemplates jumping off the railing and ending it all.[40] Even when Christine receives a Cinderella-style makeover and begins to experience life in the hotel as a fairy tale, Zweig emphasizes that her short-lived happiness is tied to economic exploitation, a bubble caused by the status-conscious guests' widespread speculation that Christine is a wealthy aristocrat. When the bubble bursts, an embittered Christine has to go through the Cinderella transformation in reverse, dressing in her old rags (what she thinks of as a dead woman's skin), and returning to a rural Austrian town that is still devastated by the effects of post-World War I inflation.

Anderson has spoken extensively about his love for Zweig's work in his promotional interviews for *The Grand Budapest Hotel*, yet his film feels like a reinterpretation of Zweig's fiction through the monomaniacal eyes of an interior design fetishist, someone who picks up only on the sumptuous period details and somehow misses the larger point. Anderson's signature "dollhouse" aesthetic works to erase any awareness of economic deprivation, as wealthy and poor characters alike occupy the same meticulously art-directed dollhouse; the poor ones just receive smaller rooms with a décor that tends more to the rustic than the rococo. But they never show the primary signs of poverty—the marks that cause Zweig's poor characters such shame—dirt, dust, grease, grime, clothing that is stained and smelly, worn and torn. Such marks would be indications of "matter out of place," and Anderson has made his brand as an auteur by arranging every detail in the cinematic frame in perfect order, with nothing left to chance.

Furthermore, consider the film's closest analogues to Zweig's deprived characters, young bellhop Zero (Tony Revolori) and his love interest Agatha (Saoirse Ronan), a baker's assistant. Mentioned above is Gondry's use of non-professional actors in films like *The We and the I* and *Microbe & Gasoline*, and how this attests to his championing of amateur creativity. The few unknown actors in Anderson's films, like Tony Revolori, who was plucked from obscurity to play Zero in *The Grand Budapest Hotel*, serve a different function. Surrounded by a cast of established stars, many of whom regularly appear in Anderson's films, Revolori plays a similar role to his character, a poor orphan who is deemed worthy by a discriminating benefactor and is thus given entry to an exclusive club; as we learn in the latter-day scenes, Zero has inherited the hotel, and the grown-up version of Revolori is played by Oscar winner F. Murray Abraham. Although Anderson cites European

Figure 4.2 Zero (Tony Revolori) and Agatha (Saoirse Ronan), Wes Anderson's picturesque lower-class workers in *The Grand Budapest Hotel* (Fox Searchlight Pictures, 2014)

literary inspirations for his film, the Zero plot seems rooted in a quintessentially American tale, that of the Horatio Alger story. Alger (1832–99) became a bestselling author in the United States at the turn of the century, a period also known as America's "Gilded Age," which was an era defined by obscene income inequality, with stories about poor young men (including *Ragged Dick*, *Tattered Tom*, and the lesser-known *Joe the Hotel Boy*) who are each singled out by a wealthy adult male benefactor who admires the poor boy's good manners and thus gives him the resources necessary to climb the class ladder and attain professional respectability.[41] In a time of intense nepotism and cronyism, when the rich were growing richer and the poor were growing poorer, Alger's fictions placated readers, reassuring them that through trickle-down acts of charity, young men of quality would rise to the top of American society. Economic historians have drawn parallels between the 2010s and the Gilded Age, and I would suggest that Anderson's narrative in *The Grand Budapest Hotel* serves a similar function to Alger's, since it reassures audiences by shifting the focus toward the wealthy individual's charitable treatment of a "worthy" poor individual (and away from any consideration of how the poor as a class are systematically disenfranchised).

Anderson's aesthetic is also all about fine craftsmanship; in *The Grand Budapest Hotel*, this even becomes part of the plot, as his heroes are all first-class artisans or members of exclusive guilds. Hence, it is not enough for Zero's love interest Agatha to be a girl who works at any bakery; she has to work at Mendl's, the country's most renowned confectioner, making her a suitable match for Zero, who feels honored to work in the country's finest hotel. This is a recurring theme in Anderson's filmography, dating back to his earlier works, including *Rushmore* (1998) and *The Royal Tenenbaums*; his protagonists' professionalism is shown as a source of pride and accomplishment. His young prodigies are not just exceptional talents, but also are highly disciplined and perfectionistic aspiring professionals.

Zweig's perspective on professionalism is very different. When he notes the professional dress and demeanor of the hotel staff, he is also noting their lack of hospitality, as they coldly ignore their under-dressed guest Christine. For instance, the desk clerk

> writes notes with his right hand and fires off bellhops like arrows with every look and nod while at the same time giving out information left and right, his ear to the telephone receiver, a universal man-machine with nerve fibers forever taut.[42]

Christine is similarly mechanical and dehumanized when observing the codes of professionalism in her job as a post-office clerk. Zweig's narration sardonically notes that

> Her hand with its pale fingers will raise and lower the same rattly wicket thousands upon thousands of times more . . . Probably the wrist will even learn to function better and better, even more mechanically and unconsciously, detached more and more completely from the conscious self.[43]

For Zweig, then, professionalism is a code of conduct that deadens the human spirit and helps perpetuate a social system that regards individuals as cogs in the machine. His protagonists, like Christine and her eventual lover, Ferdinand, are those who are willing to throw off the shackles of professionalism and decorum in order to re-invent themselves and explore new worlds. This is the opposite of Anderson's worldview. As Richard Brody observes, *The Grand Budapest Hotel* lingers on the signifiers of professionalism, depicting staff "whose uniforms and fashions are nuanced to the buttons, and whose behavior is self-controlled to the glance," in order to make a case for "the spiritual heritage and the political force of those long-vanished styles."[44] Anderson is telling "the story of a tradition of personal nobility—a severe and self-imposed code of conduct that proves, in the face of historically terrifying and catastrophic trouble, to be a rock of steadfast decency."[45] That story just happens to be almost diametrically opposed to what we find in Zweig's fiction, his ostensible inspiration.

GONDRY, ANDERSON, AND THE STATE OF THE FILM INDUSTRY

As in Zweig's *Post-Office Girl*, the characters in *Mood Indigo* move quickly from boom to bust, from luxury to poverty, with little room in between. The film itself does something similar, as it appears to have spent the bulk of its effects budget in a burst of irrational exuberance in the first thirty minutes, so that the rest of the film is comparatively drab and visually impoverished. What the film is missing, then, is both a middle-class ethos of moderation and a depiction of the middle class itself. There is, however, one notable exception. In the opening shots of the film, we see a darkened office overlooking a large auditorium full of well-dressed typists, who are apparently typing out the film's script; a close-up on the typed words "Colin was finishing washing" leads directly to the first shot of Colin, submerged in his bath. Several times, the film cuts back to this typing pool; when Colin and Chloé have a picnic on their honeymoon, the viewer sees the workers having a packed lunch at their desks, then after a shot of Colin announcing that "the picnic's over," Gondry cuts back to the typists clearing their desks and returning to work. Their menial white-collar labor thus appears intimately tied to the extravagance, and later the austerity, depicted in the film's main storyline. These scenes are Gondry's own invention, with no analogue in Vian's novel, so why might the director be so interested in showing us these images of typists laboring behind the scenes? In his book *Flickers of Film*, Jason Sperb critiques Hollywood's recent spate of nostalgic movies about moviemaking for the way they gloss over the economic transformations Hollywood has undergone, given that the transition to the digital era has eliminated numerous middle-class jobs in the industry.[46] *Mood Indigo*, I would suggest, might constitute a rare exception, because so much of the film's nostalgia is focused on those scenes of the typing pool wearing 1970s-style business casual clothing as they work on vintage machines. These comfortably middle-class workers, involved in the production of the story that we see unfold on screen, are precisely the kinds of film industry worker who have now largely been made redundant by new technology.

Gondry's *Mood Indigo* might also be read as a lament for something else that is rapidly vanishing from the industry: the midbudget film. In the late 1990s, when both Gondry and Anderson began making films, studios were far more likely to take risks on $10 or $20 million independent and art films;

even if these films flopped in theaters, DVD sales and other ancillary revenues would often make up for that. Today, however, Hollywood (not unlike the rest of the United States) has moved to a "winner takes all" economy, split between a few megabudget blockbusters at the top and many microbudget indies (often shot using digital video and requiring minimal production design work) at the bottom. Only a select few directors are given the budget they need to create lavish visual spectacles. Anderson, who has been skillful in turning himself and his style into an instantly recognizable global luxury brand, is among this "1%," while Gondry's position is far more tenuous. *Mood Indigo* made only $303,000 at the North American box office, but that was more than the *combined* gross of Gondry's three other recent movies: *The We and the I*, *Is the Man Who Is Tall Happy?* (2013), and *Microbe & Gasoline*.[47] Anderson's *The Grand Budapest Hotel*, however, was far more profitable: although it had the same estimated production budget as *Mood Indigo*, it made nearly $60 million in North America and $175 million worldwide.[48] This disparity is perhaps not surprising, given that Anderson's movie benefited from months of pre-release hype and a much wider theatrical release (playing in 1,467 theatres at its peak, compared to *Mood Indigo*'s 37).

Anderson's cinematic work is thus perhaps what one would expect from one of the victors of our current "Gilded Age" of filmmaking. He seems largely unbothered by economic issues, and his aesthetic seems designed to lull audiences into a similar state of complacency by feeding them little pieces of eye candy. Gondry's work, however, is more self-aware, and his films, such as *Mood Indigo*, aim to jar the viewer into an equally uncomfortable state of awareness. For all that Gondry celebrates about whimsy, he also raises some critical questions about how whimsy is a privilege—the privilege of having the time and resources to indulge in flights of fancy as well as the luxury of producing "useless" work for art's sake—and how this privilege is distributed unequally.

NOTES

1. See, for example, Mark Spitz's analysis of Wes Anderson's work in *Twee: The Gentle Revolution in Music, Books, Television, Fashion, and Film* (New York: HarperCollins, 2014), and numerous features such as Rachel Redfern, "14 Whimsical Motifs That Every Wes Anderson Film Has in Common," *MIC*, last modified March 10, 2014. Available at <https://www.mic.com/articles/84731/14-whimsical-motifs-that-every-wes-anderson-film-has-in-common.SEe> (last accessed February 26, 2020). Similarly, reviews of Gondry's work often use these terms, such as Geoff Pevere's look at *The Science of Sleep*, "Stuck in a Child's Dream," *Toronto Star* (Toronto, Ontario; December 22, 2006), C6, in which Pevere describes the film as "toxically twee" and featuring "gorgeously hand-crafted whimsy."

2. A. A. Dowd, "Even for a Michel Gondry film, *Mood Indigo* suffers from whimsy overload," *The AV Club*, last modified July 17, 2014. Available at <https://film.avclub

.com/even-for-a-michel-gondry-film-mood-indigo-suffers-from-1798180942> (last accessed February 26, 2020).
3. Sianne Ngai, *Our Aesthetic Categories: Zany, Cute, Interesting* (Cambridge, MA: Harvard University Press, 2012).
4. For example, Joel Stice, "25 Wes Anderson Movie Facts to Fill You with Whimsy," *Uproxx*, last modified March 4, 2014. Available at <http://uproxx.com/filmdrunk/25-fascinating-facts-might-know-wes-anderson-movies/> (last accessed February 26, 2020).
5. *Cambridge Dictionary*, s.v. "whimsical." Available at <https://dictionary.cambridge.org/dictionary/english/whimsical> (last accessed December 14, 2017).
6. *Merriam-Webster Dictionary*, s.v. "whimsical." Available at <https://www.merriam-webster.com/dictionary/whimsical> (last accessed December 14, 2017).
7. Dave Itzkoff, "Casting Shadows on a Fanciful World," *The New York Times*, last modified February 28, 2014. Available at <https://www.nytimes.com/2014/03/02/movies/wes-anderson-evokes-nostalgia-in-the-grand-budapest-hotel.html> (last accessed February 26, 2020).
8. Marc Spitz, *Twee* (New York: HarperCollins, 2014), 12.
9. Spitz, *Twee*, 230.
10. Spitz, *Twee*, 228.
11. Ryan Lamble, "Michel Gondry Interview: Mood Indigo, Eternal Sunshine, Ubik," *Den of Geek*, last modified July 28, 2014. Available at <http://www.denofgeek.com/movies/michel-gondry/31451/michel-gondry-interview-mood-indigo-eternal-sunshine-ubik> (last accessed February 26, 2020).
12. Jason Guerrasio, "Michel Gondry: 'I'm Doing Movies My Own Way,'" *Esquire*, last modified July 23, 2014. Available at <http://www.esquire.com/entertainment/movies/interviews/a29455/michel-gondry-mood-indigo-interview> (last accessed February 26, 2020).
13. Anett Böttger, "Hollywood zu Gast in Görlitz," *Frankfurter Rundschau*, last modified February 20, 2013. Available at <http://www.fr.de/panorama/the-grand-budapest-hotel-hollywood-zu-gast-in-goerlitz-a-752491> (last accessed February 26, 2020).
14. Mathilde Cesbron, "*L'Écume des jours* prend l'eau," *Le Figaro*, last modified April 25, 2013. Available at <http://www.lefigaro.fr/cinema/2013/04/25/03002-20130425ARTFIG00615--l-ecume-des-jours-prend-l-eau.php> (last accessed February 26, 2020).
15. Alex Suskind, "Interview: Michel Gondry on 'Mood Indigo,' Fancy Props, and the Future of Stop-Motion Animation," *IndieWire*, last modified July 16, 2014. Available at <http://www.indiewire.com/2014/07/interview-michel-gondry-on-mood-indigo-fancy-props-and-the-future-of-stop-motion-animation-274445/> (last accessed February 26, 2020).
16. Nora, "Pieces from the Grand Budapest Hotel in Dublin," *The Art of Exploring*, last modified March 10, 2014. Available at <https://theartofexploring.com/2014/03/10/pieces-from-the-grand-budapest-hotel-in-dublin> (last accessed February 26, 2020).
17. Suskind, "Interview."
18. "The Darjeeling Limited: Luggage by Louis Vuitton," *Classic Driver*, last modified January 25, 2008. Available at <https://www.classicdriver.com/en/article/collectables/darjeeling-limited-luggage-louis-vuitton> (last accessed February 26, 2020).
19. "Stop Everything, the Wes Anderson inspired Luggage Collection is Here," *Messy Nessy*, last modified February 27, 2015. Available at <http://www.messynessychic.com/2015/02/27/stop-everything-the-wes-anderson-inspired-luggage-collection-is-here> (last accessed February 26, 2020).
20. *Society of the Crossed Keys*. Available at <https://www.thesocietyofthecrossedkeys.com/collections/sck> (last accessed December 14, 2017).

21. Anne Quito, "The Graphic Designer Behind Wes Anderson's 'The Grand Budapest Hotel,'" *Quartz*, last modified February 22, 2015. Available at <https://qz.com/348179/the-graphic-designer-behind-wes-andersons-the-grand-budapest-hotel/> (last accessed February 26, 2020).
22. Lamble, "Michel Gondry Interview."
23. Michel Gondry, *You'll Like This Film Because You're In It: The* Be Kind Rewind *Protocol* (New York: Picturebox Books, 2008).
24. "Michel Gondry's Home Movie Factory," Garage. Available at <https://garagemca.org/en/exhibition/michel-gondry-s-home-movie-factory> (last accessed December 14, 2017).
25. Sonia Zjawinski, "Michel Gondry Builds Video Store at Deitch Projects," *Wired*, last modified February 13, 2008. Available at <https://www.wired.com/2008/02/michel-gondry-b> (last accessed February 26, 2020).
26. "Michel Gondry Talks New Film, *Mood Indigo*," *DIY*, last modified July 31, 2014. Available at <http://diymag.com/2014/07/31/interview-michel-gondry-talks-new-film-mood-indigo> (last accessed February 26, 2020).
27. "Peter Lloyd and Tony Moon/Three Chords," *Eyestorm*. Available at <http://www.eyestorm.com/Pages/Product.aspx/Peter_Lloyd_and_Tony_Moon/Three_Chords/4580463> (last accessed December 14, 2017).
28. John Flower, *Historical Dictionary of French Literature* (Lanham, MD: Scarecrow Press, 2013), 522.
29. Alexandra Schwartz, "Whimsy and Spit: Boris Vian's Two Minds," *The New Yorker* (August 12, 2014). Available at <https://www.newyorker.com/books/page-turner/whimsy-war-boris-vian-two-minds> (last accessed February 26, 2020).
30. Schwartz, "Whimsy and Spit."
31. Dowd, "Even for a Michel Gondry Film."
32. Dowd, "Even for a Michel Gondry Film."
33. Marlow Stern, "Michel Gondry on 'Mood Indigo,' Kanye West, and the 10TH Anniversary of 'Eternal Sunshine,'" *Daily Beast*, last modified July 19, 2014. Available at <http://www.thedailybeast.com/michel-gondry-on-mood-indigo-kanye-west-and-the-10th-anniversary-of-eternal-sunshine> (last accessed February 26, 2020).
34. Dowd, "Even for a Michel Gondry Film."
35. Schwartz, "Whimsy and Spit."
36. Max Nelson, "Wes Anderson's Elegy to Stefan Zweig," *Los Angeles Review of Books*, last modified March 14, 2014. Available at <https://lareviewofbooks.org/article/wes-andersons-elegy-stefan-zweig-grand-budapest-hotel/> (last accessed February 26, 2020).
37. Nelson, "Wes Anderson's Elegy to Stefan Zweig."
38. "The Society of the Crossed Keys," *Pushkin Press*. Available at <https://www.pushkinpress.com/product/the-society-of-the-crossed-keys/> (last accessed December 14, 2017).
39. Stefan Zweig, *The Post-Office Girl*, trans. Joel Rotenberg (New York: New York Review of Books, 2008), 40.
40. Zweig, *The Post-Office Girl*, 40–1.
41. Michael Moon, "'The Gentle Boy from the Dangerous Classes': Pederasty, Domesticity, and Capitalism in Horatio Alger," *Representations*, 19 (Summer 1987): 87–110.
42. Zweig, *The Post-Office Girl*, 38.
43. Zweig, *The Post-Office Girl*, 7.
44. Richard Brody, "'The Grand Budapest Hotel': Wes Anderson's Artistic Manifesto," *The New Yorker*, last modified March 7, 2014. Available at <https://www.newyorker.com/culture/richard-brody/the-grand-budapest-hotel-wes-andersons-artistic-manifesto> (last accessed February 26, 2020).
45. Brody, "'The Grand Budapest Hotel.'"

46. Jason Sperb, *Flickers of Film: Nostalgia in the Time of Digital Cinema* (New Brunswick, NJ: Rutgers University Press, 2015).
47. "Michel Gondry," *Box Office Mojo*. Available at <http://www.boxofficemojo.com/people/chart/?id=michelgondry.htm> (last accessed December 14, 2017).
48. "The Grand Budapest Hotel," *Box Office Mojo*. Available at <http://www.boxofficemojo.com/people/chart/?id=michelgondry.htm> (last accessed December 14, 2017).

PART II
French Cinema and Identity

CHAPTER 5

L'Amour fou Revisited: The Surrealist Poetics of Michel Gondry

Sian Mitchell

In 2011, the Criterion Collection released a new DVD version of *The Complete Jean Vigo* that included a short animated tribute to the titular director by Michel Gondry. This short opens with the sketched figure of Jean Vigo (1905–34), who is recognizable via his characteristic tall mass of hair, as he raises his hands to his eyes, representing the universal shape of the directorial frame. He peers through to see the well-known barge from his film *L'Atalante* (1934) appear, suggesting the connection between his cinematic imagination and arguably his most renowned work: in other words, what he sees in his head is what manifests on screen. The barge begins to float down a river before flipping upside down, after which an early twentieth-century film camera evolves from underneath the boat. Vigo appears inside the camera's body, frantically running around while images from his film emerge and project themselves to the outside world, reinforcing Vigo's unique, artistic vision and suggesting the importance of positioning his films within, at least, the canon of French film history.

This animated short, however, also serves another important purpose in relation to Gondry's films: it illustrates Vigo's influence on him, which Gondry has acknowledged. In an interview with Eric Kohn for the *New York Press*, Gondry confessed that *L'Atalante* is one of his favorite films while referring to Vigo as a surrealist influence on how he approaches the visual style of his own work.[1] Although not directly part of the early surrealist movement, Vigo and his film have been seen as sharing a similar romantic and poetic spirit.[2] This is evident in the way that Vigo visually interprets the story of newlyweds Jean (Jean Dasté) and Juliette (Dita Parlo) in *L'Atalante*. The couple are separated by Juliette's desire for life in the exciting and sophisticated city of Paris rather than on the barge with Jean, but the newlyweds are drawn back together by a love that transcends the realities of the everyday world.

The word "surreal" is often used as an adjective to describe the aesthetic feel of Michel Gondry's work, whether referring to his films or to his considerable catalog of music videos. Gondry has mentioned that, when he was growing up, he worshiped surrealism,[3] acknowledging both Vigo and surrealist filmmaker Luis Buñuel (1900–83) as having a considerable impact on him as an artist. The dreamlike worlds that Gondry creates throughout his body of work play host to the marvelous, the fantastic and sometimes nightmarish images that are analogous to the illogical projections of our unconscious while we sleep. An iconic and compelling example of such surrealism finding its way into Gondry's visual style is seen in the music video for the Foo Fighters' "Everlong," in which the gigantic hands of the band's lead singer, Dave Grohl, are foregrounded while he dreams of defending a woman from harassment. Enormous hands are also found in Gondry's film *The Science of Sleep* (*La Science des rêves*, 2006) when Stéphane (Gael García Bernal), anxious and fighting his work colleagues during a nightmare and again at age six, is lying in bed and is convinced that his hands are giant blocks. Both these examples interweave reality with the fantasy of dreams and their narratives are based upon this premise. This recalls how Gondry conceives and explores concepts and ideas. Gondry has described how the act of dreaming has influenced his creative process: "I feel that every night, when I dream, I have this kind of filmothèque, a ciné-club that I visit and I can dig anything I want for free, and use it for my work."[4] Consequently, we not only can describe the "look" of Gondry's work as surreal, but need to consider his relationship to surrealism, its association with dreams, and his subjective experiences in terms of how they influenced him as a filmmaker.

The convergence of influences from early avant-garde art and cinema find their place in Gondry's visual aesthetic and, as a result, he straddles the seemingly disparate domains of fine art, history, and popular culture. This may have to do with his upbringing, during which, prior to his film career, Gondry explored other artistic media: namely, visual art and music. He grew up in a household which he describes as "an artistic environment":[5] his father was a fan of jazz and so, from a young age, music was a constant and familiar presence for Gondry. As a child, Gondry would experiment with animation, making flipbooks and building a "zoetrope with drawings inside and slots outside."[6] At sixteen, he went to an experimental art school in Paris for a short time and ended up living with his friend, Jean-Louis Bompoint, who would eventually become the cinematographer on some of his films.[7] It was also Bompoint who introduced Gondry to *L'Atalante*, along with other films from the 1930s and 1940s. Gondry was interested in the early surrealists' method of taking inspiration from their dreams and placing emphasis on logic that stems from something other than the intellectual.[8] Between music, crafts, animation, visual art, and film, Gondry's creative experiences meld and find shape in his own filmic style. He recognizes how these experiences from a young age find form in his films. In an interview with Stephan Littger, Gondry stated:

> I use those emotions and those thoughts I had at a young age as blocks to build what I am constructing now, whether it is a video or film. It could be slightly retarded things, but then I mix it with my experience and my observations which I had over the years. But I feel my brain was imprinted strongly at a young age on my taste, on my desires, and my vision was shaped very early on when everything was just about observing things.[9]

Such a description of how Gondry perceives the impact of his childhood and formative years on his later creative process recalls discursive approaches to creativity and its psychoanalytic underpinnings. There is an awareness in these comments as to how aspects of the conscious and unconscious self, along with fantasy and desire, play a role in the creative experience.

Psychoanalytic studies of creativity, particularly from the perspective of self-formation, have stemmed from Sigmund Freud's initial postulation on creative writing and his readings of artists Leonardo da Vinci and Michelangelo. In his work on creative writing, Freud's main consideration of how an artist creates is through the concept of fantasy and its origins in childhood play. He argues that "he [the creative writer] creates a world of phantasy which he takes very seriously—that is, which he invests with large amounts of emotion—while separating it sharply from reality."[10] The implication here is that, while fantasy is an important element of the process of being creative, creative writers place a large portion of themselves and their emotions within their work. Fantasy in creative writing (and, more broadly, creative practice) is considered by Freud to be a combination of conscious and unconscious activities, as both arise from a latent wish that finds an outlet through the mental processes of condensation, displacement, and sublimation, similar to dreams. What marks the difference between these two forms of fantasy, one in dreams and the other in daydreams, is that in the latter an event in the present will provoke that wish and the subject will be reminded of an earlier experience where the wish was fulfilled. The subject will then create a daydream about the wish being fulfilled once again in the future, rather than the wish located in the dream as never having the opportunity to be fulfilled. It is interesting, then, that Gondry appears to recognize and perhaps even exploit these psychological processes in how he discusses his practice, but also in how these ideas are closely expressed through his key protagonists, such as Stéphane, Joel in *Eternal Sunshine of the Spotless Mind* (2004), and Colin in *Mood Indigo* (*L'Écume des jours*, 2013).

To focus on Gondry's films, the influence of early surrealism and its interest in Freudian dream-work has permeated not only his visual style, but also his thematic interests. Of note is how Gondry aesthetically explores the surrealist concept of *l'amour fou* (mad love), which appears in the way he depicts the intimate relationships of his protagonists. This chapter examines Gondry's films *Eternal Sunshine of the Spotless Mind* and *Mood Indigo* for traces of this influence and draws connections to Vigo's *L'Atalante*, thus positioning these films in the lineage of cinematic depictions of mad love, both revisiting and revising it.

SURREALISM, ROMANTICISM, AND *L'AMOUR FOU*

L'amour fou is a central concept in surrealist discourse and connects with a number of theories established in the writings of the early surrealist figure André Breton (1896–1966), most clearly in his homonymously titled book. Focusing on this concept in its various artistic incarnations in *L'amour fou* (*Mad Love*, 1937), Breton wrote of *l'amour fou* as a personal journey punctuated by his interactions with poetry, sculpture, and the unique found object of desire. Throughout, he focuses on fantasies of his lover, a woman who is the central figure of the penultimate chapter; his prose poetically describes their connection through time and space, ending in the suffering of love lost.

Breton was enamored of a kind of love that could surpass the ordinary or transform the ordinary into the extraordinary. His idea of love is one that completely derails the senses, where the realities of time and space do not exist and where the object of desire motivates existence. The discovery of the object, the lover, is central to Breton's discussion and provides a clear connection to the surrealist interest in psychoanalysis and dreams. For Breton, it is by chance that the object is found, but there is an inescapable connection to it, so that even when it may seem lost or becomes separated, its essence still lingers in an almost metaphysical way. As Michael Richardson observes, *l'amour fou* is represented through "a moment of rupture when the identity of the individual self is brought into doubt through an encounter with an other who holds a possibility of effecting its transformation."[11] The way in which surrealists describe the power of *l'amour fou* suggests that any transformation that occurs to the subject is so overwhelming that it has the potential for a more mystical transcendence, or a sense of other-worldliness.[12]

The fascination that Breton and surrealism have with *l'amour fou* also illustrates the connection and admiration they had with/for the legacies of nineteenth-century romanticism. In the *Second Manifesto of Surrealism* (1929), Breton positions surrealism as the prehensile tail of romanticism,[13] similarly privileging poetic aesthetics and imaginations, and seeing romanticism and themselves as sharing a sensibility and "state of mind."[14] The surrealists identified with the romantics' revolutionary challenging of the Enlightenment's prioritization of rationality, seeing individuals as completely controlled by conscious reason, thus defining each person as an autonomous human being.

Rather than attempt to create a poetics of imagination that opened up "a path to the great abstractions; to God, Beauty, Truth" and nature,[15] the surrealists, drawing from Freud's topology of the mind and the split between the conscious and unconscious, aimed to harness the poetics of irrational desire. Citing the romantic poets Percy Bysshe Shelley, Gérard de Nerval, and Achim von Arnim, Breton identifies a similarity in the uniqueness of mad love and the loved being that is formed through irrational means, the image of the loved one in one's mind shaped by desire as well as potentially destroyed through the reality of social conditions.[16]

As a medium of images, the cinema seems best poised to facilitate the visual exploration of *l'amour fou* and its otherworldliness. The surrealists saw potential in filmmaking to create works that were as close to a dream—a visual presentation of unconscious desires—as possible. Buñuel argues that surrealist film "does not attempt to recount a dream, although it profits by a mechanism analogous to that of dreams":[17] namely, its ability to capture the symbolism evident in the psychic processes Freud described in his theory of dream-work such as condensation, displacement, consideration of representability, and secondary revision. This inspired surrealist filmmakers not simply to imitate the dream on film, but to comprehend the ways in which systems of verbal and visual communication differ from one another, in order to produce films created from a process similar to that of dream analysis.[18]

Two schools of thought developed within the surrealist collective on how film should be engaging with dream-work. Antonin Artaud and Jean Goudal promoted the first of these positions, arguing that film's formal elements produced the ability to more accurately create a dream film.[19] This included the illogical changing of settings and locations, which deconstructs spatial relationships, and is similar to the way in which images in the dream change. The second school of thought, promoted by Robert Desnos, takes a position more interested in the basic thematic structure of film. Linda Williams identifies this interest as the "development of a wish-fulfilling content of amour fou [sic]."[20] This description of *l'amour fou* strongly associates with Freud's notion of latent desires that emerge and are visualized via symbols and images in dreams. It is the combination of these formal and thematic concerns, however, that is important to the overall surrealist aesthetic, and subsequently provides a starting point from which to examine the surrealist influence and exploration of *l'amour fou* evident in Gondry's films.

L'amour fou is visually and thematically represented in both *Eternal Sunshine of the Spotless Mind* and *Mood Indigo*'s romantic trajectories. In many ways, it becomes more than just romance between two individuals in a conventional sense. *L'amour fou* takes the romance further, to a metaphysical dimension where each film's pair of lovers—Joel and Clementine, Colin and Chloé—are still connected to one another, even if physical distance separates them. It is a poetic love that rises above the mundane aspects of existence and which is not impeded by societal expectation. Visual motifs also draw parallels to the ways in which Vigo addresses *l'amour fou* between Jean and Juliette in *L'Atalante*. Gondry's films each engage with these early investigations of love that inject the romantic, the poetic, and the surreal into their filmic worlds.

PROJECTIONS OF LOVE: TRANSCENDENCE AND TRANSFORMATION

Like Juliette's misplaced desire for a better life in Vigo's *L'Atalante*, both Gondry's *Eternal Sunshine of the Spotless Mind* and *Mood Indigo* position their lovers in situations where they are separated from one another and must overcome obstacles to be together. In *Eternal Sunshine of the Spotless Mind*, it is the memory erasure procedure performed by Lacuna Inc. on a distraught Joel Barish (Jim Carrey). Joel attempts to have his memories of his ex-love, Clementine Kruczynski (Kate Winslet), eradicated entirely from his mind via a process that Clementine had already undertaken. While unconscious during the procedure, Joel lucidly realizes he has made a grave mistake and attempts to resist it. He and his memory projection of Clementine attempt to outrun Lacuna Inc.'s technicians, hiding in the various recesses of Joel's mind, including memories of his childhood. All of Joel's memories of Clementine are eventually erased and, due to the non-linearity of the film's storytelling, the pair unknowingly meet for a second time, drawn together once again without fully understanding why.

In *Mood Indigo*, a mostly faithful adaptation of Boris Vian's 1947 novel, it is the illness that Chloé (Audrey Tatou) contracts that threatens her relationship with Colin (Romain Duris). Before encountering Chloé, Colin is obsessed with finding love and is susceptible to falling for almost any woman he sees. However, one night at a party he meets Chloé, her name a sign to him that she is the one, as only moments before he was introduced to the Duke Ellington song of the same name. They fall in love and get married, and all is seemingly perfect until Chloé falls gravely ill due to a water lily lodging itself in her lung. Colin tries to save her by paying for a series of medical treatments that means he must give up his wealthy lifestyle and find work. As her condition grows worse, everything around them starts to reflect the effects of Chloé's *maladie*, including their apartment slowly becoming disheveled, dark, and claustrophobic. Even after an operation removing the water lily, Chloé does not survive. The film's tragic ending contrasts with the hopeful one of *Eternal Sunshine of the Spotless Mind*.

Visually, *Eternal Sunshine of the Spotless Mind* and *L'Atalante* present their love stories as elevated beyond the ordinary by depicting versions of social or psychological realism as juxtaposed with moments of the surreal. This reinforces the nature of *l'amour fou* as a kind of love that transcends the normalcy of everyday existence. William Earle describes the convergence of the real and surreal as a celebration of the "wonder of the everyday . . . to elevate it to poetry, as though the everyday were itself a wild dream of the poetic imagination."[21] The relationship between Joel and Clementine in *Eternal Sunshine* is introduced through the revisiting of and reflection on their worst moments together, including the boredom and resentment they end up feeling, before the viewer gets to learn how much they really love one another. In one of Joel's initial memories of dinner at a Chinese restaurant, the two clearly have been together for some time as Clementine criticizes him for leaving hair on the soap and Joel thinks about how she becomes stupid when drunk. There are hints of Joel's awareness that this is a memory, such as pre-empting the words Clementine uses to describe the "repulsive" hair. However, the scene completely shifts from a representation of a memory to something more akin to lucid dreaming. While still from within his unconscious, Joel becomes aware of sounds happening externally: specifically, a phone call between Clementine and Patrick (Elijah Wood), one of the Lacuna Inc. assistants. Upon hearing her distraught voice, Joel's memory changes from the restaurant to the bookstore where Clementine worked. As if walking between memories, and still carrying his chopsticks, a confused Joel approaches the counter where Clementine is sitting and speaking to a male figure. Joel bumps into himself leaving and then futilely attempts to find out who the figure is, grabbing him on the shoulder and spinning him around. Instead of seeing the figure's face, the back of his head keeps turning towards the camera, a bizarre and somewhat disturbing image that we witness from Joel's perspective. We have moved from the ordinary into the strange. The reality of a long-term dysfunctional relationship shifts to a surreal depiction of jealous twinges born from Joel's desire and subsequent realization that he needs to keep his memories of Clementine, good or bad, romantic or dull.

Similarly, in *L'Atalante*, Jean and Juliette's post-wedding life settles into the mundane day-to-day running of a cargo barge. We see Juliette take up the role of dutiful wife, washing clothes and looking after Jean, his first mate, *le père* Jules (Michel Simon), and their cabin boy (Louis Lefebvre). As Juliette spends yet another day washing clothes, she begins to recount to Jean a myth she was once told by her mother about being able to see one's true love by opening one's eyes in the water. Jean immediately tries this, plunging his head into a bucket of water—believing he will see Juliette—but he does not. Juliette reinforces that he should be able to see her, that she was able to see him many years before they had even met when she had tested this myth as a young girl. Slightly manic, Jean takes to the rowboat and thrusts his head into the river, but still cannot see her. The scene is visually presented naturalistically with little poetic stylization, illustrating that at this stage in the pair's relationship there is a question mark over their future together. Documentarian John Grierson described Vigo's film thus: "at the base of it is a sense of documentary realism which makes the barge a real barge . . . but on top of the realism is a crazy Vigo world of symbols and magic."[22] Jean's inability to see Juliette plants seeds of doubt in her mind about life with Jean on the barge. It is not until she leaves and they are separated that Vigo visually explores the transcendent potential of *l'amour fou*, the symbols and magic.

In contrast to Vigo's *L'Atalante*, Gondry's *Mood Indigo* is, from the outset, the visually surreal experience expected of a Gondry film. The puppetlike, elongated legs of the characters as they dance the *biglemoi*, TV chef Gouffé offering Colin's personal chef Nicholas (Omar Sy) cooking advice from various appliances in the kitchen, and the cloud car that Colin and Chloé drive on their first date all introduce a dreamlike world of happiness and pleasure. This is a world where couples race in dodgem cars for the chance to be married by a priest who arrives by spaceship. Much like the absurdist moments described in the first half of Vian's novel, the insertion of incongruent imagery serves as a satirical social critique of authoritative institutions such as religion,[23] as well as a symbol of *l'amour fou*. It is as if to say that even in a world full of corruption and hypocrisy, human connection and intimacy makes this world livable. The environment is intertwined with Colin and Chloé's relationship, the former transforming to reflect the events in the latter. Instead of juxtaposing moments of realism, the film maintains a visually stylized representation of its love story, from Colin and Chloé's meeting with a vibrant color palette through to Chloé's passing and pauper funeral. The image slowly desaturates as her illness progresses until it becomes black and white. The ending's aesthetic is perhaps more reminiscent of German expressionism with its high-contrast lighting and vignetting.

Gondry's two films draw from both Vigo's *L'Atalante* and surrealist cinema in their temporal and spatial deconstruction as symbolic of the transcendence of *l'amour fou*. Inez Hedges has commented on the use of different spaces in surrealist film, on and off screen, as a metaphor for "love's capacity to conquer time and space."[24] As described at the beginning of this section, in both *L'Atalante* and *Mood Indigo* the pair of lovers are physically separated by circumstance. Their emotional connection to one another, however, continues beyond their physical distance, becoming something that can be described as metaphysical. In *L'Atalante*, after Juliette has left Jean for Paris, the two lovers are getting ready for bed in their separate locations. This scene is erotically charged as they consummate their love for one another, although they are physically and geographically apart. The parallel editing employed in this scene shows Jean and Juliette moving towards the climax of their desire for one another. The framing of their faces is the same as if they were physically taking pleasure in one another's bodies. This kind of erotic love transcends the physical.

In the final dreamlike sequence in *Eternal Sunshine*, we see the first time Joel and Clementine had really met. Before this moment, we are under the assumption that they met on a train coming home from Montauk. Instead, this memory is of them meeting on Montauk's beach, when they were both attending a mutual friend's party. Sitting on the stairs, they discuss their first meeting, what they thought of one another, how awkward they felt, but how they also seemed to feel a sense of comfort with each other. Acknowledging that this is the last memory to be erased, they walk to an empty beach house that Clementine suggests would be perfect for them, pretending that, just for the night, they are David and Ruth Laskin (the house's actual owners). Joel apprehensively goes to leave, triggering a moment of reflection on the memory for both them. In the real-world event, he left; however, in the memory he stays, and they talk about what they both wanted to have happened that night:

Clementine: I wish you'd stay.
Joel: I wish I'd stay. Now I wish I'd stayed. I wish I'd done a lot of things.

The house begins crumbling around them while the sand and water intrude around Joel's feet. The scene becomes darker, with Joel lit only via torch spotlight. As the house crumbles around Joel, Clementine's voice is heard off screen, but still within the diegesis. The focus slowly becomes softer as they speak of what they should have done and what they should have changed in that moment, until Clementine asks, "What would happen if you stayed this time?" The memory almost erased, they meet at the bottom of the stairs to say goodbye to one another. The focus becomes softer still until they are out of focus entirely and Clementine whispers, "meet me in Montauk." Time and space are visually destroyed, but their love still connects them beyond this final erasure. It is after this moment that all of Joel's memories of Clementine are erased and he finally wakes up to the urge to skip work and catch a train to Montauk, meeting Clementine all over again. Not normally an impulsive or spontaneous person, Joel has been transformed, although he has no memory at this point as to why. This feeling comes from the transcendent connection between the two, reinforced by Clementine's trip to Montauk on the same day.

Although much of the focus is on Joel as we work through his memories, there are moments where we also see hints of Clementine's own transformation post relationship and memory erasure. As this takes place in the "real world," we do not have the same insight into Clementine's psychological reflections as we do into Joel's. Rather, we see the physical symptoms of her psychological disturbance manifesting themselves externally. Clementine progresses into a state of melancholia, evidenced in teary outbursts contrasted with quiet introversion. After she calls Patrick in tears, asking him to come over, she then drags him to the lake where she and Joel had gone before. Like Joel's spontaneous truancy from work to go to Montauk, an inexplicable compulsion draws Clementine to that spot, but this time it does not feel the same. The image of her lying on the lake, as she once did with Joel but now with Patrick, is a reminder that she is there with the wrong person. The bond between Joel and Clementine is strengthened through her affective transformation and the unease of difference.

When separated by distance, these lovers are presented as still mystically connected, still appearing to one another across space. Similarly in *Mood Indigo*, when diagnosed with her lung water lily, Chloé travels to a clinic in the mountains to have it removed. At the same time, Colin goes to sell his "pianocktail" (a piano that makes cocktails when played) at a local antique store to pay for her treatment. The shop owner begins to play and sing a melancholy, bluesy ballad, with Colin eventually joining in before we then see Chloé on a daybed at the clinic beginning to sing the same song with them. The scene cuts back and forth between Chloé and a close-up of Colin singing before it shifts to Chloé lying in the operating theatre, fully awake and attached to a stringed machine raiding her chest for the water lily. As the camera pans up from her body, the faces of Colin and the shop owner appear in the room, superimposed onto the heads of two shadowy figures. Colin looks down at her for a moment and begins to smile, still singing as Chloé joins in. Although we are saddened by their circumstances and the distance apart, the use of music and visual superimposition emphasizes their interconnectedness.

The use of superimposition in the scene from *Mood Indigo* is an interesting choice by Gondry, particularly as it is used in a similar way to illustrate the metaphysical union between Juliette and Jean in *L'Atalante*. Their separation has driven Jean into a deep depression, where his behavior alternates between catatonia and hysterical fits. Remembering Juliette's story of seeing one's true love in water and clearly feeling a deep loss without her, Jean jumps into the river in the hope of seeing Juliette's face. Jean opens his eyes and the image of Juliette in her wedding dress appears before him. The shot-reverse-shot reinforces Jean's perspective and that he is indeed visualizing his true love. The shot then transforms to both the lovers in the frame, superimposed over one another, and reinforcing their connection as not just physical, but metaphysical: their love exists outside the boundaries of their own bodies as they float together through the water.

Much has been written on the symbolism of water across artistic and cultural disciplines. Walter Benjamin, for example, refers to water as an entity that is at once life-giving and purifying, but can also be considered in relation to chaos and death.[25] This understanding of water as metaphor associates it with the romantic privileging of nature and its reflection of the spectrum of human emotion: rough seas connote emotional turmoil while being immersed in water can provide a sense of calm, akin to regressing to the comfort of the womb. Gaston Bachelard suggests similar symbolic references to water found in poetry and literature. His study *Water and Dreams*, informed by early psychoanalytic frameworks, analyzes the different images of water that translate across from reveries to the artistic medium. For instance, clear waters emphasize natural beauty while deep or dormant waters signal death, maternal water, or purifying water.[26] In the cinematic context, Gilles Deleuze has considered how images of water contain properties that unveil and inform film movement, so that the film itself becomes an embodiment of the water's characteristics.[27] Combining these images with other filmic effects, such as superimposition and out-of-focus cinematography, adds to the dreamlike aesthetic and expressive possibilities of the image. When referring to *L'Atalante*, Deleuze argues that water lends to the film and its lovers a sense of gracefulness, thus differentiating it from the "clumsiness" and fixed nature of movement on land:

> a clairvoyant function is developed in water, in opposition to earthly vision: it is in the water that the loved one who has disappeared is revealed, as if perception enjoyed a scope and interaction, a truth which it did not have on land . . . it now reveals the softness and strength of the loved one's body.[28]

Deleuze's description of water—in this case, the sea—suggests a specific fluid aesthetic that conjures the poetic and emphasizes the visual difference between the surrealism of water as opposed to the realism of land.

Water is an important image in *Mood Indigo*, similarly performing as a signifier of emotion and visibly reinforcing the dreamlike aesthetic of *l'amour fou*. Throughout the film, water is representative of life and death, as directly related to Chloé's illness via the water lily in her lung. Her cure requires her to abstain from drinking more than 2 tablespoons of water a day, essentially drying out the water lily until it shrinks and dies. However, perhaps the most poignant images of water in the film recall *L'Atalante*'s lovers meeting in the sea. Chloé and Colin's wedding shifts from the carnivalesque to the poetic as they share their first kiss as husband and wife. They become immersed in water, which fills the entirety of the frame as they float together and embrace one another. They are the only ones who float, elevated above their guests, as they move down the aisle towards the church's doors while their friends stay connected to the ground, walking out as normal. The water is calm and ethereal, softening the image and expressing the uniqueness of their love, as it surrounds only them and no one else. Water, therefore, is a significant symbol of their journey together, nurturing their love as it is born, but ultimately playing a part in its tragic ending.

By juxtaposing Gondry's *Eternal Sunshine of the Spotless Mind* and *Mood Indigo* with Vigo's *L'Atalante*, a clear picture of how Gondry's films engage with early poetic, romantic, and surrealist cinema is revealed. Gondry's professed admiration for surrealist cinema, and his awareness of how dream images are, for him, cinematic inspiration, proliferate his visual aesthetic and style. Specifically, it is the connection between how Gondry's style, informed by early moments of film history, assists in a visual interpretation of *l'amour fou* that highlights its transcendent and poetic nature.

NOTES

1. Eric Kohn, "Dreaming Awake," *New York Press*, September 27, 2006. Available at <http://www.nypress.com/dreaming-awake/> (last accessed December 18, 2018).
2. Graham Fuller, "Artist of the Floating World," *Sight and Sound*, 22, no. 2 (2012): 43. Fuller argues that "*L'Atalante* built a bridge between the 1920s Surrealist cinema . . . and the poetic-realist cinema of the mid and late 1930s."
3. Kohn, "Dreaming Awake."
4. *Imagine*, season 9, episode 4, "It's the Surreal Thing," presented by Alan Yentob, directed by Tim Kirby, aired May 29, 2007, on BBC.
5. Stephan Littger, *The Director's Cut: Picturing Hollywood in the 21st Century: Conversations with 21 Contemporary Filmmakers* (New York: Continuum, 2006), 194.
6. Littger, *Director's Cut*, 198.
7. Bompoint was cinematographer on *The Science of Sleep*, *The Thorn in the Heart* (*L'Épine dans le cœur*, 2009), and a number of Gondry's music videos, including those for Gondry's band Oui Oui in the late 1980s.
8. Walker Art Center, "Michel Gondry: Regis Dialogue with Jonathan Rosenbaum," YouTube video, 1:28:35, posted September 16, 2011. Available at <https://www.youtube.com/watch?v=REux_z1Wo-E> (last accessed December 18, 2018).
9. Littger, *Director's Cut*, 197–8.
10. Sigmund Freud, *The Standard Edition of the Complete Psychological Works of Sigmund Freud*, ed. James Strachey, vol. 9. 24 vols (London: Hogarth Press, 1994), 144.
11. Michael Richardson, *Surrealism and Cinema* (Oxford: Berg, 2006), 64.
12. Richardson, *Surrealism and Cinema*, 64–5.
13. André Breton, *Manifestoes of Surrealism*, trans. Mary Ann Caws (Ann Arbor: University of Michigan Press, 1969), 153.
14. Michael Löwy, "The Speaking Flame: the Romantic Connection," in *Surrealism: Key Concepts*, eds Krzysztof Fijalkowski and Michael Richardson (Abingdon: Routledge, 2016), 82.
15. C. W. E. Bigsby, *Dada & Surrealism* (Abingdon: Routledge, 2017), 59.
16. André Breton, *Mad Love = L'Amour fou* (Lincoln: University of Nebraska Press, 1987), 7.
17. Luis Buñuel, "Notes on the Making of *Un Chien andalou*," in *Art in Cinema*, ed. Frank Stauffacher (San Francisco: San Francisco Museum of Art, 1947): 29–30, cited in Stuart Liebman, "Un Chien andalou: The Talking Cure," *Dada and Surrealist Film*, ed. Rudolf E. Kuenzli (New York: Willis, Locker and Owens, 1987), 144.
18. Linda Williams, *Figures of Desire: A Theory and Analysis of Surrealist Film* (Urbana: University of Illinois Press, 1981), 17.
19. Williams, *Figures of Desire*, 26.
20. Williams, *Figures of Desire*, 26.
21. William Earle, *A Surrealism of the Movies* (Chicago: Precedent, 1987), 12.
22. John Grierson, "Atalante," *Cinema Quarterly*, 3, no. 1 (Autumn 1934): 49, cited in Marina Warner, *L'Atalante* (London: British Film Institute, 1993), 10.
23. Boris Vian was a renowned critique of authoritarian social institutions, such as religion and capitalism. For example, in *L'Écume des jours* he calls a representative of the church where

Colin and Chloé get married a *Bedon*. The name parodically refers to someone's round (that is, fat) belly, but acts as a metaphor for the accumulation of wealth by the Church.
24. Inez Hedges, *Languages of Revolt: Dada and Surrealist Literature and Film* (Durham, NC: Duke University Press, 1983), 107.
25. Walter Benjamin, *Selected Writings Volume 1: 1913–1926*, eds Marcus Bullock and Michael W. Jennings (Cambridge, MA: Harvard University Press, 2002), 303.
26. Gaston Bachelard, *Water and Dreams*, trans. Edith R. Farrell (Dallas: Pegasus Foundation, 1983).
27. Gilles Deleuze, *Cinema 1: The Movement Image*, trans. Hugh Tomlinson and Barbara Habberjam (London and New York: Continuum, 2005), 44.
28. Deleuze, *Cinema 1*, 82.

CHAPTER 6

On the Road to Adulthood: Michel Gondry's *Microbe & Gasoline* and the French Road Movie

Marcelline Block and Jennifer Kirby

Perhaps as a result of his well-known reputation as an idiosyncratic auteur, Michel Gondry's works are not frequently discussed or analyzed within the context of a genre framework.[1] His most recent feature film at the time of this writing, *Microbe & Gasoline* (*Microbe et Gasoil*, 2015), nevertheless merits discussion as an example of the already hybridized sub-genre of the French road movie. The road movie has traditionally been characterized as crucial to understanding "American society's fascination with the road" and as a tool to explore the transgression of American social conventions through an escape into the wild.[2] Despite this focus in scholarship on the relationship between the road movie and American culture and mythology, some recent scholarship has addressed the European road movie, including several book-length examinations of the French and francophone road movie.[3] Indeed, as Jamie Steele posits, "the road movie in a European context has gained increased critical and academic currency as a means of analysing the fluidity and the ever-shifting notion of identity, society and community."[4] Since the road movie is a genre concerned with borders and mobility, it thus invites transnational variations,[5] and, "in the French context specifically, these films represent a polyphonic contribution to the ongoing debate about French identity."[6] Michael Gott and Thibault Schilt, editors of *Open Roads, Closed Borders: The Contemporary French-Language Road Movie*, which is the first published volume of essays focusing solely on French-language road films, argue that:

> part of the allure of these films lies in the nuanced perspectives they offer on contemporary French identity as well as on France's position vis-à-vis its own shifting identity, its former colonies, a new 'borderless' Europe, and the rest of the world.[7]

For Gott, the road movie offers French film directors "the possibility of elaborating flexible, transnational and multicultural alternatives to a monolithic version of France."[8] This evokes Gott and Schilt's earlier claim that French-language road movies often demonstrate how "in a traditionally culturally diverse France a monolithic conception of Frenchness has always been to some degree a fiction, or at least 'imagined' to use Benedict Anderson's term (2006)."[9]

Thus the French and/or francophone road movie often addresses themes of "displacement and identity,"[10] such as from the perspectives of "young people of diverse backgrounds who were born—or at least established early in their life—in France."[11] This includes immigrants to France navigating their new environment, as well as returning to explore the homeland(s) and/or cultural background(s) of their parents or grandparents.[12] According to Gott and Schilt (2013), this latter group of films forms a "subcategory of the French-language road film [which] might be grouped into a return to 'origins' category":[13]

> the majority of these films stage journeys to North Africa, but the sheer diversity of alternate destinations—including Armenia, India, Germany, Poland, the Czech Republic and Ukraine—highlights the fact that French . . . identity is always more complex and transnational than prevailing discourses of 'imagined' identity might admit.[14]

Although the mother of Théo (aka Gasoline), one of the titular characters of *Microbe & Gasoline*, speaks French with a foreign accent,[15] the film does not belong to what Gott and Schilt, as noted above, call the "return to 'origins' category" of the French-language road movie. As opposed to this group of French-language cinematic productions, which "stage journeys [to] alternate destinations" other than France, in *Microbe & Gasoline*, the road trip occurs entirely *within* the Hexagon. Thus the journey undertaken by the eponymous male teenage protagonists of *Microbe & Gasoline* does not "involve movement in the opposite direction" away from France, such as by embarking on a "voyage/quest into family or personal history" of Théo's mother's origins that would trace Théo and/or his mother's "genealogical link to a nation" other than France.[16] However, as Archer notes, even road movies that take place within mainland France's borders can enact a process of re-evaluation of the concept of home, undermining the stability of place and identity.[17] This concept of re-evaluating the notion of home forms a strong subtext in *Microbe & Gasoline*, beneath Gondry's characteristic whimsical sensibility.

Microbe & Gasoline is told through the eyes of two middle-school-aged French boys in Versailles—incidentally, Gondry's birthplace—whose social exclusion and difficult family situations lead them to take off on a road trip across France. The film draws from the conventions of the American road movie through its focus on social outsiders and rebellion, while light-hearted depictions of run-ins with the police reference the outlaw theme and emphasize male bonding.[18] In addition to these well-worn conventions, the film provides a commentary on the notion and definition of home in France. The film, which follows the two titular male teenage protagonists' picaresque journey in their makeshift house on wheels, links a coming-of-age narrative to a growing awareness of the complexities and divisions within France, as well as French cultural identity as a national construct.

While in road movies mobility is often synonymous with freedom, in *Microbe & Gasoline*, mobility is also represented as dangerous.[19] In one scene in the film, for instance, their house on wheels, which resembles an idealized European wooden cottage, must stand still by the side of the road in order to evade the police so that the boys will not be caught driving a vehicle that does not have a permit. The house is thus invested with symbolism; the boys' temporary abode must look like a stable part of France to be safe, in contrast to the spaces occupied by the transient and marginalized members of the Roma community—whose camp is torched in the film—or the character in *Microbe & Gasoline* who refers to an increasingly "tribal society." After witnessing the ruined Roma camp, the boys conclude that, "we live in a shitty world." In this film, Gondry depicts his trademark childhood play/whimsy alongside a sobering adult realization of the injustices found in the world, allowing the film to cross borders in both space and tone. Representing yet another form of border-crossing, the film's blending of conventions from the American road movie—including nods to aspects of American culture, such as American football—with the French road movie's potential for deconstructing national unity reinforces Gondry's status as an auteur whose work is frequently transnational in character.

THE ROAD ALREADY TRAVELED: *MICROBE & GASOLINE*, THE ROAD MOVIE AND REFLEXIVITY

While there are undeniably important cultural, national, and aesthetic factors that influence the road movie, it is nevertheless a genre with significant recognizable conventions and formulae, influenced particularly by seminal examples from the United States in the 1960s, such as *Bonnie and Clyde* (Arthur Penn, 1967) and *Easy Rider* (Dennis Hopper, 1969). As Archer argues, this genre familiarity partially underlies the road movie's popularity in transnational productions, which often employ "an intertextual and reflexive approach."[20] For this reason, the nationality of the film's auteur does not provide any unambiguous classification of the film because its national cinematic identity forms a dialogue with the film's "positioning within the history of the road movie genre."[21] Archer examines this interplay between the idiosyncratic style and generic self-reflexivity of the road movies of iconic European directors, including Jean-Luc Godard and Wim Wenders, both of whom exhibit a fascination with American genre cinema alongside fiercely subjective aesthetic and thematic preoccupations. In particular, Archer notes the prominence of road narratives in Godard's *A bout de souffle* (1960), *Pierrot le fou* (1965), and *Week-end* (1967). *Week-end* engages with the myth of the outlaw couple yet "resists any possibility of identification by making the couple as vicious and unattractive as possible, and by sporadically interrupting their mobile trajectory" with elements that encourage distantiation, such as political speeches, cameos by famous historical figures, and a ten-minute tracking shot depicting a traffic jam.[22] Although Gondry's style is considerably less corrosive and gentler than that of Godard, he shares an impulse towards playful recreation and adaptation of the hallmarks of the road movie genre in *Microbe & Gasoline*. In his influential analysis of road movies, David Laderman suggests that the genre is primarily comprised of two main types:

> [t]he quest road movie (descending from *Easy Rider*) and the outlaw road movie (descending from *Bonnie and Clyde*). Quest road movies emphasize roaming itself, usually in terms of some discovery; the tone suggests a movement *toward* something (life's meaning, the true America, Mexico, etc.). Outlaw road movies emphasize a more desperate, fugitive flight *from* the scene of a crime or the pursuit of the law.[23]

In *Microbe & Gasoline*, Gondry riffs upon the quest narrative, which he largely embraces, while also lovingly poking fun at the outlaw narrative. The quest narrative in this case is essentially interchangeable with a coming-of-age narrative. The protagonists of the film are two eccentric early teenage boys: talented artist Daniel (Ange Dargent), branded "Microbe" by the other children due to his diminutive stature and thin frame, and Théo (Théophile Baquet), who is nicknamed "Gasoil" (Gasoline) from the tell-tale smell of diesel fuel that lingers on him due to his interest in mechanics, such as fixing cars and tinkering with items that he finds in the scrapyard. These unflattering nicknames are bestowed upon the film's protagonists by their fellow students, who regularly bully them at school. When Théo befriends Daniel, the two boys form a strong bond, based on their shared status as outsiders in their rather limited immediate environments of home and school. As Théo explains to Daniel when he begins to question whether he has a strong personality: "You have to be an independent spirit to be my friend."[24] When the boys decide to undertake a trip across the country, one of the primary goals is simply to experience a world bigger than their families and school community. When they are deciding upon a route, they stare at a map of France, which Gondry shoots with them standing in front of it. Daniel observes that the country is "pretty big" before reading aloud some of the place names on the map, which is followed by a rapid-fire montage sequence of close-ups of the map itself. The camera pans across the map and briefly pauses at each of the places that Daniel reads aloud. Tom Conley writes that "in North America, after the western frontier had disappeared, the road map became a site where charts telling the traveler how to get there fueled the fantasy of finding alluring and strange places."[25] Conley goes on to explain how "like a folding map purchased at a gas station, a road movie could generate a desire to get on the road, to travel errantly, and to engage adventure."[26] In the map sequence in *Microbe & Gasoline*, the road map represents the possibility of exploring a France that extends beyond the borders of the boys' hometown where they are free to be themselves, evoking how, according to Gott and Schilt (2013), "the appeal of open roads can be attributed in some part to the newfound possibility of re-mapping French and European spaces [which] opens the door to a radical re-mapping of France."[27] However, as the boys later discover, this broadened experience brings both excitement and danger—including witnessing and encountering violence, as well as experiencing hunger, thirst, and homelessness—and thus the realization that they have previously been sheltered from the less pleasant aspects of the world, such as the racism, brutality, and displacement experienced by the Roma community whom they come across.

The process of the boys growing up and learning to fend for themselves mirrors their journey on the road. Towards the end of the film, the boys stumble across an art competition for children that is hosted by a regional airline company. The boys decide that they should enter the contest because Daniel, a talented artist, is guaranteed to win the first prize: a sophisticated, radio-controlled model airplane that uses real miniature jet engines, much to the boys' delight. This model airplane is a small-scale version of the real Airbus A310 jet plane that is flown by the airline company sponsoring the contest. Although Daniel, at age fourteen and a half, is too old to meet the eligibility criteria for the contest, which is reserved for children aged twelve and under, Théo convinces Daniel that, due to his new short haircut, he looks young enough to participate in the contest. Daniel in fact enters and draws a high-quality, detailed, realistic scene of an Airbus 310 traveling across a landscape. To Théo and Daniel's surprise and dismay, the judges deem Daniel's drawing "conventional" and so Daniel loses to a more imaginative drawing, made by a little girl, of children circling the earth while standing on sliced potatoes.

Daniel by this point has left behind his childhood imagination and idealism; his drawing reflects this departure, both literally and figuratively, since the second prize that Daniel wins is two plane tickets home—provided by the airline—for himself and Théo. Through his artwork, Daniel is able to provide himself and Théo with a way to return home via airplane since they are without other means of transport: their car/home-on-wheels had been burned down along with the Roma camp. Yet Théo still managed to salvage their house/car and used it to rescue Daniel from a group of men playing American football who run after him because he took their football. During this chase sequence—in which the same man (Ely Penh) who earlier had attacked Daniel in the hair salon/massage parlor episode is now the leader of the football players—Théo and Daniel's house/car rolls into a river, and is definitively destroyed.

The outlaw theme in *Microbe & Gasoline* is played for light humor, with a self-reflexive nod to the road movie filtered through Gondry's signature sense of whimsy. Before beginning their journey, Théo informs Daniel with utter seriousness that they should synchronize their watches and the two boys raise their arms, which are bare, gesturing at setting invisible watches. This moment suggests that the boys are simply playing at being outlaws in a form of make-believe. Because they need a permit to drive a homemade car, Théo and Daniel come up with the ingenious solution to instead construct a cottage on wheels that can easily be mistaken for a permanent dwelling. This conceit enables opportunities to stage light-hearted police pursuits, which diffuse the seriousness of the police chase in the outlaw road movie. For example, in one sequence the police approach the stationary car/house accompanied by dramatic strings on the score, indicating building tension, but the sequence resolves with the police officers posing outside the house/car for selfies, followed by a shot of the selfie with Théo's face in the window in the background, cowering like a frightened ghost. In another sequence, Gondry uses a distanced shot composition to generate deadpan humor. In a wide shot in the rain we see the makeshift car/home shuttle past road signs pointing to two different towns, one to the left and the right, before the car abruptly stops and a front doorstep is lowered. A police motorcycle enters the frame and passes by. Still in the same shot, Théo runs out, puts up the doorstep and jumps back in. The comical nature of the sequence is reinforced by the framing, which emphasizes the way that the police are harmlessly fooled rather than represent any real danger to the boys.

Similarly, the film makes gentle fun of the road movie's valorization of male intimacy. The road movie thrives upon the central figures of the couple, partly for the pragmatic reasons that two people are easily framed in the small space of a car and provide ongoing dialogue, and partly because the pairing of two characters on the road together in small spaces for an extended period of time allows the filmmakers to "build intimacy and plot conflict quickly."[28] This couple is sometimes figured as two platonic buddies, whether male, as in *Harold and Kumar Go to White Castle* (Danny Leiner, 2004) or female, such as in *Thelma & Louise* (Ridley Scott, 1991), and sometimes as a pair of outlaw lovers, as in *Badlands* (Terrence Malick, 1973), *True Romance* (Tony Scott, 1993), or *Natural Born Killers* (Oliver Stone, 1994). Yet even road movies centered upon non-sexual friendships frequently lend themselves to readings that emphasize the homoerotic subtext of "the male buddy with whom a man travels, eats, and shares a room in the intimacy of the road."[29] This sub-text was made explicit in a group of "new queer road movies" in the 1990s, such as *My Own Private Idaho* (Gus Van Sant, 1991), *The Living End* (Gregg Araki, 1992), and *The Doom Generation* (Gregg Araki, 1995), which embraced the road movie's offering of central "characters who choose to live and love outside the institution of the monogamous heterosexual partnership and the conventional nuclear family."[30] *Microbe & Gasoline* does not engage with queer cinema to any significant degree, although one of the film's *leitmotifs* is that Daniel is repeatedly misgendered as a girl by adult characters in the film (including a teacher at his school) because of his androgynous or "feminine" appearance that stems from his long hair, as well as his first name, which has a similar pronunciation in French whether for a male (Daniel) or a female (Danielle).

The film nevertheless highlights the platonic bond between two pubescent boys and suggests that this bond is to be valued over and above that between a heterosexual couple. The seemingly more naive Daniel is curious, although ignorant, about sex—such as when he asks Théo if he has ever masturbated—but is also infatuated with their classmate, Laura (Diane Besnier). Daniel also makes drawings of nude women that he hides in his room, although his mother (played by Audrey Tautou), discovers them and tries to discuss them—and his sexuality—with him, much to his dismay. Théo, however, unconvincingly playing the role of the world-weary cynical bachelor, advises Daniel that women only bring pain and disappointment, and are meaningless: "Forget Laura, the whore. We'll meet lots of Lauras."[31] Despite this warning, it is later revealed that Daniel has led them on their road trip journey to the exact lake where Laura and her family are vacationing for the summer. Daniel, however, does not have the courage to approach Laura and instead rejects her in a later fantasy sequence, which asserts, while comically undermining, Daniel's burgeoning masculinity. While sitting on the beach wearing a farcically oversized long-sleeved white shirt, Daniel fantasizes a vision of Laura walking seductively out of the water in a red swimsuit. She approaches him, but he pushes her off and she disappears. He motions gun shots at his groin area. Earlier in the film, Daniel has explained to Théo that Laura belongs to his heart while sex belongs "down there," yet in this sequence Daniel attempts to reject the vulnerability of love in favor of a macho display of sexuality, linking the finger gun to the male genitals. The fact that the gun is imaginary, and that Daniel is dressed only in a shirt that is clearly too big for him, emphasizes the childishness of this fantasy of the rejection of the temptation of women. Ultimately, the most significant relationship in *Microbe & Gasoline* is between Daniel and Théo, whose separation at the end of the film causes the emotional upset that Théo warns Daniel of in relation to attachment to women. Gondry's film thus riffs upon the centrality of the homosocial relationship to the road movie, while also paying tribute to the strong bonds of childhood friendship.

HOME, MOBILITY, AND FRANCE

Despite an evident affection for classic American road movies, *Microbe & Gasoline* nevertheless departs from and/or adapts their themes, most significantly that of mobility. In the American road movie, motor vehicles are most often associated with the freedom to move and thus to engage in self-discovery.[32] American road narrative frequently "sets the liberation of the road against the oppression of hegemonic norms" and transposes the mythology of the Western frontier "onto the landscape traversed and bound by the nation's highways."[33] The open road thus takes the place of a vast Western wilderness to be conquered. Yet, as Laderman explains, this particular connotation is a reflection of a specific cultural context in 1950s America, in which the car came "to signify not just socioeconomic status but personality" as a result of the increased customization options available to the automobile consumer.[34] Furthermore, the growth and development of the American highway system since the 1950s represented a modernized new frontier that not only linked disparate parts of the country, which the railroads had done before it, but embodied "both the entrepreneurial spirit of individualized freedom and the community spirit of transportation as communication."[35] The car thus became a symbol of progression for both the country and the individual. It is thus fitting that the American road movie's depiction of maverick outsiders is so inextricably linked to the image of the car or motorcycle.

By contrast, the French/European road film often features characters whose journeys take place via other means of transport, such as on foot, by public transport, or in rides with other drivers.[36] Examples include Agnès Varda's *Vagabond* (*Sans toit ni loi*, 1985) and more recent films such as *The Adventures of Felix* (*Drôle de Félix*, Olivier Ducastel and Jacques Martineau, 2000) and *Exiles* (*Exils*, Tony Gatlif, 2004).[37] This difference in mode of transport is not merely a variance in convention, but points towards a fundamental shift in thematic emphasis: in the French road movie the individual is often "not to be understood simply in terms of 'individualism', but in terms of the complex and often antagonistic relationship to the social body."[38]

In Gondry's *Microbe & Gasoline* these two approaches to the relationship between the individual and the geographical/social space that he or she traverses appear to merge. The trip undertaken by Daniel and Théo functions to some degree as an assertion of individual rebellion, but it is also a trip on which the boys learn about the precarity of home for numerous sections of French society and begin to understand the privilege of free mobility. Their coming-of-age journey involves not only greater self-awareness, but also greater understanding of the complexities of French identity.

Gondry utilizes the house/car that the boys build as a starting point to explore the privileges and benefits of a stable home in modern France. The boys construct the house on wheels, which can pass for a stationary structure when necessary, primarily to circumvent restrictions on driving a vehicle without a permit, but Gondry invests the house/car with greater and less pragmatic significance. Michael Gott notes a small but nevertheless relevant sub-section of road movies set in motor homes, which, Gott argues, imply that "the vehicle in which the voyage is undertaken represents an extension of home," thus confirming "that road movies are fundamentally about home."[39] In *Microbe & Gasoline*, the car/house resembles an idyllic European house, with the main body made up of a garden shed. In designing the vehicle, Daniel questions Théo's choice to place geraniums in the front windows, but Théo responds, "No, let's play up the house thing." It is this ability of their "house" to look like a permanent home that enables the boys to evade the police. Although this evasion is played for laughs (as analyzed above), the boys eventually learn about the dire consequences of not having a home for those whose place in French society is more precarious. They decide to park their vehicle near a Roma camp and leave to explore. Upon returning, they find that the police have burned down the camp, destroying the possessions of the Roma community, along with their vehicle. Although Théo grieves for the comparatively insignificant loss of his ruined, charred jacket, Daniel chastises him, noting that "a whole Roma community was wiped off the map . . . it's so unfair . . . they are always chased away and no one cares." He goes on to point out that "their relatives were in death camps," and once they arrive in the seemingly safe, multicultural France, "we treat them like criminals."[40] Interestingly, here Daniel uses the first-person plural, implying a feeling of personal culpability and identifying himself with the (adult) French public/society. His coming of age here is also a realization that he has taken the stability of home for granted and that the loss of his house/car is meaningless when compared to the injustice suffered by the Roma. Daniel's conclusion, after seeing the Roma camp burned, that "we live in a shitty world" signals the moment that he loses his childhood innocence and idealism, but also undermines the sense of freedom of the road movie.

The film also problematizes the unity of France as a nation in a rather bizarre sequence set in a massage parlor. Daniel decides that he needs to have his hair cut very short so that he will no longer be mistaken for a girl (as had occurred throughout the film). In search of a hair salon, Daniel visits several traditional French barbershops, but they are all closed. Eventually he wanders into an Asian district, with shops featuring signs written both in French and in Asian characters. Daniel stumbles into a massage parlor/hair salon, where two young Asian women, speaking in accented French to him, and in French as well as in an Asian language to each other, offer him sexual favors—which he repeatedly declines—to go along with his requested very short haircut. In the massage parlor, a young Asian French man (Ely Penh), presumably the boss of the operation, is giving a video interview, in which he spells out his territory: "We don't care about the circular zone, just the north zone. We have many codes, if you leave us alone you will have no problem. But if you try to take over, watch out!" The interviewer asks him if he is exploiting the women working there and refers to "the tribal society," at which point the interviewee attacks the interviewer. In the chaos, Daniel runs away with his head only partially shaved and is beaten up by the men from the shop for his money, although the woman who cut his hair intervenes. She tells the men to take only the ten euros that Daniel owes her for his (incomplete) haircut, a request with which the men comply. The interview content exemplifies the divisions present in, and compartmentalization of, France. When the boys initially look at the map of France, they see it as a vast, cohesive country, but in fact the country is divided by informal "zones" that delineate not a modern nation but rather a "tribal society" with a seedy underbelly. The film thus draws a new cinematic map of France, through Daniel's expanded experience.

CONCLUSION: *MICROBE & GASOLINE* AND THE FRENCH-LANGUAGE ROAD MOVIE IN A TRANSNATIONAL PERSPECTIVE

In the introduction to their edited collection entitled *Cinéma-monde: Decentered Perspectives on Global Filmmaking in French*, Michael Gott and Thibault Schilt suggest that in today's global filmmaking environment, in which international co-productions dominate, the notion of "French-language" films is of limited use. Gott and Schilt instead propose the concept of *"cinéma-monde,"* in which films engage with the francophone world through "some combination of linguistic or cultural affinities, geographic contacts, production connections or reception frameworks."[41] With *Microbe & Gasoline*, Michel Gondry offers a film set in France, in the French language and funded primarily by French production companies. Despite not being a co-production, this French film nevertheless invites a complex transnational interpretation that embraces a combination of reception frameworks and cultural affinities. *Microbe & Gasoline* embraces conventions drawn from the genre of the American road movie, and while it encourages the viewer to read it in relation to this cinematic tradition, it simultaneously works to critique contemporary France and its divisions.

Just as Gondry's film *Microbe & Gasoline* crosses borders between cinematic traditions and reception contexts, it furthermore crosses borders of genre: as a road movie which is also a coming-of-age story of two "young people [who are] on a personal, cultural, or economic quest,"[42] the film links its protagonists' entries into adulthood with their growing awareness of the complexities of a globalized world beyond their previously limited scope of experience.

NOTES

1. Contributions within this volume from Ariano and Kirby prove notable exceptions.
2. David Laderman, *Driving Visions: Exploring the Road Movie* (Austin: University of Texas Press, 2002), 2.
3. See Neil Archer, *The French Road Movie: Space, Mobility, Identity* (New York: Berghahn, 2013); Michael Gott and Thibault Schilt, eds, *Open Roads, Closed Borders: The Contemporary French-Language Road Movie* (Bristol and Chicago: Intellect, 2013); and Michael Gott, *French-Language Road Cinema: Borders, Diasporas, Migration and 'New Europe'* (Edinburgh: Edinburgh University Press, 2016.)
4. Jamie Steele, *Francophone Belgian Cinema* (Edinburgh: Edinburgh University Press, 2019), 146.
5. Archer, *The French Road Movie*, 6.
6. Gott and Schilt, *Open Roads, Closed Borders*, 3.
7. Gott and Schilt, *Open Roads, Closed Borders*, 3.
8. Gott, *French-Language Road Cinema*, 4.
9. Gott and Schilt, *Open Roads, Closed Borders*, 6.
10. Archer, *The French Road Movie*, 3.
11. Gott and Schilt, *Open Roads, Closed Borders*, 5.
12. Archer, *The French Road Movie*, 3. According to Gott and Schilt in *Open Roads, Closed Borders*, 5: "films in this category include *La Fille de Keltoum/Bent Keltoum/Keltoum's Daughter* (Mehdi Charef, 2001), *Trzy kolory: Bialy/Trois couleurs: Blanc/Three Colors: White* (Krzysztof Kieslowski, 1994), *Le Grand Voyage/Grand Voyage* (Ismaël Ferroukhi, 2004), *Gadjo Dilo/The Crazy Stranger* and *Exils/Exiles* (Tony Gatlif, 1995 and 2004), *Voyage en Arménie/Armenia* (Robert Guediguian, 2006), *35 rhums/35 Shots of Rum* (Claire Denis, 2008), *Cheb* (Rachid Bouchareb, 2001), *A l'est de moi/East of Me* (Bojena Horackova, 2008), *Souviens-toi de moi* (Zaïda Ghorab-Volta, 1996), *Voyages* (Emmanuel Finkiel, 2001), *Simon Konianski* (Micha Wald, 2009) and *Bled Number One* (Rabah Ameur-Zaïmeche, 2006)."
13. Gott and Schilt, *Open Roads, Closed Borders*, 5.
14. Gott and Schilt, *Open Roads, Closed Borders*, 5.
15. In the film, Théo's mother is played by actress Jana Bitternova, who was born in Zlaté Moravce in present-day Slovakia.
16. Gott and Schilt, *Open Roads, Closed Borders*, 5.
17. Archer, *The French Road Movie*, 7.
18. Laderman, *Driving Visions*, 1.
19. Neil Archer, *The Road Movie: In Search of Meaning* (New York: Wallflower Press, 2016), 8.
20. Archer, *The Road Movie*, 60–1.
21. Archer, *The Road Movie*, 61.
22. Archer, *The Road Movie*, 63.
23. Laderman, *Driving Visions*, 20.
24. *Microbe et Gasoil*, directed by Michel Gondry (Paris: Studio Canal and Partizan, 2015).
25. Tom Conley, *Cartographic Cinema* (Minneapolis: University of Minnesota Press, 2007), 156–7.
26. Conley, *Cartographic Cinema*, 157.
27. Gott and Schilt, *Open Roads, Closed Borders*, 9.
28. Steven Cohan and Ina Rae Hark, "Introduction," *The Road Movie Book*, eds Steven Cohan and Ina Rae Hark (London and New York: Routledge, 1997), 8.
29. Cohan and Hark, "Introduction," 9.

30. Robert Lang, *Masculine Interests: Homoerotics in Hollywood Films* (New York: Columbia University Press, 2002), 245–6.
31. *Microbe and Gasoline*, directed by Michel Gondry (Partizan and Studio Canal, 2015).
32. Archer, *The Road Movie*, 8.
33. Cohan and Hark, "Introduction," 1.
34. Laderman, *Driving Visions*, 38.
35. Laderman, *Driving Visions*, 39.
36. Gott, *French-Language Road Cinema*, 12.
37. Gott, *French-Language Road Cinema*, 2–13.
38. Archer, *The French Road Movie*, 18.
39. Gott, *French-Language Road Cinema*, 68.
40. *Microbe and Gasoline*.
41. Michael Gott and Thibaut Schilt, "Introduction," *Cinéma-monde: Decentred Perspectives on Global Filmmaking in French*, eds Michael Gott and Thibaut Schilt (Edinburgh: Edinburgh University Press, 2018), 2.
42. Gott and Schilt, *Open Roads, Closed Borders*, 5.

PART III

Narrative and *Eternal Sunshine of the Spotless Mind*

CHAPTER 7

Rethinking Romantic Comedy through the Art Film: Michel Gondry's *Eternal Sunshine of the Spotless Mind*

Raffaele Ariano

INTRODUCTION

In *Sincerity and Authenticity*, literary critic Lionel Trilling argued that the normative vision of life expressed by Shakespeare's romances is at odds with the ethical taste of the modern cultivated reader.[1] Trilling was reworking his old concerns related to the incapacity of modern literature to attach a positive value to marriage, family life, and passion.[2] He was also concerned about its unwillingness to represent the "Female Principle" as "having a transcendent and on the whole beneficent significance."[3] It would be easy to object that what in Trilling's opinion literature had ceased to do, popular cinema has continued to do with unabashed boldness. But such an objection would hold true only up to a certain point. It is in fact difficult not to sense a certain embarrassment in the cinema of our age when it comes to the celebration of romantic values. If we juxtapose the glories of an earlier time, such as *Bringing Up Baby* (Howard Hawks, 1938), *A Foreign Affair* (Billy Wilder, 1948), and *Adam's Rib* (George Cukor, 1949), with many of the romantic comedies that became hits in the 1990s and 2000s, we are easily convinced that the genre is experiencing a period of crisis.

It might be that what I am articulating here is only a form of aesthetic snobbery. Drawing on Bourdieu's study on cultural capital and taste, a survey of television audiences has in fact suggested that preferences for different types of comedy are strongly influenced by levels of education, and that more highly educated people "know" that they are "supposed to" appreciate only the more highbrow forms of comedy, and to dismiss lowbrow comedy as mere entertainment.[4] If to this we add Schiermer's considerations of the relationship between nostalgia and authenticity in the late modern cultural figure known as the "hipster," we may have reason to speculate that the preference for black-and-white romantic comedies of moviegoers highly with in cultural capital is merely a way of fetishizing our cultural past and its aesthetics.[5]

Nevertheless, scholars have long discussed the historical evolution of the romantic comedy in terms not entirely foreign to the concept of crisis. As early as 1978, Henderson put forth the idea that the romantic comedies of the 1970s were proving unable to acknowledge and meaningfully reflect upon the deep social changes in family structures and sexual habits that had occurred in the 1960s.[6] Neale argues for something similar with regard to romantic comedies of the 1980s and early 1990s, such as *When Harry Met Sally* (Rob Reiner, 1989) and *Pretty Woman* (Garry Marshall, 1990), which he identifies as "new romances"; although he does not speak openly of a crisis in the genre, Neale quite frankly charges such "new romances" with conservativism and disengagement.[7] Building upon Paul and Krutnik, Grindon has identified a new cycle, running from the 1990s to the year 2009, where the crisis of the genre assumes yet another form.[8] The films of the "grotesque and ambivalent cycle," Grindon maintains, fluctuate between a parody of the conventions of romantic comedy (the Farrelly Brothers' *There's Something About Mary*, 1998) and the portrayal of characters who substitute love with professional success, parenthood, or other non-romantic forms of human relationship (*Waitress*, Adrienne Shelly, 2007).[9]

I am convinced, however, that it is possible to identify a group of romantic comedies for which such a narrative of crisis is inadequate. The purpose of my chapter is to situate and analyze Michel Gondry's *Eternal Sunshine of the Spotless Mind* (2004) in the context of a recent cluster of films that I call "art romantic comedies." These films, I argue, represent a significant asset in contemporary American cinema, as they have been able to both revive exhausted conventions and arouse the interest of audiences that would experience Bourdieusian "disgust" when confronted with more mainstream specimens of the genre.[10] In the first section of my discussion, I set out the hypothesis that, in recent years, a way to escape the crisis of romantic comedy has been found in a reformulation of its conventions on the basis of the art-film principles of authorship, realism, and ambivalence, identified by Bordwell in a prominent article.[11] In the second section, I use this hypothesis to carry out a close analysis of *Eternal Sunshine*. Although this independent "art" film seems, at first glance, far removed from mainstream romantic comedy, I am convinced that, by analyzing it through the lens of this genre, we can arrive at an understanding of its inner workings. An interpretation of *Eternal Sunshine* as a romantic comedy will, in turn, make it clear that the aesthetic strategy it exemplifies has indeed characterized, with varying degrees of clarity and awareness, a host of American films from the late 1960s to the present. This argument will be the focus of the third and final section of the chapter. I begin with general remarks concerning the ontology of film genres suggested by the existence of something like an "art romantic comedy." Finally, I will discuss a set of recurring traits characteristic of this group of films: first, individualized characters and "sensitive" protagonists; next, the expressive use of film style, formal experimentation, and implementation of metafictional devices; and finally, "open" happy endings.

RETHINKING ROMANTIC COMEDY THROUGH THE ART FILM

To my knowledge, no genre scholar to date has systematically addressed the possibility of a hybridization of romantic comedy and art film, probably because any film that displays an artistic outlook is automatically disassociated from the genre of romantic comedy. Grindon writes of "post-classical romantic comedy" and analyzes the influence of the European art film on significant examples of the genre, such as *The Graduate* (Mike Nichols, 1967) and *Annie Hall* (Woody Allen, 1977).[12] This is indeed relevant to my point, in so far as the heritage of the American New Wave is integral to what I call art romantic comedy. Grindon also states that, in the last twenty years, "'art' films" (it is worth noticing the quotation marks around the word "art") have developed romantic comedy "in a complex and sensitive fashion."[13] He seems unconvinced, however, that such films deserve to be considered separately, and chooses to include them in the section devoted to the "grotesque and ambivalent cycle." In a more general discussion of the main trends in Hollywood filmmaking from the 1990s onward, Bordwell states that major studios have become increasingly eager to satisfy the public's desire for "offbeat stories," once typical only of art and avant-garde films.[14] Similarly, Denby highlights recent American cinema's tendency towards what he calls "disordered narratives": that is, narratives which experiment with chronology, or flood the spectator with sub-plots and even parallel equally important storylines.[15] Moreover, Bordwell includes *Eternal Sunshine of the Spotless Mind*, along with such films as *Pulp Fiction* (Quentin Tarantino, 1994), *Fight Club* (David Fincher, 1999), and *Memento* (Chris Nolan, 2000), in his discussion of the contemporary filmmaking strategy in which narrative experimentation is flanked and "tamed" by the use of redundant exposition and classical genre-storylines such as noir and romance. However, in this new trend towards a masterfully governed narrative experimentation, Bordwell does not envision a specific role for romantic comedy as a genre.

As already noted, when I speak of the art film as a genre, I am referring to Bordwell, and specifically to the article in which he contends that art cinema can be seen as "a distinct mode of film practice, possessing a definite historical existence, a set of formal conventions, and implicit viewing procedures."[16] It is certainly true that the works of directors such as Federico Fellini, Ingmar Bergman, and François Truffaut exhibit a formal and thematic variety unknown to Hollywood film genres (at least to film genres as practiced in the classical studio system). Still, Bordwell's argument is that, "whereas stylistic devices and thematic motifs may differ from director to director, the overall *functions* of style and theme remain remarkably constant in the art cinema as a whole," and can be encapsulated in the principles of realism, authorship, and ambiguity.[17] To implement these principles, the art film usually loosens or even reverses the basic structures of classical Hollywood filmmaking. To varying degrees, it deviates from linear, cause–effect, goal-oriented plots, clear-cut character psychologies, and the "transparent" use of film technique. It is thus apparent that art cinema needed classical Hollywood filmmaking as a set of conventions against which to define itself. Yet the innovations of art films have, in turn, had an effect on American cinema. "In particular," writes Bordwell, "American film genres intervene to wrap art-cinema conventions in new directions."[18]

In this perspective, the art romantic comedy can be understood as yet another example of the crossbreeding of an American film genre and the art film.[19] "Art romantic comedies" can be provisionally defined as follows: those films in which the stylistic devices and thematic motifs (in other words, the conventions) of romantic comedy are re-interpreted and transformed so as to carry out the overall functions that style and theme fulfill in the genre of art cinema—that is, those of realism, authorship, and ambivalence. With such a hypothesis, it is possible to venture into a close analysis of *Eternal Sunshine of the Spotless Mind*.

ONEIRIC REMARRIAGE: *ETERNAL SUNSHINE OF THE SPOTLESS MIND*

Eternal Sunshine of the Spotless Mind is an auteur film with two authors. Charlie Kaufman provides a screenplay filled with the quirky fantasies and metacinematic structures that characterize his oeuvre, from *Being John Malkovich* (Spike Jonze, 1999) to *Synecdoche, New York* (Charlie Kaufman, 2008). Michel Gondry endows the film with the oneiric visuals that have since become one of his trademarks. If we pierce the veil of science fiction and narrative complexity, it becomes immediately apparent that *Eternal Sunshine* draws upon the conventions of the romantic comedy. The film follows the typical ten-step plot structure identified by Mernit and Grindon: Unfulfilled Desire, the Meeting, Fun Together, Obstacles Arise, the Journey, New Conflicts, the Choice, Crisis, Epiphany, and Resolution.[20] The only departures from the model are the non-chronological order in which the events are presented, and the introduction, mentioned in both reviews and academic essays, of the Cavellian theme of "remarriage."[21]

Joel (Jim Carrey) is an introverted man in his late thirties, whose life is shaken by an encounter with Clementine (Kate Winslet). She is a modern screwball heroine: beautiful, energetic, and impulsive, although plagued by a vein of self-loathing unknown to the characters played by the Barbara Stanwycks and Katherine Hepburns of previous eras. Joel and Clementine fall in love, but time passes and the stark differences between their personalities tear them apart. After their separation, they resort to a technology that allows them to selectively erase each other from their memories. But, as if moved by an unconscious desire—call it predestination—the two meet again. Despite the awareness of their differences and past conflicts, they are able to come to "genuine forgiveness" and to the sense of "a past they can admit together," and decide to be a couple again.[22] Watching the hallway scene at the end of the film, when the just reunited lovers suddenly pass from tears to laughter, a passage from Cavell comes to mind:

> It is as though you know you are married when you come to see that you cannot divorce, that is, when you find that your lives simply will not disentangle. If your love is lucky, this knowledge will be greeted by laughter.[23]

A limitation of the scholarship on *Eternal Sunshine* lies in the fact that those who notice the affinity of the film with the comedy of remarriage tend to pay too little attention to its experimental approach to narrative and style. On the other hand, it is likewise problematic that scholars focusing on the film's formal innovations habitually seem interested neither in remarriage, nor—for that matter—in romantic comedy. This limits their interpretations, because in *Eternal Sunshine* the unconventional use of narrative and style is deeply connected to the storytelling and contributes to an ingenious reinterpretation of the conventions of remarriage, as well as of the romantic comedy in general.

Referring to a well-established terminology, it can be said the narrative structures of *Eternal Sunshine* display an inventive use of the chronological order in which the plot presents the story events, the range of story information, and the depth of story information. These three aspects are carefully coordinated. The film can be divided into three main segments: the seventeen-minute opening sequence; the long middle sequence, set mainly inside Joel's head during the erasure procedure; and the fifteen-minute end sequence. In the first part spectators thinks they are witnessing the first meeting between Joel and Clem, while they are actually being shown their second meeting. The spectator's knowledge at this point is restricted to that of the characters: they are meeting for the second time, but having erased their memories, cannot recognize each other. Then, a transition to Joel alone in his car crying desperately leads the spectator to think that the narration has moved a year or more forward (it is "again" the St. Valentine's period):

the couple has broken up and Clementine has had Joel erased from her memory. In fact, the film has moved not forward, but two days back. However, despite the hints dropped throughout the oneiric central section of the film, the spectator will piece together the correct chronology only during the closing sequence, when the meeting will be repeated. Gondry even re-edits part of the same footage for the sake of clarity, because, as Bordwell writes, "the more complex the devices, the more redundant the storytelling needs to be."[24]

This interplay of non-linear chronology and restricted narration has the function of manipulating the spectator's emotions. The illusion of a time ellipsis—the abrupt jump from a love being born to a love ended—communicates a strong fatalism. Then, when Joel is mourning Clem's decision to erase him, we are spared none of his suffering. Due to realistic acting, handheld camera and low-key lighting, we assume a highly intimate perspective on Joel's pain. This sets a dramatic and realistic tone that is far from the usual choices of the romantic comedy. When, in the end sequence, we finally understand that, despite having erased each other, the two lovers will be together again, we experience a sudden rush of insight: we discover not only that they meet again, but that *they had already met again*—that, in a way, it was impossible for them not to meet again. And this is as powerful an interpretation of Cavell's "myth" of remarriage as there can be.

The most radical departures from the use of film form typical of the romantic comedy are related to the central oneiric section. Here, Gondry, drawing upon his experience as a music video director but also taking inspiration from art and experimental cinema, has the opportunity to build a highly distinctive dream imagery: over- and under-exposed cinematography, digital special effects, sound distortions, off-balance shots, speeded-up and slowed-down footage.[25] Joel is having his memory erased, so his dreams are, simultaneously, his memories. It is through his subjective oneiric filter that we learn of his first love with Clementine. The chronology here is inverted: the first memories Joel recalls come from the last acts of their relationship. All the conflicts and all the bitterness are shown first, expanding the already mentioned sense of fatalism. But then, one step at a time, Joel travels backwards in time to their first meeting. The good memories progressively unfold; the reasons for their past attachment are revealed. Joel finally decides that he wants to stop the erasing procedure, but he is asleep. From that moment, he and the dream character of Clementine forge an alliance: they will do whatever possible to hide the memory of their love in some safe part of Joel's mind that the erasing machine cannot reach. They frantically discuss a strategy in the first impulse to that renewed conversation that, as Cavell argues, is the condition of remarriage.[26]

They start jumping from memory to memory, running like playful children across beaches covered in snow, through forests and lavish parades replete with elephants. These are all "green worlds" in Frye's sense, magical spaces where the rules of everyday life are subverted through play, laughter, or sheer magic, and love becomes possible.[27] From a broader perspective, however, it is the realm of dream and memory itself that, in *Eternal Sunshine*, carries out the dramatic and symbolic functions of Shakespeare's forests. It is only in the space of memory and dream that Joel and Clementine can seize the opportunity to play, laugh, talk, dress up like children. It is in the world of dream and memory that conflicts can be resolved and desires realized. Therefore, the art film device of implementing a metadiegetic plane allows for an interpretation of some of the oldest conventions of the romantic comedy, an interpretation that is at one and the same time literal and full of symbolic depth. Childhood has a special relevance here. Cavell writes that remarriage couples need the fantasy of "having shared a childhood together," of being "brother and sister."[28] In films like *Bringing Up Baby* this is only a metaphor.[29] In *Eternal Sunshine*, on the contrary, it becomes quite literal: Joel brings Clementine into his childhood. We see the characters dressed up like children; we even see them interpreted by child actors.

The film has what I call an open happy ending. The couple is reunited, but the realism with which their conflicts and differences had been previously portrayed leaves little space for unqualified optimism. In the last shot of the film, Joel and Clementine *run* playfully on the Montauk beach where they fall in love twice. It could almost be seen as a classic "they lived happily ever after" scene, but a few details dissolve this rushed judgment. The fact that Clementine has red hair tells us that the scene comes from their first relationship, which is from the past rather than the future. Moreover, part of the shot is repeated three times in a loop that ends only when a fade to white introduces the closing credits. I interpret this subtle montage trick as a way to suggest that the couple may end up repeating their past mistakes. On the soundtrack, Beck sings that "Everybody's Gotta Learn Sometime," but we have reasons to doubt that the couple has actually learned very much, that the "miracle of change"[30]—the main outcome of love in a traditional romantic comedy—has actually taken place. Maybe they are together again only because they have erased their memory, after all. It can therefore be argued that this last scene is a placeholder for the ending Kaufman had written in a previous draft of the screenplay: Clementine, already an old woman, walks into Lacuna Inc. and has Joel erased from her memory for the sixteenth time. In this nightmarish version of the story, the two lovers keep erasing each other and falling in love again throughout their entire lives.[31] Whether this is to be read as a celebration of the relentless power of love or as an affirmation of an irredeemable aspect of human nature cannot be decided here.

To conclude, *Eternal Sunshine* uses its expressionistic audio-visual style and its metacinematic narrative structures to recast romance and the comic into the realm of dream and memory. Instead of jokes, gags, and paradoxical situations, the comic tone is achieved through the appeal to oneiric imagery in all its childish playfulness. At the same time, the realization of a romanticized relation with reality is linked not so much to a fantasy of everlasting love as to the choice of being faithful to one's own memory and feelings: in a word, to one's own biography.

"THE ART ROMANTIC COMEDY": AN ATTEMPT AT A GENERALIZATION

Gondry's *Eternal Sunshine of the Spotless Mind* epitomizes—and permits us to more clearly identify—an aesthetic strategy first realized in the late 1960s by a film that is usually taken as the starting point of the American New Wave: *The Graduate*. Numerous traits of Mike Nichols's masterpiece represent a clear break with the philosophy and aesthetics of the genre in its classical form, and an anticipation of the recent development I am discussing, especially in areas such as the casting (Dustin Hoffman as protagonist Benjamin Braddock) and characterization of the film's protagonist. Significant as well are both the degree of psychological realism and even of social criticism deemed compatible with a comedic tone (the generational conflict of the 1960s; the critique of money and fixed social roles) and, finally, the handling of the convention of the happy ending. It is worth noticing, at least in passing, that if one ending in the history of romantic comedy has been as ambivalent and touchingly open as that of *Eternal Sunshine of the Spotless Mind*, it is probably the ending of *The Graduate*, especially its two famous final shots: the long medium close-up of Benjamin and Elaine (Katharine Ross) sitting on the back seats of a bus and staring ahead of them, their faces gradually passing from laughter to a suspended feeling of uncertainty and melancholy; the same bus, seen from behind while it rides into the unknown to the notes of Simon & Garfunkel's "The Sound of Silence."

The aesthetic strategy I am discussing is consolidated in the late 1970s with Woody Allen's departure from the domain of parody with *Annie Hall*, a romantic comedy promptly understood by both audiences and critics as a kind of "high culture comedy."[32] Allen's *Manhattan* (1979) followed soon after, and ever since, Allen has remained the champion of the romantic comedy–art film strategy, creating a long series of critically acclaimed films. At least since the late 1990s, Allen has been joined by a younger group of auteur filmmakers, including Paul Thomas Anderson, Noah Baumbach, Sofia Coppola, Greta Gerwig, Michel Gondry, Spike Jonze, Charlie Kaufman, Richard Linklater, and Alexander Payne. Without attempting to compile a "list" of the art romantic comedies of the last two decades, it is worth mentioning *Being John Malkovich*, *High Fidelity* (Stephen Frears, 2000), *Adaptation* (Spike Jonze, 2002), *Punch-Drunk Love* (Paul Thomas Anderson, 2002), *Lost in Translation* (Sofia Coppola, 2003), *Eternal Sunshine of the Spotless Mind*, *Sideways* (Alexander Payne, 2004), *Before Sunset* (Richard Linklater, 2004), *Greenberg* (Noah Baumbach, 2010), *Frances Ha* (Greta Gerwig, 2012), and *Mistress America* (Greta Gerwig, 2015).

The complex dialectical relationship between this group of films and the tradition of the romantic comedy suggests some considerations concerning the ontology of film genres and their evolution. Despite what it might seem *prima facie*, what I call art romantic comedy does not fit into the (now classic) teleological conception of the evolution of film genres put forth by Schatz.[33] According to Schatz, whose theory is tailored to the Hollywood studio system, genres are systems of conventions that perform a cultural problem-solving function. Their internal evolution, he argues, can be described according to "patterns of increasing self-consciousness," ranging from the "formal transparency" of their beginnings to the "opacity" of the later phases, where conventions have "saturated" the audience, and filmmakers resort to parody and other forms of subversion of the genre's typical traits.[34] Schatz's theory, it would seem, suggests not only that film genres undergo a "natural" development, but also that there comes a moment, sooner or later, when, through irony, filmmakers and audiences alike distance themselves from the original cultural meaning of the genre. A romantic comedy such as *There's Something About Mary* seems a perfect example of the pattern described by Schatz.

However, it is clear that *Eternal Sunshine*, *Lost in Translation*, and more or less all the other films categorized above as art romantic comedies aim at neither irony nor distance. They are sometimes complex and self-aware art films, but in an age of saturation and skepticism they use complexity and self-awareness with the objective of making possible once again those same symbolic functions that the genre of romantic comedy performed in its classical, "naive" phase. In order to characterize the ontology of the art romantic comedy as a genre, then, we turn to a distinction sketched out by Cavell in *Pursuits of Happiness* and further developed in *The Fact of Television*: the distinction between "genre-as-cycle" and "genre-as-medium."[35] Films such as *There's Something About Mary* resort to parody because they conceive genre as a cycle: that is, as a set of compositional formulas (conventions) that may vary slightly, but in which repetition and recurrence prevail. On the contrary, films such as *Eternal Sunshine* conceive of romantic comedy as a "medium"—as something that "undergoes continuous definition and redefinition."[36] In this latter case, the members of a genre are engaged in "conversation" with one another about what the genre is and, for this reason, their membership of the genre itself is not only less patent, but also a continuing subject of discussion and interpretation. In a genre conceived as medium, a film can do without at least some of the traditional traits of that genre, provided it manages to "compensate" with new traits that keep the original "myth" of the genre alive.

Therefore, I would like to describe, following the cue of *Eternal Sunshine*, a few of the recurring traits of art romantic comedies. A first departure from classical romantic comedy, as well as from its mainstream contemporary representatives, can be found in character construction and comic devices. In new romances, as well as grotesque romantic comedies, romance and laughter are still obtained through characters that are strongly typified: The Modern Cinderella (Julia Roberts in *Pretty Woman*); The Charming Gay Friend (Rupert Everett in *My Best Friend's Wedding*, P. J. Hogan, 1997), The Creep (Chris Elliott in *There's Something About Mary*), The Aged Nerd (Steve Carell in *The 40 Year-Old Virgin*, Judd Apatow, 2005), The Slacker with a Heart of Gold (Seth Rogen in *Knocked Up*, Judd Apatow, 2007), and so on. On the contrary, in art romantic comedies, plotting, acting, costume, and make-up choices aim at highly individualized character construction for both main and secondary characters, thus situating the narration on a more realistic level and opening wider avenues for the exploration of psychologies and manners. At the same time, the possibilities for laughter are correspondingly narrowed. Physical comedy is superseded by more sophisticated forms of intellectual wit and self-mockery (the example of Woody Allen is obvious). Laughter is subdued, or even displaced by narrative and stylistic devices that perform the task of establishing a light "comedic" tone. Irony and satire are still important, and still target what Frye called "the blocking characters," people whose moral and psychological flaws constitute an obstacle to the fulfillment of love.[37] But the nature of blocking characters has changed in the art romantic comedy. The core dramatic conflict is no longer with the father figures of the older generation; nor does it contrast male and female mentalities, as commonly occurred in the 1950s and 1960s in "comedy of the sexes" such as *The Seven Year Itch* (Billy Wilder, 1955) and *Some Like it Hot* (Billy Wilder, 1959). Rather, the main conflict is situated at the level of the psychological problems of the leading characters. These are what truly hamper the realization of love and desire, and the humorous figures against which the satire is directed are therefore not secondary characters or an external antagonist, but the protagonists themselves.

The choice of inner conflicts as the focus of the drama is consistent with an interest in sensitive, even tormented protagonists. A typical art romantic comedy protagonist is the ironic, fast-talking, guilt-ridden New York Jewish intellectual of Woody Allen's "nervous romances," whose existential and physical uncertainty have become emblematic of masculinity in crisis.[38] Nevertheless, also worth mentioning in this respect is the more recent example of the splenetic titular character played by Ben Stiller in Noah Baumbach's *Greenberg*, whose ambivalent feelings towards himself and others almost make him a contemporary version of the main character of Diderot's *Rameau's Nephew*. At times, psychological suffering is represented in all its hideous realities, as in

Punch-Drunk Love. On other occasions, a mitigation of realism makes room for the possibility of romanticizing psychological maladjustment. It happens, for example, in *Sideways*, whose protagonist is a writer *manqué*, an alcoholic and a sensitive man. A common choice involves making such sensitive protagonists into artists or intellectuals. Allen interprets directors, stand-up comedians, and novelists. The protagonist of *Before Midnight* is a successful novelist. John Cusack in *Being John Malkovich* is a struggling street-puppeteer, who secretly yearns for his craft to be universally recognized as art. Scarlett Johansson in *Lost in Translation* is a philosophy graduate who has not yet decided what direction her adult life will take. It is noteworthy that creativity and intellectuality are treated with the same ambivalence that is reserved for psychological suffering: on the one hand they are intensely romanticized, on the other they are made the targets of satire, or realistically exposed with all their eccentricities and self-deceptions.

The romantic couple of *Eternal Sunshine* offer a good example of this penchant for individualized characters and sensitive protagonists. Within the genre of romantic comedy, neither the aggressively sexualized but insecure woman, nor the shy man tinged with resentment constitutes what could be called a character-type. Both Clementine and Joel, moreover, are portrayed through a complex mixture of likable and unlikable elements. Clementine's impulsive nature is fascinating, but also leaves her prone to cantankerous behavior that sometimes borders on sordidness. Joel, on the other hand, is not as good-natured as he would have people believe, and we sense that part of his dullness can be ascribed, as Clementine probably supposes, to a deeper existential laziness. Furthermore, Joel and Clementine are both, each in their own way, sensitive and eccentric. They are not artists or New York intellectual types, but Joel is a loner who constantly broods over a diary filled with thoughts and sketches, while Clementine, stuck in an unfulfilling job as a cashier, expresses her unwillingness to accept the boredom of a normal life through her racy enthusiasm and ever-changing hair color.

This affinity on the part of art romantic comedies for sensitive characters and psychological depth is often tied up with some form of stylistic and narrative experimentation. Bordwell writes that art cinema "is less concerned with action than reaction," that it is "a cinema of psychological effects in search of their causes," in which the "dissection of feeling is often represented explicitly as therapy and cure."[39] This is a good characterization of many art romantic comedies as well. Grindon has used the expression "existential mystery" to describe Woody Allen's *Annie Hall*,[40] a film in which, as would happen years later in *High Fidelity*, the main character breaks the fourth wall to address the audience directly and, through voiceover narration and flashbacks, tries to "sift the pieces" of a failed relationship, to examine his life and figure out "where did the screw-up come?" The unfolding of such existential mysteries often benefits from an expressive, non-transparent use of film style. Albeit in ways less overt than those of the art films discussed by Bordwell, art romantic comedies distance themselves from the use of film form typical of classical Hollywood by opting for a resolute use of *mise-en-scène*, cinematography, montage, and music as objective correlatives of the characters' inner states. *Manhattan* and *Frances Ha*, for example, use black-and-white cinematography and old-fashioned musical scores to convey the illusion of romanticism that their main characters harbor towards the city of New York and the human relations that are possible within it. *Punch-Drunk Love* uses bizarre camera angles, low-key lighting, and over-exposure, together with Jon Brion's disturbing soundtrack, to immerse the viewer in the distressed mind of its protagonist. Metafictional narrative devices, too, may play a role in the psychological inquiry these films carry out. Take *Adaptation*, for example. Its protagonist is not only a screenplay writer, but the film's writer Charlie Kaufman himself (played by Nicolas Cage), and specifically, Charlie Kaufman portrayed in the act of struggling to write the script for *Adaptation*. Such a *mise-en-abyme* is obviously an extreme case, and it should not be overlooked that Kaufman and Jonze, as Woody Allen before them in *Annie Hall*, use self-reflexivity to ironically undercut the autobiographical illusion that the film is creating.[41] However, self-reflexivity and metanarration are used not with the sole aim of post-modern irony, but also to involve the spectator more actively in the psychological inquiry of the film, and to render this inquiry more complex and layered. That *Eternal Sunshine of the Spotless Mind*, too, uses film style and metadiegetic narration to enrich the "existential mystery" it narrates should be clear from the analysis offered in the previous section. It is worth adding here that Gondry's film, with the reverse chronological order in which a large part of the story is narrated, is able to add to Woody Allen's question "where did the screw-up come?" a further and equally poignant question: "where did love come from in the first place?"

The ambivalence and open-endedness attributed by Bordwell to art cinema have a specific importance for the cluster of films I am discussing, as they characterize the treatment of both tone and the convention of the happy ending, quite possibly the two most salient traits of romantic comedy.[42] Art romantic comedies are often defined as "romantic comedy-dramas" due to their heavily mixed tone. In these films the representation of loneliness, melancholy, and pain is not only tolerated, but welcomed as part of a pursuit of psychological and existential authenticity. Certainly, if they can be still described as comedies it is because in the end the characters are rewarded with some form of human growth, and an at least partial fulfillment of their desire. But this does not always entail the literal realization of love, nor any form of "they lived happily ever after." The cultural and psychological conflicts presented in the narrative are not 'solved' in Schatz's sense but only "soothed." A typical art romantic comedy ending shows the main character finally ready to go out and seek what he/she desires in life but does not show the actual fulfillment of this desire, or, when fulfillment is portrayed, the spectator is left with justifiable doubts as to its permanence. I have called this reworking of the convention of the happy ending simply the "open happy ending." Two end scenes will provide useful examples, to be kept in mind alongside those of *The Graduate* and *Eternal Sunshine of the Spotless Mind*. The ending of *Lost in Translation* is as follows: in the middle of a crowded Tokyo street, Bob (Bill Murray) whispers something into the ear of Charlotte (Scarlett Johansson) before they part ways. We have the sense that he has said something meaningful, something that gives their story a resolution, but we are never told what it is. In *Sideways*, Miles (Paul Giamatti) knocks at the door of a woman he barely knows. Neither he nor we can be sure if she will return the warmth and understanding he lost when his wife left him two years earlier, but the mere capacity to knock at that door already feels like a substantial change.

To conclude, I would argue that the aesthetic strategy of what I have called "art romantic comedy," as displayed by a wealth of recent and less recent works by American auteur filmmakers and epitomized by Michel Gondry's *Eternal Sunshine of the Spotless Mind*, is a revealing example of what an interplay between "high" and "low," tradition and innovation, entertainment and art can produce within the realm of Hollywood filmmaking. Old cultural myths are revived by means of new narrative and stylistic devices. A seemingly exhausted genre undergoes redefinition and becomes able, once again, to offer some form of symbolic solution—what Aristotle would have called "catharsis"—to long-standing social and psychological anxieties.

NOTES

1. Lionel Trilling, *Sincerity and Authenticity* (Cambridge, MA: Harvard University Press, 1972), 39.
2. Lionel Trilling, *The Moral Obligation to be Intelligent* (Evanston, IL: Northwestern University Press, 2008), 268, 354–71.
3. Trilling, *The Moral Obligation to be Intelligent*, 438.
4. Nathalie Claessens and Alexander Dhoest, "Comedy Taste: Highbrow/Lowbrow Comedy and Cultural Capital," *Participations: Journal of Audience & Reception Studies*, 7, no. 1 (2010): 49–72.
5. Bjørn Schiermer, "Late-Modern Hipsters: New Tendencies in Popular Culture," *Acta Sociologica*, 57, no. 2 (2014): 167–81.
6. Brian Henderson, "Romantic Comedy Today: Semi-Tough or Impossible?," *Film Quarterly*, 31, no. 4 (1978): 11–23.
7. Steve Neale, "The Big Romance or Something Wild?: Romantic Comedy Today," *Screen*, 33, no. 3 (1992): 284–99.
8. William Paul, "The Impossibility of Romance: Hollywood Comedy, 1978–1999," in *Genre and Contemporary Hollywood*, ed. Steve Neale (London: BFI, 2002), 117–29; Frank Krutnik, "Conforming Passions?: Contemporary Romantic Comedy," in *Genre*

and *Contemporary Hollywood*, 131–47; Leger Grindon, *The Hollywood Romantic Comedy* (Oxford: Wiley–Blackwell, 2011).
9. Grindon, *The Hollywood Romantic Comedy*, 171–90.
10. Pierre Bourdieu, *Distinction. A Social Critique of the Judgement of Taste* (Cambridge, MA: Harvard University Press, 1984), 486–8.
11. David Bordwell, "The Art Cinema as a Mode of Film Practice," in *Film Theory and Criticism*, eds Leo Braudy and Marshall Cohen (Oxford: Oxford University Press, 2009).
12. Grindon, *The Hollywood Romantic Comedy*, 54, 139–59.
13. Grindon, *The Hollywood Romantic Comedy*, 64–5.
14. David Bordwell, *The Way Hollywood Tells It: Story and Style in Modern Movies* (Berkeley: University of California Press, 2006), 74.
15. David Denby, "The New Disorder: Disordered Narratives in Film," *The New Yorker* (March 5, 2007). Available at <http://www.newyorker.com/magazine/2007/03/05/the-new-disorder> (last accessed February 26, 2020).
16. Bordwell, "The Art Cinema as a Mode of Film Practice," 649.
17. Bordwell, "The Art Cinema as a Mode of Film Practice," 650.
18. Bordwell, "The Art Cinema as a Mode of Film Practice," 656.
19. Here, I want to stress not that the art film is not inherently American, but rather that film genres are typical of American cinema.
20. Billy Mernit, *Writing the Romantic Comedy* (New York: HarperCollins, 2000), 109–17; Grindon, *The Hollywood Romantic Comedy*, 3–20.
21. Reviews: David Edelstein, "Forget Me Not: The Genius of Charlie Kaufman's Eternal Sunshine of the Spotless Mind," *Slate Magazine*, March 18, 2004. Available at <http://www.slate.com/articles/arts/movies/2004/03/forget_me_not.html> (last accessed February 26, 2020); A. O. Scott, "Charlie Kaufman's Critique of Pure Comedy," *The New York Times*, April 4, 2004. Available at <http://www.nytimes.com/2004/04/04/arts/film-charlie-kaufman-s-critique-of-pure-comedy.html> (last accessed February 26, 2020). Academic essays: Michael J. Meyer, "Reflections on Comic Reconciliations: Ethics, Memory and Anxious Happy Endings," *The Journal of Aesthetics and Art Criticism*, 66, no. 1 (2008): 77–87; William Day, "I Don't Know, Just Wait: Remembering Remarriage in *Eternal Sunshine of the Spotless Mind*," in *The Philosophy of Charlie Kaufman*, ed. David La Rocca (Lexington: University Press of Kentucky, 2011).
22. Stanley Cavell, *Pursuits of Happiness: The Hollywood Comedy of Remarriage* (Cambridge, MA: Harvard University Press, 1981), 19.
23. Cavell, *Pursuits of Happiness*, 127.
24. Bordwell, *The Way Hollywood Tells It*, 78.
25. Carol Vernallis, "Music Video, Songs, Sound: Experience, Technique and Emotion in *Eternal Sunshine of the Spotless Mind*," *Screen*, 49, no. 3 (2008): 277–97; Matthew Campora, "Art Cinema and New Hollywood: Multiform Narrative and Sonic Metalepsis in *Eternal Sunshine of the Spotless Mind*," *New Review of Film and Television Studies*, 7, no. 2 (2009): 119–31.
26. Cavell, *Pursuits of Happiness*, 1–42.
27. Northrop Frye, *Anatomy of Criticism: Four Essays* (Princeton: Princeton University Press, 2000), 163–86.
28. Cavell, *Pursuits of Happiness*, 31.
29. Cavell, *Pursuits of Happiness*, 125. In his essay on *Bringing Up Baby*, Cavell discusses how the playful interactions between the two adults that form the romantic couple of the film and several other narrative and allegorical devices "add up to a representation of a particular childhood world, to that stage of childhood preceding puberty."
30. Cavell, *Pursuits of Happiness*, 23.

31. Charlie Kaufman, *Eternal Sunshine of the Spotless Mind: First Draft*, Undated. Available at <http://www.beingcharliekaufman.com/index.php/scripts-writing/scripts-writing/film-scripts> (last accessed September 1, 2019).
32. Alex Symons, "The Problem of 'High Culture' Comedy: How Annie Hall (1977) Complicated Woody Allen's Reputation," *Journal of Popular Film and Television*, 41, no. 3 (2013): 118–27.
33. Thomas Schatz, *Hollywood Genres: Formulas, Filmmaking, and the Studio System* (New York: Random House, 1981), 36–41.
34. Schatz, *Hollywood Genres*, 36–41.
35. Stanley Cavell, "The Fact of Television," *Daedalus*, 111, no. 4 (1982): 79–85.
36. Cavell, "The Fact of Television," 81.
37. Frye, *Anatomy of Criticism*, 166–7.
38. I take the concepts of "comedy of the sexes" and "nervous romances" from Frank Krutnik, "The Faint Aroma of Performing Seals: The Nervous Romance and the Comedy of the Sexes," *The Velvet Light Trap*, 26 (Fall 1990): 57–72.
39. Bordwell, "The Art Cinema as a Mode of Film Practice," 651.
40. Grindon, *The Hollywood Romantic Comedy*, 152.
41. K. L. Evans, "Charlie Kaufman, Screenwriter," in *The Philosophy of Charlie Kaufman*, ed. David La Rocca (Lexington: University Press of Kentucky, 2011). Peter J. Bailey, *The Reluctant Film Art of Woody Allen* (Lexington: University Press of Kentucky, 2001), 33–44.
42. Bordwell, "The Art Cinema as a Mode of Film Practice," 654.

CHAPTER 8

Apocalypse Ever After: Lifted Veils and Transcendent Time in *Eternal Sunshine of the Spotless Mind*

Sheheryar B. Sheikh

Michel Gondry loves to create parallel narrative structures. Whether he creates a music video featuring multiple Kylie Minogues concurrently interacting with each other as well as with pedestrians and vehicles,[1] or a commercial focusing on conversation full of *double-entendres* about the desirability of George Clooney and coffee in a Nespresso advertisement, the multiple narrators in *Human Nature* (2001), or other parallel structures, Gondry is fascinated with creating doubles, triples, and quintuples, all layered, in all his films.[2] In his second feature-length film, *Eternal Sunshine of the Spotless Mind* (2004), the director complicates narrative parallelism by collapsing the representation of time and space into concurrent past and present, even as most of the action takes place within protagonist Joel Barish's (Jim Carrey's) memories.

The set-up invites readers to imagine their world as manipulated by the existence of a singular science fictional novum: a device that can remove specific memories. Lacuna Inc., headed by Tom Wilkinson's character, Dr. Howard Mierzwiak, owns this proprietary technology. He sells the service of memory removal to clients looking to erase traumatic memories after they lose pets and loved ones. The film's story chronologically begins when, after two years of dating each other, Joel and Clementine (Kate Winslet) hit an ugly impasse in their relationship. Clementine decides to erase all the memories of Joel that she has accumulated in those two years. When Joel finds out, he does the same and it is at this point in the narrative that the viewer begins watching events from inside Joel's head, while the technicians of Lacuna Inc. erase Clementine from his mental record. As they are erased, in reverse chronological order to the relationship's timeline, the segments of memory that Joel has recorded of Clementine are displayed for the film's audience even as he interacts with the memories, reliving them, and thereby beginning to engage more meaningfully with his past.

An apocalyptic reading of any film would focus on the denouement (especially if cataclysmic), as well as the film's processes of revelation and uncovering of its characters' and plot's meaning-making structures. In the etymological sense of "apocalypse," which is the primary focus of this chapter, the process of erasing Joel's memories "lifts veils from" Joel and Clementine's relationship, while also adding more layers of complication to the meaning of those memories. Gondry's visual depiction of these processes is achieved through repetition, in which subtle changes are made to memories encountered repeatedly, each time complicating Joel's experience of them further. The metacommentary of this apocalyptic and concealing process argues for the need to reassess any memory, however trusted it appears.

MEMORY AS A CINEMATIC PLAYGROUND

Dreams and memories are ripe material for filmic representation, commonly represented through the use of blurred edges (in the case of dreams) and flashbacks (in the case of memories); especially in recent years, the inner workings of the imagination have become dominant, even if heterotopic, "places" for events in films to transpire. Gondry himself plays with the notion of reality-infused dreams in *The Science of Sleep* (*La Science des rêves*, 2006). Another contemporary auteur director, Christopher Nolan, has played with both memory and dreams as his subjects. The latter-themed film, *Inception* (2010), uses large-scale computer-generated effects to transform and mold urban landscapes as though they were made of wax, and to make the laws of physics upend themselves. Buildings turn on imaginary axes; a vista of a city appears to collapse until it appears bent and folded on top of itself; and within the dream sequences, extreme-slow motion is used to enhance or destabilize the idea of time, and to give credence to the film's central conceit of time passing much quicker in a dream environment. The space of dreams for Nolan is an arena for spectacle. He dazzles the audience with digital manipulation.

For his earlier, memory-themed film, *Memento* (2000), Nolan chose to eschew the flashback in order to serve his story better. The story revolves around Leonard (Guy Pearce), who has lost the ability to transfer short-term memories to long-term memory storage. He resets to the present every minute or so, and during that minute, while he retains the short-term memories, he has to leave notes for himself to update his base-level memories. Nolan starts showing Leonard's story from both ends of the narration (one thread in black and white, the other in color), and works his way to the middle in short segments. Breaking down the film into shorter, atemporal segments allowed Nolan to project Leonard's existential condition onto the audience (given that viewers now have the burden of arranging and remembering the sequence of events to work out the film's chain of causation).

Just like Nolan, Gondry plays with form to match different content requirements; he finds a way to tell a story, visually, about enforced loss of memories while the subject of those recollections is engaging with them through visual recall. When Charlie Kaufman's script for *Eternal Sunshine* calls for scenic transitions between associated memories in Joel's head, they are listed as a solid transition; for example:

> CLEMENTINE (CONT'D)
> What you doin' here, baaaaaaay-beeee?
> INT. ROB AND CARRIE'S LIVING ROOM—NIGHT[3]

But Gondry's creation of this transition and others like these bends time and space in a subtle yet quite obvious manner. Through elaborate set pieces (and explicitly *not* via digital manipulation), it appears as though a door out of the bookstore leads into Rob and Carrie's living room. Day turns swiftly to night as lights shut off in the Barnes & Noble bookstore behind Joel; he walks through a doorway, and he is in his friends' house, and the situation is a completely different one once time and space are bent. The way memory works in Joel's head is much like how the dreams of *Inception* operate, but with much more intimate scales of manipulation; only the environment immediately around Joel is transformed, and without physical laws being bent out of shape. No wonder Joel does not figure out for a long time that he is in his own head.

PAST AND PRESENT COLLAPSE

Gondry uses several transitions and juxtapositions to show how Joel's act of remembrance is either outside of time and space, or in a place other than the one in which time and space operate like waking life. He reveals in a long take the temporally impossible movement from the bookstore where Clementine works to Joel's friends' house. When they first began to be employed in film, "long takes . . . called [audience] attention to [filmmakers'] methods, exploited the possibilities of *mise-en-scène*, and asked viewers to become aware that form creates content; that stories don't exist without the telling of them."[4] The long take is a signature move, on top of which Gondry puts his own signature by transitioning between memory, recall of memory, and re-engagement and re-interpretation of memory, all at the same time.

Other scenes use similar transitions: the cracked-ice surface of a frozen Charles River, which transforms quite dramatically through lighting, changing into the large open hall of Grand Central station; the memory-removal technicians Stan and Patrick's conversation intrudes upon Joel's imagined spaces, especially incongruent for him when he is searching the streets for a vanished Clementine and when he is sitting with her in his own apartment; Clementine blurs into the background as she talks to Joel at a flea market; Joel walks into Dr. Howard Mierzwiak's clinic at Lacuna Inc. again and again, at different points in his thoughts, and finds even the faces erased when he willfully tries to engage with that memory one last time, beyond the point at which it is already supposed to be erased.

The cocktail of Joel's memories fuses discrete events into a jumble that, instead of building up and snowballing, does the exact opposite. Tarja Laine describes these overlaps and the melting of imaginary spaces as a point at which Joel's memories "get torn apart, disaggregated, and redistributed. Scenes that Joel remembers turn into scenes that focus on the act of remembering itself."[5] Eventually, the act of remembering is what Joel engages with, especially when he begins to realize that the memories are being erased even as he re-experiences them. However, at first, the collapses merely indicate how memories work; their string forms a whole trail from the end of his relationship with Clementine to their first meeting.

One of the main questions for cognitivist understanding of the film is whether Joel would realize his memories are worth keeping, if it were not for the intrusion of one memory on another and, perhaps especially, the intrusion of the technicians' voices as voiceover to his memories. Patrick's presence is especially alarming to Joel: his last few memories of her indicate that Clementine has formed a relationship with a man of that name, and the name refuses to leave his conscious thoughts; it is Patrick's connection to Clementine that begins to alarm him and make him wonder whether his memories of Clementine or her memories of him have been used by Patrick ("Tangerine . . . how does he know to call you that?") in unethical ways. Soon after that, he speaks directly to Dr. Mierzwiak from within his memory-reliving state: "Please let me keep this one." The clarity of knowing what is happening to him is already present before he states it within his recall. This makes the realization implicit for a while before it becomes explicit, and when Joel does vocalize the idea of trying to keep his memories from being erased, the audience does not remember when the realization came, thereby hiding the part that Patrick has played in disrupting the process.

Laine argues that the "memory-erasing procedure does not work, since it only focuses on thinking memory, leaving sense memory intact," but based on evidence that Patrick and his actions are disruptive, I would argue that the procedure is intruded upon from the outside, and that is why it does not work; Joel no longer wants to erase his memories once he finds out how valuable they are to anyone who wants to be an intimate part of Clementine's life.[6] Gondry's smartest move is to hide this fact from the viewer deep within the folds of spaces and times intruding upon each other.

The way that Gondry and Kaufman indicate the beginning of the memory-erasure procedures constitutes another maneuver: the first memory, in the reverse-chronology of Joel and Clementine's relationship, that needs to be erased is the erasure of Joel's visit to Lacuna Inc., where he hires Dr. Mierzwiak to conduct the procedure. This is the first memory we have of Joel realizing that he is going through the process: he sees himself in the patient's chair as an "other"—a pair of Joels exist in that memory, one that watches the Joel taking part in the procedure, and the other, conscious Joel, who predicts exactly the words that will come out of Dr. Mierzwiak's mouth as the procedure begins. After that, the memory-Joel becomes unconscious of the removal of the memories while he relives them until the invocation of "Patrick," the one character who crosses the liminal boundary between mind-space and reality, causing both to collapse.

IMMANENCE OF THE IMMINENT

Joel does not recognize how deeply Clementine is etched into his memory storage until the memory-removal procedure gets well under way. By that time, as he and the viewers both know, it is likely too late to stop the procedure; Joel is asleep and at the mercy of the entirely unethical technicians of Lacuna Inc. Within a few hours, all his memories of his romantic other half will be removed. When he becomes conscious and repentant of this fact, midway through the procedure, the rest of the memories become pervaded with a sense of loss. This suffusing sense of loss is what Frank Kermode, in his book-length essay, *The Sense of an Ending*, calls the "immanence" of the "imminent."[7] While, for Kermode, the "imminent" macro-apocalypse (the global one) is continuously delayed beyond dates on which it is predicted to happen (that is, it gets "disconfirmed without being discredited"), for Joel, the eschatological end of his Clementine-related memories is confirmed: it will happen by morning. For him, the concurrence of remembering and existence of memory are inextricably linked with the inevitability of the procedure of memory removal.

Kermode's essay is an exploration of how Western fiction deals with eschatological and teleological ends, and what revelations they bring, or are supposed to bring. He argues that "although for us the End has perhaps lost its naïve *imminence*, its shadow still lies on the crises of our fictions; we may speak of it as *immanent*."[8] As a work of fiction, *Eternal Sunshine* is in alignment with Kermode's idea; the film's focus is on a minor, intimate, and personal eschatology; no city comes to a standstill, no fire and brimstone of Judgement Day: just simple loss of recall. Gondry and Kaufman build this loss as an immanent subject with the story, but the cinematic treatment requires visual cues of the immanence of Clementine's disappearance.

Gondry permeates each of Joel's memories with the inevitable loss of Clementine from his life once he wakes up. He does this by making Clementine, as object and person, disappear from each memory in a variety of ways: blurring out of focus, suddenly vanishing when she turns a corner, or being dragged away from Joel and the camera, from light into void. The loss is compounded by the multiplicity of methods employed to make Clementine vanish from forethought. The audience is left guessing how she will disappear from this one. And none of the disappearances calls for anything more than set manipulation or change in camera focus.

For Gondry, and for Kate Winslet, the creator of a whimsical character whom the audience sees mostly through the lens of Joel's memories, the presence and performance of Clementine has to be an almost effervescent one. Todd McGowan argues that Clementine

> is never a fully present object on the screen, either for Joel or for us. As a result of this procedure, she is constantly on the verge of actually disappearing . . . her presence is always fleeting, which has the effect of reigniting and sustaining the desire for her.[9]

If Clementine disappears, the memory is a void, and not worth keeping at all, because it does not have meaning without her. It is her disappearance from each memory that indicates it is now removed or on the brink of erasure. Her lack of sustained presence is the major procedural threat that indicates that Joel's personal apocalypse is imminent.

Before each vanishing point, however, Gondry gives the memory time to play out, to unfurl fully so that Clementine is able to fully occupy the scene before she disappears. But as soon as her presence becomes established, and Joel has connected with her again, ostensibly outwitting the memory-erasing technicians, the vanishing act recurs. McGowan puts it in terms of object-removal: "the perfect moment vanishes at the precise moment one identifies it as such, and the object that creates the perfections resists any attempt that one makes to hold onto it."[10] Clementine disappears, the memory is wiped out, and the technicians move on to the next memory.

THE ISSUE WITH COGNITIVISM

Two schools of thought, which purport to be at odds when attempting to analyze a film, can actually help illuminate *Eternal Sunshine* when their approaches are applied simultaneously, while keeping in mind Kermodic thoughts about literature's teleological bent. Cognitivism, as Noël Carroll describes it, is concerned mostly with "cognitive and rational processes rather than irrational or unconscious ones" and is "a stance" rather than "a single, unified theory" that claims "to explain phenomena better than extant psychoanalytic theories."[11] Carroll states that cognitivists are concerned mostly with "film reception and comprehension," which is an area also explored "by psychoanalytic film theorists."[12]

But whereas cognitivism relates to the "how does it work?" and the logistics of filmmaking and analytic deconstruction that enables comprehension, psychoanalytic theories are the avenues of understanding—the "what does it mean?"—once the logistics have been worked out. The "how does it work?" is just as important as "what does it mean?"; at the very least, the questions are helically intertwined in each plot mechanism. But, as Carroll notes,

> Psychoanalytic theories face a special burden of proof when confronting cognitive theorists. For a psychoanalytic theory to reenter the debate, it must be demonstrated that there is something about the data of which given cognitivist (or organic) explanations can give no adequate account, and which, as well, cannot be explained by some other cognitive theory, which remainder is susceptible to psychoanalytic theory *alone*.[13]

What Carroll appears to overlook is that this film—or *any* film—is much more than its "data" points. Beyond the construction of a cause-and-effect chain, the film requires interpretation through several different lenses, which yield different ontological, if not epistemological, ways of viewing the film. There is no inherent burden of proof on psychoanalytic theory that makes it a secondary mode of understanding films, once all cognitivist approaches have been exhausted.

For example, in *Eternal Sunshine*, while cognitively it may be understood that Joel exits the bookstore and arrives at his friends' house subsequently (this, then that), the *meaning* of the chain can be understood only when psychoanalytically processing the mental leap that Joel makes: that the darkness that follows Joel out of the bookstore is indicative of him losing that memory, of Clementine not seeming to recognize him, forever; and that *this*, the session of therapy and consultation with his friends, is the next significant memory associated with Clementine, and not the passage of time it takes him to reach their place, which has been erased along with the memory of the bookstore.

Additionally, it is only possible to empathize with Joel with a degree of involvement beyond trying to merely understand the mechanism of the film. While cognitivist approaches, then, are limited to a hovering viewpoint from which to understand the audience's comprehension of the film, it is only through a psychoanalytic understanding of *Eternal Sunshine* that the cause of audience empathy with Joel can be understood. Alex Neill argues that "the imaginative activity that is characteristic of empathy involves taking another's perspective on things, imaginatively representing to oneself the thoughts, beliefs, desires, and so on of another as though they were one's own."[14] Empathy is not possible with a film's protagonist from a detached perspective, and while logical understanding of empathy is possible cognitively, an experiential understanding calls for psychological investment with the protagonist's condition and his dilemma(s).

Gondry and Kaufman appeal to universal fears with the story's essential crises: what stands in the way of Joel's love for Clementine is his fear that he is not interesting enough to keep her attention and that she may be looking for something better; what impedes Clementine's commitment to Joel is that he closes up and hides his very interesting thoughts, and remains suspicious about her aggressive way of loving—will she (even *did* she) cheat on him? The representation of the clichés of perceived "boredom" and "promiscuity" as the bases for ending relationships puts the viewers in the direct position of one or other of the characters on screen. Joel and Clementine have only their fears to blame because, as audience members who understand both sides of the story, viewers of the film know that Joel is a very interesting character, with sophisticated thought patterns and artistic inclinations, while Clementine is utterly devoted to Joel, and the passion she exhibits towards him is authentic, and not a sign of promiscuity.

At the end of the film, Gondry and Kaufman give the audience cathartic release from being the only possessors of both sides of the story. Once Joel and Clementine re-encounter each other, after having undergone the Lacuna Inc. memory-removal procedure, and once they have formed a reconnection without knowing anything about their past two-year relationship, they are suddenly confronted with tapes sent to them by Lacuna Inc. Through these tapes, Joel and Clementine are granted what James Bowman calls "a double perspective on their relationship: they simultaneously see the typically sweet, trusting, ever-hopeful beginning and the typically sour, suspicious, despairing end."[15] Bowman's use of "typically" is key here (in how it indicates the clichéd reasons for the relationship to go sour), as is the idea that the two perspectives that Joel and Clementine possess are that of the beginning and that of the end: what they do not get is the middle, on the basis of which an ending can occur.

Joel and Clementine come to terms rather rapidly with each other's flaws in a quick back-and-forth about how she may eventually find him boring, even though he is not, and he may have to trust her faithfulness. However, there is a naive hopefulness in their exchange, a giving-up of sorts, to a fate, an eventuality that has not happened this second time around in the beginning of a romance. Cognitively, it is difficult to reconcile how the two can transcend a fate that is coming straight at them. Bowman, with a cognitivist's summation, argues that "memory is also shorthand for identity: we are our memories" and that "it is precisely memory that solidifies identity"; but he fails to account for Joel and Clementine reconnecting from a point at which they had been erased from each other's lives.[16] The film argues, at least according to one psychoanalytic reading, that humans transcend their memories, even gaps in their memories. It is possible to re-engage with a person just by connecting with the feeling of them. Gondry and Kaufman are arguing against the idea that memory is what constitutes identity. Gaps in memory can be filled and the "sense of loss of self" is recoverable through meeting a person (or persons) that fill(s) an individual's personal lacunae.[17]

MAKING MEANING THROUGH ENGAGEMENT

Once Joel recognizes that the memories he is losing are worth salvaging, he attempts to communicate directly with the memory-removal technicians, meaning that he tries to communicate across the barrier of sleep and signal to Stan and Patrick, and Mary (a clinic receptionist who joins Stan and Patrick in Joel's apartment), that he wants the procedure to stop, that he wishes to "call it off." Through sheer power of will, his sleeping body briefly opens its eyes and watches his apartment as it has been lit up in the middle of the night by the Lacuna Inc. employees; he even says the name "Patrick" in a whisper that Stan hears, or thinks he hears.

The presence of a rival spurs Joel to question "how" Clementine has become entangled with someone else, but it is Joel's increased engagement with his memories, as they appear and dissipate, which causes him to recognize their worth. The act of remembering is an act of reliving and re-interpreting through (enforced) engagement with the memories; it is a confrontation. While at first he is a passive recipient of the memories, the idea of Patrick inspires Joel into a more active mode of receiving, as well as a failed attempt at negotiating with the technicians.

As audience members, viewers are not certain that the memory-removal procedure will be completed; Joel's attempts at disrupting the process may succeed. However, as Kermode points out, "we concern ourselves with the conflict between the deterministic pattern any plot suggests, and the freedom of persons within that plot to choose and so to alter the structure, the relations of beginning, middle, and end."[18] The increased engagement and investment that Joel begins to exhibit in each relived memory as the film progresses develop a pattern of increased association with and meaning from his memories for the audience as well.

For Joel, the memories, as he relives them, take on a different kind of significance than they had when he first created them by living them. In the first living, they were what Kermode calls "*chronos*," which "is 'passing time' or 'waiting time'—that which, according to Revelation, 'shall be no more,'" whereas, once he realizes the worth of each of those memories, it becomes what Kermode calls "*kairos*," "a point in time filled with significance, charged with a meaning derived from its relation to the end."[19] Even the most banal memory, such as that of the couple eating silently at a restaurant, both bored with each other, avoiding all non-monosyllabic conversation, becomes an important one for Joel; he plays guessing games with his memory, saying before Clementine the words that will come out of her mouth as she complains about his domestic habits—"gross . . . repulsive"—and he smiles at the insults he recalls while he relives the recalling.

Gondry and Kaufman not only tell viewers about the first romance in reverse chronological order, they also bookend the entire process with glimpses of the post-memory-removal re-encounter of Joel and Clementine, in which they rebegin a romance from scratch. In this rebeginning is the kindling of romance: boy meets girl is where the film begins, which is just as much *in medias res* as the point at which the credits appear, with Joel crying at the end of the relationship once a flashback leads to the point where he first learns about Clementine having undergone the Lacuna Inc. process. As Kermode points out, great works of literature contain "beginnings, ends, and potentiality," especially novels, which "concern themselves only with human time, a faring forward irreversibly into a virgin future from ecstasy to ecstasy . . . from *kairos* to *kairos*."[20] Like deft writers of one of the most skillfully constructed works of literature, Gondry and Kaufman are careful to keep Joel and Clementine's story mostly in the arena of Kermodic "potentiality." Even as Joel realizes the potential of his own memories to mean more than he first gave them credit for, the audience is entranced, by the bookendings that promise fresh love and a new start, to surrender at first, along with Joel, to the idea that "awkward romance is the only possible kind in our post-modern condition" and at the end of the film to wonder whether soulmates do really exist, as the film seems to argue. Alternative—even opposite—readings of the ending are possible, of course, especially after the very last shot of the film, but more on that later.

For now, let us consider what kind of romance does not succeed. Patrick uses Joel and Clementine's erased memories to try to become Clementine's significant other. But even though, as McGowan points out, "Patrick knows exactly what Clementine wants" and is "able to reproduce the scenes from her past that have given her the greatest enjoyment . . . the more Patrick gives Clementine what she wants, the more Clementine finds him a repulsive figure."[21] McGowan asserts the psychoanalytic reading that although Patrick says the words—Joel's words—in "the proper way . . . he fails because the words, when he says them, lack nothing" while, "in contrast, when Joel says the same words, [Clementine] hears his desire, his uncertainty about her desire and about how she'll respond to what he says."[22] While McGowan's cognitivist reading of the scene is appropriate, the psychoanalytic part fails to acknowledge that Patrick is trying to fill the gaps in Clementine's self with pieces that do not belong to him; he is impersonating Joel. The incongruity, rather than any "lack of desire," is what makes Clementine question what Patrick is saying—it is his lack of passion and authenticity, and not the kind of "proper" delivery of his lines that causes Clementine to suspect Patrick; he is a phony, and she senses it. When Joel says the lines, originally, they had a creative aspect to them; they came out unrehearsed and not recurring, incongruously, with speech patterns that could not possibly be associated with anybody but his own character.

The past does not simply disappear because Lacuna Inc.'s process promises it will. Though Dr. Mierzwiak has tried to give his patients "freedom from the past," only a reset Joel is able to appeal to Clementine once she has undergone the memory-removal process.[23] They do not repeat dialogue from their first meeting; and it is not the same memories that they re-create, so they are not filling gaps that were removed in memory; what they fill up, once they meet again, both as supposed *tabula rasa*, is the lack of each other's presence in their lives.

An inevitable question arises: while the process of memory removal is being conducted on Joel (and on Clementine), does his renewed interest in his memories, even though they are slipping away, change him? In other words, does his associating deeper meaning with his initially banal memories, even though they are being erased, make the meaning he associates with them *count* for something? According to one rather obvious reading, the film argues—through the last words within Joel's memory-removal process, when the Clementine of his imagination tells him to meet her "in Montauk"—that, yes; despite the removal of Clementine from his storage bank, Joel sets himself up for another beginning with her and so does she, even though the audience does not witness it. This reading is especially supported by the psychoanalytic reading that gives credence to the "soulmates" theory that Gondry and Kaufman leave up for debate.

What is indisputable about cognitivist and psychoanalytic readings of the film is the argument put forward by Gondry that the past is not static. Gondry shows Joel's engagement with his own memories as he keeps switching point of view from one memory to the next, and even sometimes within the same memory. In his review, Chris Norris describes succinctly Joel's manipulations of his own memory:

> Joel wanders through his own psyche from memory to memory, reexperiencing his true love, realizing his folly, and then trying to circumvent the erasing process by fleeing the synaptic marauders with his damsel, ever deeper into his labyrinthine memory. It's an intracranial action/romance.[24]

But it is not always full of action, this romance. And not always is the action of the memories full of romance. Only once Joel begins to re-evaluate the worth of his memories, and to regret the procedure, does it turn from a low-key science fiction film to a film with both action and romance.

REVELATION: THE LIFTING OF THE VEIL

Apocalyptic thinking does not necessarily have to be tied to eschatological notions within a work of literature. While Frank Kermode argues that literature is ends-oriented, if not End-oriented, Erich Auerbach associates revelations with a different kind of "lifting of the veils" (the etymological meaning of the Greek word "apocalypse") than one linked only to end-based *exposé*. In *Mimesis: The Representation of Reality in Western Literature*, Auerbach lists two styles prevalent in narratives. The first, the "Homeric style," is able "to represent phenomena in a fully externalized form, visible and palpable in all their parts, and completely fixed in their spatial and temporal relations."[25] In other words, the Homeric style, which creates epic stories such as the tales of Odysseus, produces "closed texts" that are linear in narration, and have a beginning, a middle and an end.

The other style, Revelation, is characterized by "the externalization of only so much of the phenomena as is necessary for the purpose of the narrative" while "all else [is] left in obscurity; the decisive points of the narrative alone are emphasized, what lies between is nonexistent; time and place are undefined and call for interpretation."[26] As Kermode interprets the style of Revelation, he cites Auerbach's use of the example of the sacrifice of Isaac: this "story has continually to be modified by reference to what is known of the divine plan from the Creation to the Last Days: it is perpetually open to history, to reinterpretation."[27] In other words, though there is a divulgence of details within the story of Isaac's sacrifice, they are scant enough for it to remain an "open" text: the meaning of the narration can be constantly revised according to new contexts within which the story applies. Auerbach argues of the writer of the biblical story that "what he produced ... was not primarily oriented toward 'realism' (if he succeeded in being realistic, it was merely a means, not an end); it was oriented toward truth."[28]

Something similar is at work in *Eternal Sunshine of the Spotless Mind*. Gondry's visual crafting of scenes that re-create Joel's memories in the middle of the process of their erasure borrows heavily from "realistic" processes of erasure. Note the disintegration of the house on Montauk beach during the final act of erasure as an indicator of the process of removal, as well as the Barnes & Noble shelf lined with blank spines as color and titles are removed from Joel's memory. But these "realistic" notions of tangible material undergoing collapse and deletion are merely representations of abstract ideas that signify what is happening to Joel's memories: the removal of neural connections is gestured at while the meaning of them is an "open text," left undetermined, and open to interpretation. That the house collapses while Clementine merely vanishes or goes out of focus should indicate how open to interpretation Lacuna Inc.'s process of erasure is. Similarly, for many of the memory scenes, Gondry uses very limited, one-bulb lighting to illuminate just enough details for the visual aspect of the memory to become illuminated, while keeping the borders of the scenes in relative, if not complete, darkness.

Eternal Sunshine is a more reflective film than even the "intra-cranial action/romance" description allows. Deeper reflections on its "message" can yield ethical positions beyond merely the overt ones, like *do not use other people's memories to entrap them in romantic relationships with you!* For instance, should human beings "have to hang on to the bad memories as well as the good" because "the bad ones are somehow *included* in the good ones and are redeemed by them," as Bowman argues?[29] What about memories of trauma—and who is to decide what is traumatic for any one person, even if it is not for another? Of course, to grow and to become stronger one must learn to cope and contextualize the meaning of memories. Bowman argues that "if you come to forget the bad times, the good times go too,"[30] and acceptance of the bad indicates development. Joel undergoes this process of maturation through deeper engagement with his memories, and that growth seems to last him even beyond their erasure, when he refuses to let flaws in their personalities prevent Clementine and him from starting a relationship, even after their previous one did not work out. He chooses to sacrifice what Christopher Grau calls "contentment" because he places more value on "veracity"; he values knowing what happened in the past, because it allows Clementine and him to move past their previous mistakes.

Ethical dilemmas complicate the viewing of films, and take the audience to a cerebral space where they contemplate whether (as in *Memento*'s case) revenge is so important that it does not matter on whom it is enacted, as long as the avenger is able to achieve closure; and whether it would be right to erase someone from memory if the memories or the association with that person triggered feelings of trauma.

Films with ethical dilemmas that require cerebral effort on the audience's part usually attract niche audiences, but both *Memento* and *Eternal Sunshine* have grossed between $25 and 40 million at the box office; they are cult films, with a good following within a sub-section of the mainstream audience. The decoding of the logic of these films (a cognitivist understanding) does require more effort from their audience than is explained through a nearly tutorial-like introduction in films like *Inception*.

Revelation does not come without cerebration, though. Intricacies must be understood cognitively as well as psychoanalytically. The intricate plot of *Eternal*

Sunshine weaves the world of memories into the conscious one in very subtle ways; without one, the other would not exist, and the plot would not move forward. For instance, it is because of Mary, the receptionist at Lacuna Inc., that Joel and Clementine find out about their past relationship. It all pivots on an ethical choice that is quickly made without the reader's overt attention being brought to the point at which it has been made. When Joel decides he wants to keep his memories of Clementine, and tries to hide her in memories where she does not belong—humiliating ones from childhood, especially—the technicians have to call in Dr. Mierzwiak to salvage the operation. Mary flirts unabashedly with Dr. Mierzwiak after Stan and Patrick leave, and the doctor and receptionist kiss. It transpires that this is not the first time they have become intimate; Mary has previously requested a memory erasure, so she does not remember the original affair that she had with Dr. Mierzwiak. She makes an ethical choice not only for herself, but for all patients of Lacuna Inc. She mails out all the recordings of pre-erasure patients who list the reasons why they want their memories erased.

In effect, Mary is forcing the patients to face their past. For some patients, the effect could be devastating, but the film glosses over the ethical implications of Mary's choice to drive forward the main plot. Revelation comes at a cost; in the case of *Eternal Sunshine*, the cost of truth is that the film's focus is restricted to Joel and Clementine at the expense of other patients that the viewer does not even know about. Gondry deftly hides the dilemma, which cannot be mulled over once it becomes a plot point in the past and yields positive results, at least for Joel and Clementine.

"ANXIOUS HAPPY ENDINGS" AND THE LAST SCENE

The ending of *Eternal Sunshine of the Spotless Mind* has been read on a spectrum that ranges from considering that Joel and Clementine's relationship will fail with an "agonizing breakup" to believing that they have achieved a happily ever after.[31] While this can be said of many films, Gondry highlights ambiguity in multiple ways with the final two scenes of the film. Just after they receive their own pre-erasure cassettes from Mary at Lacuna Inc., Joel and Clementine are able to listen to each other explain why they want to have their memories of the other removed: the reasons, promiscuity and boredom, rear their heads again in the voices of their past selves. Both want to escape the hurtful words of the ex- and future romantic partner. But after Clementine leaves Joel's apartment while he is listening to himself say hurtful things (and negating them in the present), he hurries after her, to tell her to "wait." Clementine tells him that she is not a "concept" but a "fucked-up girl" who is looking for her "own peace of mind." Joel does not argue back. He says the one word: "Okay," with a shrug and a relenting smile, after which they both say that word again, and laugh, just before one final shot of them playing in the snow, after which credits roll.

In that tension-releasing shrug, and that simple, reassuring word "Okay," Gondry and Kaufman set up the possible interpretations for the ending. Already ambiguous as an ending, the scene is further complicated by what Gondry depicts just before the credits roll: Joel and Clementine are running on the snow-covered Montauk beach, and as they run further away from the camera, the shot repeats from the middle of their run, moves forward, and then cuts again to further along in their run, and moves forward. This could be read in several ways that respectively sentence Joel and Clementine to either eternally recurring happiness, or multiple memory-erasure processes, or, simply, reliving their memories from whichever point they like. It could also just be a game on Gondry's part, putting an opening into the ending, mimicking what Richard J. Allen calls the condition of "post-modernity: not wanting the game to end."[32]

As Laine puts it, readings of the film depend on the viewer's "central assumption" regarding the idea of "'true' love" and whether it can be "geared to one person only, and cannot be administered in variable degrees."[33] Laine sees the potentiality of where Gondry chooses to leave the narrative—"perhaps the ending can also be seen as a possible origin of authentic love between Joel and Clementine"—and here, perhaps, Laine wishes to label the original romantic association a "naive" kind of love rather than an "authentic" one.[34] Certainly, it can be inferred from Kaufman's interviews regarding *Eternal Sunshine* that he was trying to create in this script a more authentic version of romance than the "damaging" fairy tales that mainstream cinema had been selling to its audiences.

To consider Joel's growth is perhaps a much more fascinating locus of ethical concern than the final frames of the frolic in the snow, but both yield interesting variations in reading. Joel has matured through the process of memory removal; even though something has been taken from him, perhaps the simultaneous juxtaposition of the beginning of romance and the end of romance that is afforded to him enables an optimistic glance past the flaws that threaten the relationship. Maybe he needed to see the ending with the vulnerability and openheartedness that a new romance brings with it; maybe this was the only way forward for Clementine and Joel. Howard Hampton agrees that Joel shows "behavioral cues we can all profit from" when viewing our own memories.[35] When the audience views its own memories as matter for re-engagement and material for drawing further lessons, the self-reflection is much like the audience-inclusive self-reflection that Joel experiences.

Joel's singular experience, influenced as it is by the "Patrick" factor (which permeates both sleeping state and wakefulness), does not mean, however, that the process guarantees growth. In fact, Joel is the outlier, and, as Tracey K.

Parker argues, "Joel and Clementine's problems are never solved."[36] Parker goes on to state that *Eternal Sunshine* is among "examples of art whose form and content work together to impart this message to the viewer [that] . . . self-help culture and postmodern art concern themselves with the individual's loss of a concrete identity."[37] While there is no *happily ever after* in the film, Parker's reading seems unsound, based on Joel and Clementine's relief at having moved past their problems, and accepting that they are flawed individuals. Their growth guarantees that the problem has been faced, if not eliminated, and they are ready for a complex relationship that does not deal only with binaries. In *Eternal Sunshine*, the ending is more of what Michael Meyer calls an "anxious happy ending" than an eternal recurrence or happily ever after; and Joel and Clementine, by vocalizing their "Okay"s at the end, both perform "an act of acceptance that 'living happily ever after' takes the form of 'living uncertainly ever after,' but doing so in a spirit of memory, forgiveness, and reconciliation."[38] Similarly, Laine labels the repeated frames of the snow frolic a "recurrence": "for a Nietzschean spectator the 'eternal' aspect indicates the innumerable times that Joel and Clementine will have to live through their past relationship."[39]

Gondry's work is firmly in Revelation rather than Homeric territory because of his decision to leave the cognitivist interpretation open to debate. Plantinga points out that

> Gondry's imaginative visual style . . . represents both memory and its disappearance, making use of elaborate set pieces and lighting changes . . . offer[ing] a surprisingly cogent thought experiment that raises fascinating questions about memory, romantic relationships and the nature of attraction and other issues.[40]

That he does not answer the questions is a credit to the director; the ethics and visuals of *Eternal Sunshine* can mean different things, even evolving things, just like Revelation.

CONCLUSION: THE AVANT-GARDE AND THE ANTI-CAPITAL FILM

Gondry consciously eschews a "realist" cinematic depiction of Joel's dilemmas to create something closer to truth in *Eternal Sunshine*. While *Inception* targets spectacle, Gondry's aim seems to be creating veracity rather than entertainment through scaling of experience. Gondry creates a mode of revelation and concealment that is simultaneous, much like the real-life reliving of memories

In an introductory chapter to *The Film Studies Reader* (edited by Hollows et al.), the editorial note lists how:

> Adorno and Horkheimer ... present a "pessimistic thesis" about the fate of culture under twentieth-century capitalism. For them, the only source of political optimism is found in avant-garde art, which transcends all-encompassing control of the culture industry because it refuses to become a commodity and so maintains both its aesthetic and political freedom. Whereas mass culture reconciled its audience to the system, avant-garde art showed its audience the contradictions within the system. Unlike the masses who passively consumed the product of the culture industry, the audience for avant-garde art were 'enlightened outsiders' who struggled to make meanings from art forms that refused to let themselves be easily consumed.[41]

Tracey K. Parker points out how "fresh starts are commodified" in Lacuna Inc.'s technology.[42] That the procedure does not work, or seems to fail, is the individual's fight against the system of capital succeeding. And that the film does not have a commodified happy ending makes it more stimulating. Along these lines, Sheryl Vint points out that "the film 'transcends' both romantic comedy and sf because it refuses to provide the expected ending built into each genre's formula."[43] It is the narrative of a cautious triumph of a reticent individual over technological intervention's influence on a tenuous relationship. The cataclysm and apocalypse in this narrative are on the individual level—world-changing only on a micro scale. Therefore, quite appropriately, Gondry's visual treatment via subtle and nuanced visualizations of memory's simultaneous obfuscation and revelation is unlike *Inception*'s spectacular treatment of visualizing mental processes. The larger implication of struggles against capitalism are left to viewers' imagination to unfold as they contemplate how the recipients of Mary's letters and the memories on their own tapes will react to being faced with the memories they wished to have erased. Whether the technology will triumph over individual will is an unanswered question—except in Joel and Clementine's case, where Gondry shows that humans (at least temporarily, but significantly) triumph over technological intervention.

NOTES

1. *Kylie Minogue—Come Into My World*, directed by Michel Gondry, performed by Kylie Minogue. YouTube.com, April 6, 2010. Available at <https://www.youtube.com/watch?v=63vqob-MljQ> (last accessed August 1, 2018).

2. *Nespresso Commercial—George Clooney—What Else*, directed by Michel Gondry, performed by George Clooney. Youtube.com, July 5, 2006. Available at <https://www.youtube.com/watch?v=DfyeXrdZZ10>(last accessed 1 August 2018).
3. *Eternal Sunshine of the Spotless Mind*, screenplay by Charlie Kaufman, directed by Michel Gondry (London: Momentum Pictures, 2004).
4. John Hill and Pamela Church Gibson, eds, *Film Studies: Critical Approaches* (New York: Oxford University Press, 2000), 19.
5. Tarja Laine, *Feeling Cinema: Emotional Dynamics in Film Studies* (New York City: Continuum, 2011), 136.
6. Laine, *Feeling Cinema*, 138.
7. Frank Kermode, *The Sense of an Ending* (Oxford: Oxford University Press, 2000), 25.
8. Kermode, *The Sense of an Ending*, 25.
9. Todd McGowan, *Out of Time: Desire in Atemporal Cinema* (Minneapolis: University of Minnesota Press, 2011), 94.
10. McGowan, *Out of Time*, 95.
11. David Bordwell and Noël Carroll, eds, *Post-Theory: Reconstructing Film Studies* (Madison: University of Wisconsin Press, 1996), 61–2.
12. Bordwell and Carroll, *Post-Theory*, 62.
13. Bordwell and Carroll, *Post-Theory*, 65.
14. Bordwell and Carroll, *Post-Theory*, 186.
15. James Bowman, "Memory and the Movies," *The New Atlantis*, 5 (2004): 89.
16. Bowman, "Memory and the Movies," 85.
17. Bowman, "Memory and the Movies," 89.
18. Kermode, *The Sense of an Ending*, 30.
19. Kermode, *The Sense of an Ending*, 47.
20. Kermode, *The Sense of an Ending*, 138–9.
21. McGowan, *Out of Time*, 95.
22. McGowan, *Out of Time*, 96.
23. McGowan, *Out of Time*, 97.
24. Chris Norris, "Charlie Kaufman and Michel Gondry's Head Trip," *Film Comment*, 40, no. 2 (2004): 20.
25. Erich Auerbach, *Mimesis: The Representation of Reality in Western Literature*, trans. Willard R. Trask (Princeton: Princeton University Press, 1974), 6.
26. Auerbach, *Mimesis*, 11.
27. Kermode, *The Sense of an Ending*, 5–6.
28. Auerbach, *Mimesis*, 14.
29. Bowman, "Memory and the Movies," 90.
30. Bowman, "Memory and the Movies," 79.
31. Bart Cardullo, "Review: Falling in and out of Love, Again," *The Hudson Review*, 60, no. 2 (2007): 302.
32. Richard J. Allen, "Beginning, Middle, End of an Era: Has Technology Trumped Aristotle?," *Journal of Film and Video*, 65, nos 1–2 (2013): 12.
33. Laine, *Feeling Cinema*, 135.
34. Laine, *Feeling Cinema*, 139.
35. Howard Hampton, "True Romance: On the Current State of Date Movies," *Film Comment*, 40, no. 6 (August 2004): 30–4.
36. Tracey K. Parker, "Do I Lie to Myself to Be Happy?: Self-Help Culture and Fragmentation in Postmodern Film," *Interdisciplinary Literary Studies*, 10, no. 1 (2008): 5.
37. Parker, "Do I Lie to Myself to Be Happy?," 13.

38. Michael Meyer, "Reflections on Comic Reconciliations: Ethics, Memory, and Anxious Happy Endings," *The Journal of Aesthetics and Art Criticism*, 66, no. 1 (2008): 82.
39. Laine, *Feeling Cinema*, 139.
40. Carl Plantinga, "Reviewed Work(s): *Eternal Sunshine of the Spotless Mind* by Christopher Grau," *The Journal of Aesthetics and Art Criticism*, 68, no. 4 (2010): 419.
41. Mark Jancovich, Peter Hutchings and Joanne Hollows, eds, *The Film Studies Reader* (London: Arnold, 2000), 2.
42. Parker, "Do I Lie to Myself to Be Happy?," 6.
43. Sheryl Vint, "Review: Possibilities for a Science-Fiction Cinema," *Science Fiction Studies*, 43, no. 3 (November 2016): 570.

PART IV

Gondry in/on America

CHAPTER 9

The Reel and Surreal of Race in America: Michel Gondry and the African–American Identity Crisis of Dave Chappelle

Monique Taylor

OUTSIDER(S) LOOKING IN

Throughout its history, America has been the subject of observations by outsiders whose perspectives can offer a window into the American psyche. From classic texts such as *Democracy in America* (1835) by French political scientist Alexis de Tocqueville (1805–59) to *An American Dilemma: The Negro Problem and Modern Democracy* (1944) by Swedish sociologist Gunnar Myrdal (1898–1987), the trope of the outsider-looking-in has been a longstanding source of socio-political commentary about America. Especially concerning America's "Achilles heel" of race, outsiders' perspectives such as these often approach fractured identities as social constructions. In many of Michel Gondry's transnational/transatlantic cinematic collaborations, including those with screenwriter Charlie Kaufman, public intellectual and scholar Noam Chomsky, and—most importantly for the purposes of this discussion—actor and comedian Dave Chappelle, Gondry plays the role of outsider-looking-in as both a participant in and an observer of aspects of American cultural conversations on memory, identity, and language.

In his commercial advertisements as well as music videos and films, Gondry showcases a recognizable visual style that often makes use of windows, mirrors, and other glass mediations and boundaries of perception to frame as well as to focus a gaze from an outsider's perspective. At times, the viewer floats into windows that could be portals through ears, eyes, and noses in a quest to reach the neural origin of stories that add up to interiority. Gondry's works, in which dreams and being wide awake collide and unfold in flights of fancy, are often called whimsical and playful, as well as surreal and imaginative. As the director of African–American comedian Dave Chappelle's concert documentary, *Dave Chappelle's Block Party*

(2005), Gondry enters the American discourse on race, to which he brings his unique vantage as a French visual artist who makes films in both his native France and the United States.

By way of a neighborhood block party staged in a gentrifying community in Brooklyn, New York, *Dave Chappelle's Block Party* documents the intersection of music, popular culture, and race, which are forces that are simultaneously cohesive and disruptive. Using a documentary format, Gondry's film depicts the titular block party, hosted by Chappelle, that brings together artists including ?uestlove, Mos Def, Kanye West, Erykah Badu, and Jill Scott, as well as Lauryn Hill in a reunion with The Fugees. Just as in his subsequent feature film, *Be Kind Rewind* (2008), in *Dave Chappelle's Block Party* Gondry places memory at the center of multiple visions and construction(s) of community. Through the same fragmented and non-linear approach that Gondry had previously employed in *Eternal Sunshine of the Spotless Mind* (2004), in *Block Party* he confers instability of memory and narrative onto the real and surreal of race.

While *Dave Chappelle's Block Party* has been compared to the 1973 documentary *Wattstax* (Mel Stuart), a soul-stoked celebration of Black Pride in post-Watts Los Angeles, Gondry's film is better read as a "post-soul" construction. As defined by Mark Anthony Neal, the post-soul aesthetic is a "meditation on contemporary issues such as deindustrialization, desegregation, the corporate annexation of black popular expression . . . and the general commodification of black life and black culture."[1] However, whereas *Wattstax* ended with a freeze frame of a fist raised in the Black Power salute, in *Block Party* the black nationalist image is presented as a more commodified signifier sported on the tongue of Chappelle's canvas sneakers. In another moment in *Block Party*, Erykah Badu's performance under her mushroom cloud of an afro recalls that of Angela Davis during the 1970s. Never mind that the wind carries Badu's wig away: the afro as a marker of Black Pride consciousness is playfully laid bare rather than being airbrushed out or left on the cutting-room floor. Badu jubilantly continues to perform and appears to take flight when she exits the stage by being carried away as a crowd surfer. This emphasis on the construction, performance, and commodification of race both distinguishes *Dave Chappelle's Block Party* from other documentaries about aspects of the African–American experience, such as the above-mentioned *Wattstax*, and intersects with Chappelle's own persona as star and performer.

Dave Chappelle's Block Party was released in 2005 during the time of Chappelle's highly publicized flight from Comedy Central but before his departure from the United States for South Africa. When Chappelle shocked the world by walking away from a $50-million renewal contract for *Chappelle's Show*—his successful Comedy Central sketch comedy program—at the start of the show's third season, rumors swirled about drugs, criminality, and mental illness. Walking a fine line between edginess and mainstream success, the humor in *Chappelle's Show* had often flirted with controversy. Indeed, Chappelle's sketches could be innovative and controversial, such as the critically acclaimed skit, "Frontline: Blind Hatred," featuring the character of Clayton Bigsby, the blind African–American who is a white supremacist (Bigsby is played by Chappelle).[2] The show's sensibility was characterized as displaying "liberatory impulses,"[3] but at times Chappelle was also accused of trafficking in "stereotypical tropes."[4]

The success of *Chappelle's Show* birthed an existential crisis for Chappelle. When he overheard white crew members on the set laughing, he famously wondered, "are they laughing *with* me or are they laughing *at* me?"[5] This was Chappelle's own case of DuBoisian "double consciousness," a moment of existential angst when racism forces black Americans to see themselves through the eyes of white others. Ironically, at the start of the second season of *Chappelle's Show*, Chappelle had introduced a three-sketch series entitled "When Keeping It Real Goes Wrong,"[6] whose title is a play on a well-known watchword ("keeping it real") in the hip hop community. In Chappelle's hands, the premise laid bare African–American angst over protecting and projecting one's authenticity in the face of success. Keeping it real, Chappelle had warned in setting up the sketches, is not as easy as it seems.

It is worth noting that Chappelle's edgy and complicated depictions of race in *Chappelle's Show* were shared creations with a *white* writing partner, Neal Brennan. Media scholar Bambi Haggins has noted that Chappelle's work "interweaves multiple threads of American popular culture"[7] and brings a "sense of fluidity" that "embodies the movement in his life across communities and regions."[8] Therefore Chappelle is, according to Haggins, imbued with dual credibility and crossover appeal. In part, Haggins attributes these qualities to the collaboration between Brennan and Chappelle as co-writers with a "comic strategy that is purposefully multiple."[9] I would argue that this multiplicity characterizes Chappelle's collaboration with Michel Gondry as well.

REEL AND SURREAL: CRAZY AND FANTASTICAL WITH CHAPPELLE AND MICHEL

In film, a surrealist attitude is marked by a logic that is illogical. Dreams and flights of fancy disturb and disintegrate reality. In contemporary American life, where a post-racialist desire to reach beyond the past now sits uncomfortably alongside a race-filled present, surrealism strikes the right note for probing analysis. In so far as *Block Party* joins the post-soul sensibility of an African–American comedian with the surreal eye of a French filmmaker, it reveals a distinctive visual vernacular that channels the highly publicized angst associated with Chappelle's struggle to "keep it real." Chappelle and Gondry bridge the real and surreal by constructing a virtual community that is hybrid and hyper-real. As a hybrid construction, the film mixes and matches documentary, stand-up comedy, and music video techniques. Its hyper-reality builds to an end product that functions as a sign and a simulation of community.

The concert at the center of *Dave Chappelle's Block Party* happens at a specific time (a summer Saturday afternoon) and in a specific place (the Bedford–Stuyvesant neighborhood of Brooklyn). But the event begins only after the film has moved back and forth in time and place between the state of Ohio—where Chappelle spent part of his youth, and where he maintains a residence—and New York City. By unfolding across multiple temporalities and locations, the documentary offers a behind-the-scenes glimpse of Chappelle's own efforts at community-building by trailing him as he promotes a hip hop experience that will be cross-generational as well as multiracial. The camera films a range of moments when Chappelle invites people to join up: he is seen knocking on doors as well as entering homes, apartments, and shops. The camera follows Chappelle into these spaces, thus creating an important sensation of bonding that Gondry can construct and control visually. The dialogue is chatty and intimate. Chappelle is in search of ideas that are otherwise elusive: solidarity, identity, belonging. With The Roots as a house band that anchors the experience and provides back story in some of the film's intimate backstage moments, ?uestlove and his players lend a touch of authenticity. But a close analysis of the film reveals when and how the viewer enters a world of fantasy and make-believe.

BEHIND THE MASK: BLACK IDENTITY IN POST-SOUL AMERICA

The viewer is thrown into this world of play from the moment that *Dave Chappelle's Block Party* begins. While the screen is still black, the spluttering of an engine that will not start is heard. The sound invites worry, along with anticipation about what is to come. The scene opens with Chappelle watching two elderly African–American buddies trying to start a car, one behind the wheel while the other hovers under the hood. The glass of the car's windshield makes it difficult for them to hear each other and the misfires of their questions and responses lend a comic twist to their repartee. Their (mis)understandings are not helped by the blaring horns of a marching band, which provides the aural wallpaper of the film's opening. Chappelle steps in with a megaphone, a prop that will accompany him throughout the film and which establishes him as the translator, director, and guide who can cut through the confusion. Words spills forth from the bullhorn, announcing the show's performers. The bullhorn and the apostrophe that joins *Dave Chappelle* with *Block Party* in the film's title focus attention not on Gondry, but rather on Chappelle as author of this post-soul tale.

Born in 1973 in Washington, DC, and raised in its suburbs as well as in rural Ohio, Dave Chappelle solidly belongs to a generation of African–Americans whose experience of life in black America is distinct from the Civil Rights struggles of their parents and grandparents. Chappelle's return to DC to launch his stand-up career coincided with the city's crack epidemic in the 1980s and 1990s. Haggins defines twenty-first-century African–American comedians and writers like Dave Chappelle as "post soul . . . media babies": that is, "post-Civil Rights, post Black-Arts products of fixed and fluid cultural imagery circulating through various old and new media outlets: film, television, video, the internet."[10] Chappelle's big-screen presence ranged from roles in Mel Brooks's comedy *Robin Hood: Men in Tights* (1993) to the rom-com *You've Got Mail* (Nora Ephron, 1998) where his side-kick, slacker, and stoner roles bolstered his crossover appeal. He was also a cable regular on HBO's *Def Comedy Jam* and is a featured artist on Okayplayer, the on-line hip hop collective founded by ?uestlove, whose collaboration with Chappelle continues in *Block Party*.

Dave Chappelle, argues Kimberly Yates,

> caters to a black standard while creating broader debate about racial inequality. He creates a sense of nation precisely by challenging this nation's mainstream to consider the ways in which it is not living up to its ideals of democracy, equality and inclusiveness.[11]

In *Block Party*, Chappelle is able to achieve this, although not as a practitioner but rather an advocate of hip hop, and with Gondry as the visual architect of the film as a post-soul collaboration:

> MG: I think it was important that we talk about communities and this type of music. In a way I was flattered that I was asked to do that, but for me, being an outsider, I didn't think I could have a lot of view on that. But the positive thing about that . . . I don't like a documentary that has a lot of views that are stronger than what you actually experienced making the documentary. I think you have to find your truth as you go along. Not to say that I was distant, but the fact that I didn't know this community so well protected me from trying anything being too directive. What I knew, as I said before, I wanted to try and distant [*sic*] myself, but I wanted to listen to people to see what they have to say.[12]

Throughout the film Chappelle and Gondry flirt with notions of nostalgia and authenticity, holding out the possibility that each can be mined from imaginative longing.

Gondry's collaboration with Chappelle can be read as a revelation of black identity politics in an era of crack, gentrification, and the lingering ravages of the Ronald Reagan 1980s. As an observer, Gondry's eye for detail frames black iconographic figures (Mumia, Tupac, Biggie Smalls), fashion (political messages telegraphed through T-shirts and tennis shoes), raised Black Power fists, and celebrity call-and-response music against police brutality. Throughout *Dave Chappelle's Block Party*, the performative aspects of race are highlighted. Both Gondry and Chappelle are storytellers, and the film's many stage spaces become full with arranged set pieces in a work that is ultimately read as a visual/narrative construction of community, identity and race:

> MG: I think that in documentary film, you have to break down the same layers, because when you start to shoot somebody, they first put on a show. And they are not necessarily natural, because they think too much about how people will think of them, how they will be perceived. So I found out during the shooting that it is not in the first five or ten minutes of shooting that you get anything interesting . . . But to shoot a film without exactly knowing the story as you shoot, and finding the truth of it all as you go along, was something that was very interesting to me.[13]

In *Block Party*, Gondry's camera captures several instances of simultaneous masking and unmasking. The conscious juxtaposition of the behind-the-scenes footage and the stage of the show itself offers important glimpses of Chappelle and the other performers, especially given that Chappelle has famously struggled with preconceived notions of who he is that arise from his comic creations. In one moment the camera trails Chappelle as he wanders through a Salvation Army. In the Salvation Army shop Chappelle picks out a suit and jacket, poking fun at himself and striking a playful tone with the storekeeper, who is asked whether this costume choice would be a good outfit for a rap show. Chappelle preens in front of the mirror. The camera hovers so that the props have their own close-up (the suit, the fedora) and we laugh along as Chapelle delivers the stock lines of a pimp, as performed from the mad mind of Dave Chappelle. Playing with a deconstruction of the pimp image allows Chappelle to unloose himself from one of the professional straightjackets of his highly public persona. Untethered from stage and screen, the catchphrase "I'm Rick James, Bitch!"[14] from the *Chappelle's Show* segment "Charlie Murphy's True Hollywood Stories: Rick James"—in which Chappelle plays James—is a quotation that hounded and haunted Chappelle when spit back at him from the mouths of hecklers or fans.[15] Indeed, in the DVD of *For What it's Worth* (2004), Chappelle's stand-up comedy special that aired on Showtime, Chappelle confides to a theatre audience that he once had to ask exuberant fans at Disney World not to call him a bitch in front of his kids.[16]

Other backstage and greenroom moments in *Dave Chappelle's Block Party* become a running feature of the film's narrative mixing in meandering cuts crossing time and space. Though filmed as behind-the-scenes shots, these scenes are equally front and center stage within the film and are given a whimsical treatment by Gondry. "I'm the lady Jill Scott," coos the performer Jill Scott, who looks closely into the camera as she introduces herself. "I'm a poet and a singer and a lot of other things," she offers in a slow drawl before adding playfully, "and this is my pimple Herbert. He arrived today and he decided to stay so we will see his performance tomorrow."[17] Gondry uses this moment to zoom in on Scott at the hands of hair and make-up, patting her nose before the camera lands with her mid-performance on stage.

Several signature Gondry elements develop the post-racial aspects of *Dave Chappelle's Block Party*. According to Holly Willis, Gondry's Smirnoff vodka commercial from 1997 is one of the prime examples of his use of hybrid space creation or "the ways in which the 'mediated' world aligns with the 'immediate' world, and the sense that our experience of the two is increasingly difficult to separate."[18] The Smirnoff commercial famously weds music video and visual storytelling to disrupt an unfolding spatial narrative through a screen of glass: namely, the bottle of vodka. When Gondry directs the viewer's gaze in, out, and around glass, the bottle becomes a slippery frame of reference between the blurring of here and there, one space and another, real and not real sitting side by side.[19] Lynn Hirschberg noted in a *New York Times* profile that:

> Gondry creates highly imaginative worlds that seem to exist somewhere between the conscious and the unconscious; again and again, states of waking and dreaming clash and collide and, finally, create a new sort of reality. All of this is a little chaotic, but Gondry understands the appeal of disorientation, of the audience's not immediately understanding what it is seeing.[20]

Early in *Dave Chappelle's Block Party*, the viewer sees Chappelle on stage and the concert seems to be in full swing. Suddenly, Gondry cuts to a group of people gathered in prayer in the empty concert space, which splits into a number of frames on the screen depicting open sky, sunshine, and a line of concertgoers entering the empty space that the viewer has just seen full. It is as if the viewer is watching the process in reverse. Also running in the frame with the prayer is a tilt shot from ground level that captures two figures standing on a balcony in front of an open window. The prayer shot closes and suddenly moves to Ohio. A vision of green grass shot through the window of a moving car replaces the concrete jungle. Brooklyn is left behind, only to be replaced by the Midwest. "Three days before," reads a rare caption that provides some orientation to traveling here/there through time and space.

THE HOUSE OF HYPER-REALITY: WELCOME TO THE BROKEN ANGEL

The window on the house in Brooklyn is on the façade of the second floor of a building with a stylized graffiti script that tags it as "The Broken Angel."[21] It takes multiple viewings to make sense of the central and important role that this house plays as a symbolic core of the entire Gondry/Chappelle enterprise. The viewer first meets the home's owners on the street as they are standing in front of the house. Chappelle plays interested interviewer and draws forth a story about how they met, when they fell in love, and why they got married. The viewer is invited in. Both husband and wife are eccentric and offer a winding shaggy dog story that is the auditory backdrop for a spiraling, dizzying visual climb filled with twists and turns that, from the inside of the house, mirror the building's unusual exterior. The camerawork locates dislocation. This sensation is the point of the film.

Gondry takes viewers through a door. It is dark. The narrator is seen from the front and then from behind. As she climbs, viewers are directed by following the sweep of her hand to take a peek. But, when she points left, the camera pans up into an expanse of empty space, as if offering a pause to clear the mind and vision, but then spirals, spirals and turns with Gondry, who focuses close up on the narrator as she gestures above, again forcing a look up as the climb continues with the camera following over her shoulder and then close up on her, but soon back down one level, pulled by her husband's voice, before the climb continues upward again. The camera carries the viewer higher until reaching level ground at the top of the house. Here, the brilliance of the sunlight flooding the frame raises the question of whether it signals an epiphany or a moment of awareness.

The film cuts to Chappelle regaling his performers/musicians in another of *Block Party*'s backstage moments: "It's like looking through a pipe," he says, bringing cupped hands to his eye as if raising a pretend telescope. "It is an illusion," he cackles. Viewers are brought outside, then back inside, and finally arrive again at the front door of the house, when the shot moves away and back to Chappelle as he continues to recount the "madness" before concluding. "If I were a location scout and I needed a crack house I might refer this place," he jokingly tells the camera. Knowing Gondry's love for the surreal and affirming Gondry's role as Chappelle's dream weaver, the viewer concludes that the faux crack house is but a prop, bringing a whiff of authenticity to the urban concert. The kaleidoscopic swirling around and upwards through the house disorients while suggesting a heightened state of mind. This produces the visual effect of swirling, *Cabinet of Dr. Caligari*-like, as in Robert Wiene's 1920 film that frequently introduces the moments of dream, madness, or insanity in film and television. The shots inside the house create the sensation and image of a corkscrew biting deep and deeper with each turn to gain purchase in the cork of a wine bottle.

THE GEOGRAPHY OF BLACKNESS(ES)

The geographical range of Gondry's kaleidoscope of a film carries one across a landscape of African–American cultural meaning throughout Brooklyn, including such sites as a barber shop; the corner store; a day-care center named for the late hip hop legend Biggie Smalls (1972–97); the iconic Junior's Restaurant; and a basketball court. There is even a gathering of talking heads in lawn chairs on the street, which is an image well known to anyone brought up in the black community or familiar with the black Greek chorus in Spike Lee films such as *Do the Right Thing* (1989), *Jungle Fever* (1991), or *Crooklyn* (1994). When asked whether he was influenced by Spike Lee, Gondry replied,

> Yeah, of course. I remember when I was preparing *Block Party* I saw him . . . and he sort of gave me his approval, his moral support. But it was nice that he seemed very nice . . . and he said, "It's good you're doing *Block Party*."[22]

It is important that the film takes place in Bedford–Stuyvesant (known colloquially as "Bed-Stuy") in Brooklyn, an historic home to hip hop. Not only was hip hop was born there, but so were many of the performers featured in *Block Party*. The film's viewers, however, arrive as outsiders. But they are also equally members of the community that Gondry constructs through staging. When the film was released, Gondry stated to a *Washington Post* interviewer that it was his suggestion to move the concert from Central Park (which Chappelle had suggested) to Brooklyn: "that was my first contribution. I said we should bring it to people for whom it means more."[23] But this is not a neighborhood block party thrown down for neighbors. This is a ticketed event with advance publicity that is being hosted by a well-known comedian and featuring internationally acclaimed performers. In a rooftop interview, the viewer is reminded that a rooftop scene is obligatory in any New York City movie.

As *Dave Chappelle's Block Party* moves backward and forward in time and place, central to the film are the events that take place on the Saturday afternoon of the concert. The action on the stage on Saturday intercuts between audience and artists. The documentary serves up classic concert footage, but beyond the stage, the bifurcation of black America is a recurring theme. Midway through the film, Mos Def shares his memories as well as his fondness for Bed-Stuy. From an elevated tree-level shot in the sky the camera scans the neighborhood's rooftops while Mos Def talks about what is and what was: "it's actually better now than it has been in a long time," he says quietly, pensively, and matter-of-factly. The camera pans a garbage dumpster and a figure slumped in a decrepit doorframe. "Some of it," interjects Chappelle, "looks like when *The Cosby Show* comes back from commercial break. And some of it," he continues by way of offering a contrast, "some of it looks like when *Good Times* came back from commercial break." Chappelle's observation captures a fissure of class and race in the black experience that the film tries to visually reflect: dislocation and belonging, the impact of poverty, the creep of gentrification.

"Like it could be in the same block," Chappelle stresses, joined by a voice from the side of the room, which adds "you turn the corner," and Gondry cuts from musings in the backroom to Chappelle walking past a car. The viewer is looking out of the windshield of a car, with the Broken Angel House straight ahead. Another portal. With subtle optical management, Gondry experiments with a familiar framing device: narratives that unfold through glass or bring watchful eyes into buildings by way of invisible and non-existent panes of glass. The viewer pauses to consider how the mind's eye view is mediated, focused, and refocused through windows. In this scene, Chappelle walks across the front windshield while the camera pans and redeposits him out through the side window, where the narrative shifts the viewer's frame of reference.

Through the side window, Chappelle arrives at the Biggie Smalls daycare center. An earlier scene showed Chappelle rolling along a boulevard of brownstones while yelling through his megaphone, "attention, Huxtables."[24] Through these visual dislocations the possibility emerges that one can hold several versions of geography and blackness. At the Biggie Smalls Daycare Center the viewer is introduced to the school director, who offers her views on the legacy of rapper Biggie Smalls, who was shot to death at the age of 24, and the possibilities of the next generation. This is a quick moment, though not deeply delved into, of memory and nostalgia. The film devotes some moments to Chappelle spending time with the kids ("I love kids," he says). Again, the viewer embarks on a climb as the camera follows Chappelle up and through a few staircase landings and the viewer arrives on the rooftop.

Here again, the camera provides a vantage point that offers another perspective from above to take in the stage, which will be below. Eventually, because the film will capture the space both empty and full, the audience can contemplate how time and circumstance (and Dave Chappelle) bring people together. A more perfect *mise-en-scène* could not have been set, especially where the space of the stage is more broadly an opening onto the community that surrounds the performance. In each place that is visited (the roof, the daycare center, a restaurant, the Salvation Army, a basketball court, a barber shop), viewers are taken along for a ride. Viewers come to the realization that the geographic locations of Ohio or New York are realities that are subtly destabilized, supporting C. Riley Snorton's claim that the significance of the documentary

Block Party lies in its role as "a piece of semi-ethnographic evidence on urban life, black political thought and cultural expression."²⁵

BUSLOAD OF FAITH

> CSU Campus, Ohio
> 1 day before Block Party
> —scene caption at 35′40″

In an interesting prefiguration of a later Gondry film, *The We and the I* (2012), which was shot on a bus, *Block Party* moves from Ohio to New York with the Ohio State University marching band, whose members Chappelle has invited early on in the film to attend the concert in Brooklyn. Gondry's camera lingers at the side of the bus under a light drizzle while musical instruments and items of luggage are loaded below. By shooting from inside of the bus, Gondry captures the energy of youthful exuberance with a dash of silliness. "We are dating," says a young couple, as they mug and kiss for the camera. A nearby seatmate teases them about how long they have been dating: how many months, weeks, days, and hours? The camera quietly tiptoes across other travelers sleeping in uncomfortable knots along window and aisle seats. The drops of light rain dapple the bus windshield while accompanied by the soft tinkling of Dave Chappelle playing Thelonious Monk's "Round Midnight" (1947), a reminder of the scene earlier (or later?) when Chappelle was seated at the piano in the Salvation Army. Time and place collapse, with the two scenes connected via the nostalgic embrace of jazz. Camaraderie is contained within the bus, and the community spirit delivered along the highway is another prop that will add to the scene that is being staged in Bed-Stuy.

This ethos serves as a thread woven into the tapestry of *Dave Chappelle's Block Party* and makes the multiple visits to other sites and places beyond the concert an integral part of the whole. As the viewer rides with the band, they experience once again arrival and departure via the windshield, as well as from inside and outside of the bus. The majesty of the Brooklyn Bridge signals entry via a portal. Through a marker of belonging, the destination is framed by one of the most instantly recognizable, iconic images of New York City. Gondry offered a similar Tocquevillian gesture in the 2011 music video that he directed for French musician Lacquer's song "Behind," in which he hurtled the viewer across the American landscape, speeding from LA to NY through the windshield of a car.²⁶

Off the bus, the band assembles at its hotel and then joins in line with the crowd of others waiting for tickets to the mystery location of the show. Soon the viewer will see, and hear, the band strutting through the street, with their booming drums, joyous horns, and laughter. Their uniforms are pomp and circumstance, and the school's maroon and gold colors pop in the sunshine and the eye of the camera. The band's arrival is interwoven with shots that deliver viewers back to the concert.

JESUS WALKS: REAL MEETS HYPER-REAL

Kanye West is up and he is all energy. The *Block Party* viewer is about to be hit with a blend of the real and virtual that is reminiscent of how Holly Willis described Gondry's 2012 video for the Chemical Brothers' song, "Star Guitar":

> a landscape [that] seems to be linked directly to the beats and sounds in the music; [. . .] trees appear and then reappear in a subtle iteration of the music, the landscape embodying the sound . . . While the landscape appears to be "real", there is no way that it could "naturally" appear in synchronization with the music the way it does . . . the real becomes virtual.[27]

In Gondry's concert film *Dave Chappelle's Block Party*, the viewer has to watch closely for these moments of hyper-reality.

On the stage, Kanye West is lanky, all arms and legs, pumping as he performs his 2004 song "Jesus Walks." With a syncopated slicing of the air, he paces the stage like a manic thespian. The camera takes the viewers close up and fills their ears with blaring horns. Gold glints of light shoot from the horns' sensuous curves. This is a loud number and the audience feels it, as it is deep and booming. The camera is close up tight on members of the crowd mouthing "Jesus Walks," one syllable at a time. Now Gondry plays with the viewer by cutting back and forth between different shots. The audience is on the stage, then in the streets with the band. Back to the stage. In the streets. Then West is on the street and watching the band rehearse/perform "Jesus Walks." West is a witness to the band director's baton, as he claps his approval of the majorettes shimmying their hips, twirlers twirling, and flag girls kicking their knees up high. The music is West's, but it belongs to them as well. The line is blurred in a way that recalls Willis's observation about that moment when the audience is guided into a hybrid space: "it is simultaneously flat and deep, unitary and dispersed, near and remote, real and fake, miniature and gigantic, live and recorded, reflective and immersive."[28]

At the end of a long day (the show ran for over eight hours) the concert ends on a high note: the reunion of the band The Fugees. The band's lead singer, Lauryn Hill, belts out a bit of nostalgia with The Fugees' cover of "Killing Me Softly with His Song," Roberta Flack's 1973 Atlantic records hit song. The crowd shots are a sea of hands waving in unison and close-ups of lip-synching fans. By now, night is a dark embrace for the collective. The Broken Angel's jagged graffiti peeks through from behind the musicians. A colorful crowd shot from above the dancing mass looks like a giant bowl of gumballs. Backstage, Lauryn Hill opens up about the *Block Party* reunion and her suburban origins, and reminisces about style and fashion back in the days when The Fugees first met. If this seems a bit magical, then Michel Gondry's sleight of hand has been a success. Hybrid and hyper-real, the hip hop community assembled for Gondry's *Dave Chappelle's Block Party* will live on forever with the click of rewind.

NOTES

1. Mark Anthony Neal, *Soul Babies: Black Popular Culture and the Post-Soul Aesthetic* (New York: Routledge, 2002), Kindle, 2.
2. Segment "Blind Hatred," *Chappelle's Show*, season 1, episode 1, "Popcopy & Clayton Bigsby," directed by Rusty Cundieff, written by Neal Brennan and Dave Chappelle, featuring Dave Chappelle, aired January 22, 2003, on Comedy Central.
3. Bambi Haggins, *Laughing Mad* (New Brunswick, NJ: Rutgers University Press, 2007), 203.
4. Haggins, *Laughing Mad*, 214.
5. Dave Chappelle, interview by Oprah Winfrey, *The Oprah Winfrey Show*, February 3, 2006.
6. Segment "When Keeping It Real Goes Wrong," *Chappelle's Show*, season 2, episode 6, "The Internet & Moment in the Life of Lil Jon," directed by Rusty Cundieff, written by Neal Brennan and Dave Chappelle, featuring Anthony Hamilton, aired February 25, 2004, on Comedy Central; Segment "When Keeping It Real Goes Wrong," *Chappelle's Show*, season 2, episode 7, "World Series of Dice & Mooney on Movies," directed by Rusty Cundieff, written by Neal Brennan, Dave Chappelle, Celina Lorenz, Paul Mooney, and Allison Walton, featuring Common and Kanye West, aired March 3, 2004, on Comedy Central; Segment "When Keeping It Real Goes Wrong," *Chappelle's Show*, season 2, episode 8, "I Know Black People & When Keeping It Real Goes Wrong," directed by Rusty Cundieff and Andre Allen, written by Neal Brennan and Dave Chappelle, featuring Erykah Badu, aired March 10, 2004, on Comedy Central.
7. Haggins, *Laughing Mad*, 182.
8. Haggins, *Laughing Mad*, 179.
9. Haggins, *Laughing Mad*, 182.
10. Marvin McAllister, "Embodied and Disembodied Black Satire: From Chappelle and Crockett to Key and Peele," in *Post-Soul Satire: Black Identity After Civil Rights*, eds Derek Maus and James Donahue (Jackson: University of Mississippi Press, 2014), 241.
11. Kimberly A. Yates, "When 'Keeping It Real' Goes Right," in *The Comedy of Dave Chappelle: Critical Essays*, ed. K. A. Wisniewski (Jefferson, NC: McFarland, 2009). Kindle, location 2092 of 3684.
12. Kara Warner, "Interview with Michel Gondry," FilmJerk.com, February 25, 2006. Available at <http://www.filmjerk.com/interviews/2006/02/25/interview-with-michel-gondry/> (last accessed February 26, 2020).
13. Scott Thill, "'How My Brain Works': An Interview with Michel Gondry," *Bright Lights Film Journal*, August 1, 2006. Available at <http://brightlightsfilm.com/brain-works-interview-michel-gondry/#.WItSpckUnIU> (last accessed February 26, 2020).

14. Segment "Charlie Murphy's True Hollywood Story: Rick James," *Chappelle's Show*, season 2, episode 4, "The Love Contract and True Hollywood Stories: Rick James," directed by Neal Brennan and Andre Allen, written by Neal Brennan and Dave Chappelle, featuring Ludacris, aired February 11, 2004, on Comedy Central.
15. Elahe Izadi, "The 20 Defining Comedy Sketches of the Past 20 Years," *The Washington Post* (October 23, 2019). Available at <https://www.washingtonpost.com/arts-entertainment/2019/10/23/defining-comedy-sketches-last-years-rick-james-lazy-sunday/?arc404=true> (last accessed February 26, 2020).
16. *For What it's Worth*, directed by Stan Lathan (Showtime, 2004).
17. *Dave Chapelle's Block Party*, directed by Michel Gondry (2005; Universal City, Rogue Pictures, 2006), DVD. All future references come from this primary source.
18. Holly Willis, *New Digital Cinema: Reinventing the Moving Image (Short Cuts)* (London: Wallflower Press, 2005), 57.
19. Michel Gondry, "Smirnoff--Smarienberg (1996, UK)," Bing (Microsoft, May 1, 2012). Available at <https://www.bing.com/videos/search?q=gondry+the+vodka+commercial&ru=/search?q=gondry+the+vodka+commercial&go=Submit+Query&qs=ds&form=QBLH&mmscn=vwrc&view=detail&mid=3654F240F3D0066DF8DF3654F240F3D0066DF8DF&rvsmid=E790709D4586A043083CE790709D4586A043083C&FORM=VDQVAP> (last accessed February 26, 2020).
20. Lynn Hirschberg, "Le Romantique," *The New York Times* (September 17, 2006). Available at <http://www.nytimes.com/2006/09/17/magazine/17gondry.html> (last accessed February 26, 2020).
21. The address of this house was 4/6 Downing Street, Clinton Hill, Brooklyn. It was demolished in 2014.
22. Jada Yuan, "Michel Gondry on *The We and the I*, Bronx Kids, and *Mood Indigo*," *Vulture* (March 15, 2013). Available at <http://www.vulture.com/2013/03/michel-gondry-the-we-and-the-i-mood-indigo-interview.html> (last accessed February 26, 2020).
23. Jen Chaney, "Michel Gondry Gets the 'Party' Started," *The Washington Post* (March 3, 2006). Available at <http://www.washingtonpost.com/wp-dyn/content/article/2006/03/02/AR2006030200705.html?noredirect=on> (last accessed February 26, 2020).
24. "Huxtable" is the name of family on *The Cosby Show* (1984–92), which was a landmark sensation of the 1980s when Bill Cosby's "buppie" (black urban professional) family for the first time brought the black middle class into the living rooms of television viewers who had grown up on the ghetto, urban poverty, and sitcom characters like those in *What's Happening!!* (1976–9), *Sanford and Son* (1972–7), and *Good Times* (1974–9).
25. C. Riley Snorton, "The Artistry of Ethnography in Dave Chappelle's Block Party," in *The Comedy of Dave Chappelle: Critical Essays*, ed. K. A. Wisniewski (Jefferson, NC: McFarland, 2009), Kindle, location 1530 of 3684.
26. lacquerVEVO, "Lacquer—Behind (Clip Officiel)," YouTube (YouTube, March 17, 2011). Available at <https://www.youtube.com/watch?v=FQ1F29btH4c> (last accessed February 26, 2020).
27. Willis, *New Digital Cinema*, 58.
28. Willis, *New Digital Cinema*, 58.

CHAPTER 10

Memory *à la* Americana: From *Eternal Sunshine of the Spotless Mind* to *Be Kind Rewind*

Yu-Yun Hsieh

French filmmaker Michel Gondry stages playful and reflexive representations of memory in two of his American-themed films, *Eternal Sunshine of the Spotless Mind* (2004) and *Be Kind Rewind* (2008). In *Eternal Sunshine*, protagonist Joel Barish (Jim Carrey) arrives at Lacuna Inc. with mementos that remind him of his ex-girlfriend, Clementine Kruczynski (Kate Winslet), for the technician to reconstruct the circuit between each item and its corresponding emotional core in Joel's brain before degrading those connections. One such item, a snow globe of Boston, prompts Joel to speak about the story behind it, but the technician instructs him to focus on memories without using verbal description. In *Be Kind Rewind*, the townspeople of Passaic, New Jersey, make film adaptations and fabricate a glorified history of the town in order to save the last VHS rental shop in town and keep their nostalgia alive in the age of digitalization. While the main character in *Eternal Sunshine* is asked to focus on remembrance, this premise is overturned in *Be Kind Rewind* when characters freely act out any sort of visual and auditory representation of the past without possessing memories in the first place.

Characters in both films are given the choice to forget, through either voluntary or involuntary memory erasure, and then to re-imagine and remember their new memories. In *Eternal Sunshine*, individual memory is malleable and erasable; it can be mapped out on screen and erased by a censor at Lacuna. Memory is also transferable: for example, when a Lacuna employee appropriates Joel's memories of love with the hope of winning Clementine over. In *Be Kind Rewind*, the town residents gather to invent their cultural icon, jazz musician Fats Waller, and construct their own collective memory from the past in another fabrication. Although Gondry adapts the time loop to both films about memory, his interest has evolved from personal emotion and individual memory in *Eternal Sunshine* to community sentiment and collective memory in *Be Kind Rewind*. While Joel's different states of mind are presented as fractured and fragmented slices of memories, the locals of Passaic in *Be Kind Rewind* negotiate amateurism and kitsch by making adaptations of Hollywood movies from their mediated memories. As Gondry represents characters' remembrances in a tangible manner via musical repetition and visual association, he evokes characters' memories of the past as well as the audience's nostalgia for cinema.

ETERNAL SUNSHINE OF THE SPOTLESS MIND

Michel Gondry, a seasoned music video director, ventured into feature film and examined how memories of experience influence human behavior with his 2001 directorial debut, *Human Nature*, written by Charlie Kaufman. *Eternal Sunshine of the Spotless Mind*, also co-written by Kaufman, would mark their continuing collaboration.

Eternal Sunshine, with its titular allusion to Alexander Pope's poem and the Prospero-like character of Dr. Howard Mierzwiak (Tom Wilkinson), was touted upon its release as the "latest Charlie Kaufman flick."[1] The film's complicated narrative structure and pointed *exposé* of moral ambiguity are reminiscent of Kaufman's previous critically acclaimed mind-game scripts for the Spike Jonze-directed films *Being John Malkovich* (1999) and *Adaptation* (2002). In his comparison of *Eternal Sunshine* and *Adaptation*, Chris Dzialo suggests that Kaufman's attempt to "frustrate" time by adopting non-linear narrative indicates the screenwriter's resistance to the "irreversible nature of projector time."[2] The intricate writerly attempt might have been compromised regardless, since some puns and intertextual references in Kaufman's script were either edited or removed from the final product; even Clementine changes from a cerebral book lover to a lively magazine-reading girl in the film.

What makes *Eternal Sunshine* unique and still resonant, beyond its rich intertextuality, is the film's demand that the audience focus on memories, paying attention to any visual and auditory description offered by the film. Dzialo ascribes the film's success to Kaufman's script and argues that its complex temporal structure changes our reading process into the resulting interactive "self-organization."[3] However, *Eternal Sunshine* delivers its intended effect via its stylized utilization of audio-visual techniques, such as musical repetition and parallel editing, which clearly indicate Gondry's contribution and background as a music video director. Carol Vernallis notes that music video directors are susceptible to "intensified audiovisual aesthetics" and are more accustomed to working with performers who "possess a hypermobility."[4] From casting physical comedian Jim Carrey to play the lead to presenting the dreamlike visual–aural rendering of memories, Gondry's aesthetic is present throughout *Eternal Sunshine*.

MEMORY AND FORGETTING

The director's self-referential note emerges in the Lacuna technician's instruction to Joel: "I'll get a much better readout if you refrain from any sort of verbal description of the items. Just please try to focus on the memories." The instruction functions as a premise that shifts the audience's attention from words (written by the screenwriter) to the subsequent representation of memories (rendered by the director). *Eternal Sunshine* unfurls like a convoluted loop story on Valentine's Day: the memories that Joel needs to focus on expanding over a period of two years, starting from the day he met Clementine to the night before he lies down in bed to undergo the memory-erasure procedure. But the frame narrative begins with the future when the couple has erased each other from memory, before time moves backwards—in synch with Joel's memories—to retrieve the motivation behind the erasure and reconstruct these lost memories. The convoluted presentation of time here is neither the conventional narrative, nor the "forking-path movie" that provides future possibilities in linear order.[5] The cumbersome layers that differentiate states of the future, the present, and the past are intertwined in a non-linear order that exemplifies a structure close to the "mind-game film." This is because the mind-game film either comprises characters playing games with or without knowing it, or emphasizes characters' states of mind when caught between illusion and reality.[6] Joel is caught between his current state of sleep and his remembrance of things past, except that his memories are susceptible to change.

Eternal Sunshine presents the malleability and adaptability of personal memory through deliberate forgetting—the erasure procedure—in a United States of America sci-fi setting. Dr. Mierzwiak, founder of Lacuna in New York, can create a map of Joel's mind via everything that has some association with Clementine, and then wipe Clementine from Joel's life by eradicating the corresponding emotional cores in Joel's brain. Joel wonders if this would cause brain damage, but Mierzwiak reassures him with, "Well, technically speaking, the procedure *is* brain damage, but it's on a par with a night of heavy drinking. Nothing you'll miss."[7] The traces of memory in our mind are like those words written on the wax paper of Sigmund Freud's "Mystic Writing-Pad": one can easily erase the words on the double covering-sheet from the wax slab with a light pull, because the Mystic Pad functions in the same way as "the perceptual apparatus of our mind."[8] That a Prospero-like character has the power to overwrite and erase other people's writing pads is symptomatic of the dominance of consumerism in late capitalist society.

At Lacuna, memory is susceptible to erasure and adaptation not only because the substance of remembering can be reified and consumed, but also because the resulting emotional response is thought to hinder productivity at work and in life. The truth is, the people working at Lacuna seem nonchalant about the potential loss of personal memories and even downplay the aftermath of memory erasure on individuals: Dr. Mierzwiak describes undergoing the procedure as being "in a dream upon waking"; Stan (Mark Ruffalo) wants to wipes Joel's memories as clean as he likes; the nurse, Mary (Kirsten Dunst), extols Dr. Mierzwiak's contribution to society as a way of giving people a chance to begin over. The rationale behind wiping out one's memories and authentic feelings in order to make one blend in and start over again reflects the public obsession with efficiency and productivity in late capitalist society.

The parallel editing adopted in *Eternal Sunshine* marks and then fractures linear time in order to recreate characters' different states of mind. For example, Joel is conscious when his two-year-old memories of Clementine unfurl in front of him in his dream. Even though Joel commits to his "voluntary forgetting" by having his memories of Clementine erased, he changes his mind in the middle of the procedure after hearing Patrick (Elijah Wood), the young Lacuna assistant, steal Clementine from him. Joel's two states of mind, one in his dream and the other in his memories, are presented via parallel editing. After consulting Mierzwiak, Joel goes home, takes the pill, and waits in bed for the Lacuna technicians to arrive. The camera cuts to the two technicians working at Joel's apartment, and then cuts to Joel talking to Mierzwiak at the clinic. The two repetitious clinic scenes are only four minutes (of the running time) apart, which can be read as a cue to read the sequence as part of Joel's dream sequence, since he is already in bed. But even in his dream, Joel is awed by an uncanny sense of *déjà vu*, because he simultaneously sees the image of Mierzwiak talking to him about the brain damage at the other end of the room and the image of himself in pajamas standing by another Mierzwiak. The appearance of two Joels in the same frame blurs the marker of linear time, yet it realistically reflects the situation as Joel oscillates between two states of mind: he perceives the flow of real time and, like the audience, observes his memories unfurl in his lucid dream.

If the complexity of the editing in this film indicates the visual description of personal memories, the use of repetition, reiteration, and reverberation supplements the auditory track. The past and the present are depicted as a spatial–temporal conflation with a series of crosscuts and intercuts. As Joel in his dream is awed by his own memories of lip-synching himself, Stan notices that he cannot erase certain light spots on the map of Joel's brain and asks for Patrick's help. The name Patrick ironically prompts Joel to remember visiting Clementine three days before Valentine's Day, only to find she no longer remembered him, and instead, endearingly kissed a man named Patrick. The name Patrick reverberates and creates a bug in the circuit of Joel's memory that delays and interrupts the erasure procedure; every time Joel hears the repetition of Patrick's name, he remembers his frustrated relationship with Clementine and nearly wakes up. Despite the comic effect, the repetition of the name serves as an auditory reminder of Joel's repressed memories.

A nostalgic attempt to protect one's individuality is given a post-modern twist when Joel, afraid of losing his authentic memories, decides to react against the machine by making up memories that never existed in the first place. An incoming phone call from Clementine interrupts the erasure procedure and awakes Joel, who is desperate to stop Patrick from stealing Clementine from him and to persuade her to see through his trick. Remembering Clementine's vulnerability makes Joel determined to stop the procedure of memory erasure. In his dream, Clementine confesses to Joel her childhood fear and they make love under the bedsheet; however, as the erasure continues, the image of Clementine slips away and gradually disappears from his memories. Joel, half-awakened by disappointment, starts to question the purpose of the memory erasure, yelling, "Mierzwiak, please let me keep this memory!" He crawls out of bed but finds that no one on the side of the monitor can really hear him. Once Joel decides to protect his memories from elimination, he invents new memories with Clementine to avoid the machine's detection. As a strategy to resist the unwanted, involuntary forgetting facilitated by the machine, Joel imagines Clementine as his childhood playmate or as a trigger of his experience of humiliation, thus creating inauthentic personal memories from the past.

APPROPRIATION AND PASTICHE

Both Clementine and Mary are victims of memory erasure in *Eternal Sunshine*. If the name "Patrick" brings Joel back to reality, then the adjective "nice" has the same reverberating effect on Clementine. In real time, while Joel lies in bed, Mary and Stan enjoy a short period of debauchery at Joel's apartment and Patrick takes Clementine to Boston to see the frozen Charles River. Before emptying Joel from her mind, Clementine, shown in Joel's memories, likes teasing Joel for his overuse of the bland adjective "nice." Joel thinks she is nice and wants to be nice to her. Apart from the commonality of their fast-developing relationship, the two lovers are fundamentally different. Clementine is impulsive and wants to live her life to the fullest; Joel, timid and passive, would rather wait for someone like her to come and change his life. In real time, Patrick keeps Joel's journal close by so that he can appropriate and re-use Joel's memories with Clementine. But Clementine needs to have proof of love before she can ascertain her feelings. Asking Patrick to go to the Charles River with her is her way of understanding her own feelings. On the frozen river, Patrick recites the lines he has memorized from Joel's journal and says, "This is exactly where I want to be," but Clementine, sensing doubt, abruptly decides to go home. Patrick's failed effort on the frozen river appears four minutes after Joel, who, while dreaming, remembers the night of lying on the frozen surface of this very river with Clementine. The proximity of the two Charles River episodes highlights the contrasting dynamics between the two pairs: Clementine and Joel versus Clementine and Patrick. The thematic resonance here leads the audience to reach the conclusion that memory may be erased, but unconscious love cannot lie. On their drive home, when Clementine asks Patrick why he loves her, Patrick unsuspectingly repeats Joel's favorite adjective "nice": an answer that bursts the bubble of Clementine's feelings and finally, she wakes up from this illusion of love.

Mary, like Clementine, comes to her realization late because of memory erasure, and unlike Clementine, her memories are always already mediated via her deliberate remembering. Mary likes to memorize quotations, not from books she likes, but rather, from *Bartlett's Familiar Quotes*. To better understand the organization where she works, Mary focuses on remembering quotations associated with forgetting. At Joel's apartment, she uses Nietzsche's words to describe the sleeping Joel: "Blessed are the forgetful, for they get the better even of their blunders." However, she quotes Nietzsche from *Bartlett's* rather than from the actual text, *Beyond Good and Evil*. Mary's vicarious memories of the original text are fragmented, bridged, and mediated from secondary sources. There is no primary source behind her references, and worse, there is no hint of self-conscious irony.

In *Postmodernism, or The Cultural Logic of Late Capitalism* (1991), Fredric Jameson writes: "The disappearance of the individual subject, along with its formal consequence, the increasing unavailability of the personal style, engender the well-nigh universal practice today of what may be called pastiche."[9] Pastiche is "like parody, the imitation of a peculiar or unique, idiosyncratic style," but it is "a neutral practice of such mimicry, without any parody's ulterior motives, amputated of the satiric impulse, devoid of laughter" and thus "blank parody."[10] Mary's memorization of quotations from a quote book trenchantly resonates with Jameson's notion of pastiche, for it has neither roots nor authenticity. Nor does Mary have any historical awareness when she recites the quotations. Her characterization is like a post-modern jest, and even her full name, Mary Svevo, is a playful derivative of Italian writer Italo Svevo (1861–1928), whose notable work, *Zeno's Conscience* (1923), is protagonist Zeno's fictional memoir published by his psychiatrist. Mary forgets that she once had an affair with Dr. Mierzwiak and let him erase their troubled past for her to live her life. Forgetting her past, Mary reveals to Stan her admiration for Mierzwiak without any satiric impulse: "I think Howard (Mierzwiak) will be in *Bartlett's* one day."

In comparison to her oblivious past, Mary's recitation of her favorite poem—also memorized from *Barlett's*—Alexander Pope's *Eloisa to Abelard* (1717), seems genuine and self-referential, and it brings out the original source of the film title:

> How happy is the blameless vestal's lot!
> The world forgetting, by the world forgot.
> Eternal sunshine of the spotless mind!
> Each pray'r accepted, and each wish resign'd . . .[11]

As Mary recites the poem, the non-diegetic image on screen is a slice of memory that Joel and Clementine once shared, when they walked along the streets of New York and watched the circus in town. Mary would not know it, and neither would she notice the parallel between herself and protagonist Eloisa in Pope's original verse epistle: there is a lacuna in her mind where the torments of love have been erased without trace. Mary still loves Howard, even when she is oblivious of their past. She becomes nervous around Howard, mistakes Alexander Pope for Pope Alexander, and rushes to make a pass at him. Her reading of the line "eternal sunshine of the spotless mind" points to her forgetting mind and the collective forgetting facilitated by the machine at Lacuna. Therefore, after retrieving her erased memory in the clinic from a cassette recorded with her confession, Mary decides to end Lacuna's absurd service by returning these records of personal memories to all the clients who underwent the erasure procedure. Memories may be erased, but real feelings of love can return in various forms and deserve to be remembered.

Sounds and images of memories to be erased are rendered through association and repetition, visually and aurally, like music videos, and thus, the film also creates an open space for the audience to comprehend their cinematic memories and organize the narrative during the viewing. After watching the film, the audience will remember Joel's bittersweet memories of Clementine, remember Jim Carrey shrinking to fit into the sink, the scene of the lovers playing on the snow-clad beach in Montauk. The frozen surface of the Charles River that appears three times has a symbolic role in the film. Joel and Clementine have met each other on the Montauk beach on Valentine's Day and Clementine invites Joel to the Charles River with her the following night. In a stylized rendition we see the couple walking on the frozen surface; Joel fears that the river might crack and Clementine teases him. A high-angle shot shows the two of them lying on the frozen river, looking at the stars, with cracks on the side of Clementine that attest to Joel's concern about cracking ice. Since "a crack is a lacuna,"[12] the crack here not only epitomizes their erased memories, but it heralds the impending crack in their newly resumed relationship.

Figure 10.1 Joel and Clementine watch stars on the frozen surface of the Charles River in *Eternal Sunshine of the Spotless Mind* (Focus Features, 2004)

After watching *Eternal Sunshine*, nearly every viewer will remember Beck Hansen's rendition of the Korgis' 1980 single "Everybody's Gotta Learn Sometime,"[13] for it appears as the main title theme, background noise, and the end title theme to conclude the film. The title theme is inserted after Patrick knocks on Joel's car window, asking him "Can I help you?" and it creates a lacuna in the narrative. The title theme begins on the rainy night when Joel drives the car, listening to Beck's performance of "Everybody's Gotta Learn Sometime" on the cassette. He is crying so hard that he needs to stop the music and throw the cassette out of the window. This insertion presents an undetermined lacuna in the narrative, for the cassette is often read as the one delivered by Mary, which records his confession at Lacuna. I read this insertion as having happened on the day when Joel went to the bookstore and found that Clementine had forgotten him, because Beck's rendition is used as a diegetic element in this sequence. As soon as Joel takes out the cassette, the singing stops, which is an episode so short that it leaves little room for ambiguity. The motif of "Everybody's Gotta Learn Sometime" once again appears when Joel remembers Clementine's childhood fear and starts to resist the erasure procedure. Audio mixing effects are used to distort the rhythm and add an eerie feel when the non-diegetic image shows Joel and Clementine visiting Charles River. Lying on the frozen river, Joel says this is exactly where he wants to be. As he turns around to look at Clementine, she slips away. The floor of Grand Central Station in this cross-cut replaces the frozen river. The various adaptations of the same piece of music evoke Joel's memories and reinforce the message of the lyrics—Joel has to learn something from the process. The recognizable refrain prompts the audience to remember what they have seen in the film. Kaufman might have attempted to overturn the irreversible nature of projector time, but Gondry is entrusted with the task of recreating the visual and auditory memory of the character, as well as that of the audience.

BE KIND REWIND

While the protagonists of *Eternal Sunshine* silently focus on memories, to have them read by the machine, the characters in *Be Kind Rewind* fabricate stories and act out any manner of visual and auditory description without possessing such memories in the first place. *Be Kind Rewind*, set in Passaic, New Jersey, poses the issue of the fabrication of collective memory and cultural identity. Protagonist Mike (Yasiin Bey) is working at the Be Kind Rewind video store, whose owner Mr. Fletcher (Danny Glover) treats him like a surrogate son. Mike believes a bedtime story told by Mr. Fletcher, to the effect that the world-famous jazz pianist Thomas "Fats" Waller (1904–43) was born on the site of the store (in reality, Fats Waller was born in New York City). Fascinated by this history, Mike and his mechanic friend, Jerry (Jack Black), listen to jazz standards and paint murals of Fats Waller beneath the overpass. While Mr. Fletcher journeys to the sixtieth anniversary of Fats Waller's death, he ponders over how he can transform his business to save the building from demolition by the city. The store is left in Mike's care, but Jerry, after an electrical accident, has the power to magnetize anything he touches and wipes out all the contents of the videotapes on the store's shelves. To save the business, Mike and Jerry use a camcorder to shoot their customized remakes of Hollywood movies: in other words, their "sweded" adaptations, which are based on their faint memories of the content or a rough impression of VHS cover art. However, their sweded business grows too fast and attracts FBI attention. In order to replace the unauthorized remakes, Mike and Jerry invite the town's residents to create a movie entitled *Fats Waller Was Born Here* to commemorate a fictionalized version of the life of this (not) native son of Passaic.

Be Kind Rewind is a star vehicle for comedian–musician Jack Black and Yasiin Bey, the hip hop artist known as Mos Def. Casting two musicians with comedic sensibilities to play the duo exemplifies Gondry's strength in exploring musicality in comedy, which is also shown in his documentary *Dave Chappelle's Block Party* (2005). In 2004, Gondry joined comedian Dave Chappelle to shoot this documentary about a free street concert organized by Chappelle and his friends in Bedford–Stuyvesant, Brooklyn. The documentary reads like Gondry's reflection on the format of *cinéma vérité*, as well as being a shout-out to Spike Lee's

Do the Right Thing (1989), which was filmed in the same neighborhood. In a backstage scene, Chappelle elaborates his belief in the common ties between musician and comedian. He looks at the camera and says, "Comedians and musicians are like this," interlocking his fingers; he continues, "Every comic wants to be a musician. Every musician thinks they're funny. It's a very strange relationship we have. Some musicians are funny. Some comedians can play. I'll give you an example, Mos Def, funny guy."[14] Chappelle's comments apparently resonate with Gondry's casting decisions for the Mike–Jerry duo in *Be Kind Rewind*.[15] Mos Def and Jack Black are expected to expand their thespian images and evoke our memories of them as two musical comedians, two funny musicians.

AMATEURISM, KITSCH, DIY FILMMAKING

The contrasting personalities of the Mike–Jerry duo recall the conventions of the buddy film. Mike dreams big but is stuck in a small place: a VHS rental store in Passaic, New Jersey. Jerry is an inventive mechanic who creates problems for the storyline: after being electrified, he has acquired magnetizing power and has erased all the contents of the VHS tapes in the store. Miss Falewicz (Mia Farrow) wants to borrow a tape of *Ghostbusters* or she will report their negligence to Mr. Fletcher. Mike travels the town to look for a tape of *Ghostbusters*, but to no avail, so he decides to shoot his own version, since Miss Falewicz only knows the movie from the cover. Drawing from his unreliable memories of the film and limited resources, Mike persuades Jerry to join the team, offering "I'll be Bill Murray; you be everyone else," and they are going to "swede" (their neologism) the film by making their own Hollywood adaptation.

This slightly anachronistic episode in the storyline illustrates the rarity of analogue signals in the age of digital transmission. The transition that spurs the characters on to launch their moviemaking demonstrates nostalgia for analogue memories. Mike travels the town to look for a VHS tape, but finds that the erased tape at Be Kind Rewind is the only one he can locate in one day. The old-fashioned videotape symbolizes a sentimental item of cultural memory that seems to have been forgotten by the digital era and represents a trace of memory embodied in a physical object, much like the cassette tapes that reveal lost memories to the former patients in *Eternal Sunshine*. Working at a presumably "historic" building, Mike is nostalgic both for the jazz era in which he never participated and for the Hollywood movies that he has consumed over the years. With jazz and Hollywood as two cultural indices, Mike, a native son of Passaic, obstinately preserves regional history and cultural memory. His resistance to the fast wave of digitalization is to hold on to a camera to record new memories on erased tapes, just as Joel resists erasure by escaping into fictional memories in *Eternal Sunshine*. Later in the film, Mike decides to make a movie to create a fictional history of Fats Waller; he uses a cassette recorder to tape others' accounts of their hero. Their fabrication of Fats Waller's life, compared to Mary's recitation of Alexander Pope's poem in *Eternal Sunshine*, is authentic yet not truthful. Behind their fanciful search for a cultural icon is a nostalgic attempt to evoke the community's history and collective memory against the backdrop of the digital age.

If the Be Kind Rewind video store is the last site in Passaic that preserves analogue memories, it is also *the* place to celebrate amateurism and kitsch. The film continues the surreal undertone and handmade aesthetics of Gondry's previous film, *The Science of Sleep* (*La Science des rêves*, 2006).[16] In Passaic, all the tapes that are made by Mike and Jerry are recycled, because the tapes have been erased and rewritten with new contents. Mike and Jerry's remakes of Hollywood films are not original at all. The inauthentic contents are adapted from their mediated memories of Hollywood films or, at least, from their impressions of VHS cover art. Not only is their memory content ersatz, but also their art medium—the retaped cassette—is second-hand. The Be Kind Rewind video store is like a lacuna in the linear time of late capitalist society, a utopia of cinephiles perhaps, for it remains the rare place that allows moviemakers to recycle ideas and to recreate their cinematic memories with everyday objects on the already erased medium. Akin to the human brain depicted in *Eternal Sunshine*, the erased tape in *Be Kind Rewind* is the medium that testifies to memory's malleability and adaptability. While in *Eternal Sunshine* one pays the price for undergoing a severe manner of voluntary forgetting—the deliberate memory erasure at Lacuna—moviemakers may find an easier solution for rescuing memories erased by mistake: to rewind and retape.

With no money, low technology, and non-professional acting, Mike and Jerry's off-key remakes are the products of amateurism and DIY aesthetics. All their "sweded" remakes of Hollywood films are made with everyday objects, limited resources, and no budget. They recruit Alma (Melonie Diaz) to play the female lead in every homemade movie. In sweded movies, clothes hangers and Christmas tinsel are the substitutes for strange things in the air, a full pizza symbolizes a pool of blood in a shooting scene, and watercolor-painted pieces of cardboards are used for a lion skin. Mike and Jerry switch to the negative mode to shoot night scenes during the day, but they have to wear Xeroxed masks or their faces become negative in the frame. To recreate the famous "Chinese bamboo" scene in *Rush Hour 2* (Brett Ratner, 2001), Mike and Jerry film at a children's playground, on rooftops and piles of trash bags. The very strong Chinese bamboo is recreated first with playground monkey bars for high-angle shots, and subsequently with a plastic tube for the low-angle shot. The sweded movies with amateur aesthetics farcically boost the rental business because Mike and Jerry can "shoot any genre." Jerry even creates a slogan for their customization service at Be Kind Rewind: "Be Kind Rewind, videos à la carte. You name it. We shoot it."

A real-life comedian, Jack Black brings his thespian image to his character, Jerry, who transforms from an amateur to a self-taught professional in Passaic. Black is a physical comedian and performs as a singer for his mock rock duo Tenacious D, a cult band that mixes rock music with satire and self-mockery. In *Be Kind Rewind*, Black needs to perform the part of an uncertain amateur and starts by playing "everyone else" in Mike's adaptation of *Ghostbusters* before reaching stardom in DIY filmmaking. During the shoot in the public library, Jerry shies away from shooting because he "look[ed] right into the lens": a common trait among non-professional actors who suddenly realize the existence of the camera. Mos Def, also a newcomer to acting, knows how to encourage Jerry to continue acting, telling Black's character that he is "doing fine." Black feels encouraged and resumes his blithe confidence in front of the camera, performing Ray Parker, Jr.'s "Bustin' Makes Me Feel Good": a moment that makes the audience wonder if they are watching Jack Black play Jack Black, or Jack Black play Jerry of Passaic. However, once the amateur realizes how the camera has liberated him from his old self and given him a new identity, this newly acquired freedom manifests as offensive behavior, hinting at the instigation of populism. Black acts out unacceptable racial prejudice by appearing in blackface to cast the role of Fats Waller, or by wearing a dress to "stay in character" as an obnoxious Daisy Werthan from *Driving Miss Daisy* (Bruce Beresford, 1989)—a role he knows only from the VHS box—and is rightfully condemned for his offensive rhetoric and unacceptable behavior in both instances.

Criticisms of late capitalism are smuggled in through characters' resistance to analogue-to-digital conversion, the mass-produced sweded films, and the impending gentrification of the neighborhood. Mr. Fletcher faces time pressure exerted by City Hall, to the effect that the building will be demolished if it is not repaired in six weeks; he plans to adopt a "progressive transition to a modern medium: the DVD" to boost the business. He observes the competing West Coast Video Store, where he finds only comedies and action-adventures, and "no specific knowledge required" on the part of the clerks. Meanwhile, Mike and his team need to mass-produce many of the shorter sweded movies in order to save the building and invite customers to act in their movies. However, since authorized DVDs are prevailing, sweded tapes based on mediated memories by the community cannot woo customers in a short period of time and are subject to destruction: an outcome that nearly overturns the film's celebratory depiction of amateurism and DIY filmmaking.

In contrast to pirated DVDs, however, moviemaking in *Be Kind Rewind* is both a self-reflexive art and a communal experience. Mike and Jerry demonstrate how to adapt to their circumstances and transform everyday objects into spectacles. They may be amateurs but they are also cinephiles. During the shooting of *Ghostbusters*, when Mike wants to give up the idea of shooting the night scene during the day, Jerry scolds him: "All you need is a minimal amount of professionalism." This ironic call for professionalism reminds the audience that the amateurs learn their trade from imitation. They know the tricks a camera can play by changing its position and angle. They draw on a diverse array of cinematic references during their daily conversation and believe deeply in the democratic essence of moviemaking. After taking money from some juvenile delinquents, Mike, Jerry, and Alma celebrate their little victory in a restaurant, wondering how to remake the Disney animated film *The Lion King* (Roger Allers and Rob Minkoff, 1994). As they discuss the synopsis, the waiter and the customer at the next table jump into their discussion. They are awed by how "Shakespearean" *The Lion King* is without mentioning *Hamlet* once, as if the name of Shakespeare is a shorthand for its nominal cultural capital. The rootless cultural reference is emblematic of the lacuna of memory in Passaic.

Be Kind Rewind is a metafilm that shows how amateurs reflect on film history by moviemaking. In a stylized *mise-en-scène*, Mike and Jerry shoot five movies in a long take: *When We Were Kings* (Leon Gast, 1996); *2001: A Space Odyssey* (Stanley Kubrick, 1968); *King Kong* (Merian C. Cooper and Ernest B. Schoedsack, 1933); *Carrie* (Brian De Palma, 1976), and *Men in Black* (Barry Sonnenfeld, 1997). Mike and Jerry are now the stars and the talk of the town. As Jack Black walks out of his trailer in blue boxers to play Ali in the boxing ring, his performance reminds the audience of his wrestler role in the sports comedy *Nacho Libre* (Jared Hess, 2006). These long takes exemplify the mix-and-match of high concept and kitsch: a whirling dryer drum is the substitute for Kubrick's spaceship; a bucket of ketchup is used to humiliate Carrie; and toy cars are used to create perspective. Moreover, some juvenile delinquents are recruited to perform teenage gangsters in the sweded version of *Boyz n the Hood* (John Singleton, 1991). Still wearing Afro wigs, they gather together to watch themselves on TV and laugh out loud. The educational function of filmmaking is manifested in the celebratory portrait of the communal experience of the amateur community. Ultimately, an FBI agent, played in a cameo by Sigourney Weaver, busts Be Kind Rewind and insists that all of the "black-market videos, pirates and bootleggers" need to be destroyed because of "copyright infringement." As the locals witness a steamroller flatten all their sweded tapes on the street, Fats Waller's rendition of "Swing Low, Sweet Chariot" fades in as the background music to this melancholy moment. All the re-recorded cassettes made in Passaic are destroyed, and so are their mediated memories of Hollywood. But Weaver's parodic cameo triggers the audience's cinematic memory, since she did appear in the real *Ghostbusters* film in 1984.

MEMORIES AND FABRICATIONS

Making a fictionalized movie of Fats Waller's life in Passaic epitomizes the adaptability of collective memory. Akin to Jameson's discussion of the postmodern situation, in which "the survival, the residue, the holdover, the archaic, has finally been swept away without a trace," and "the past itself has disappeared (along with the well-known 'sense of the past' or historicity and collective memory),"[17] the locals have lost their mediated memories of Hollywood. After a day of group mourning, the town's residents gather outside of Be Kind Rewind, demanding that Mike make new movies. Mike plans to make a movie about Fats Waller but needs Mr. Fletcher's approval. Mr. Fletcher, after confessing to fabricating Fats Waller's life story, feels embarrassed and reluctant to approve this project. But Miss Falewicz, standing by Mike and Jerry, proudly announces: "Our past belongs to us. We can change it if we want." She makes up an anecdote about Fats Waller's fabricated life in Passaic, saying, "My mom saw Fats Waller playing piano right here in the Passaic Theater. Sure, anybody want to say anything about that?" Akin to a chain of word associations, a string of nuggets about Fats Waller bursts out from the crowd, and the pianist's fictitious life is brought to life. Through the power of narrative, Fats Waller was born right here in the Be Kind Rewind building in Passaic, New Jersey, and the fabricated collective memory is and will be shared by the community.

In *Be Kind Rewind*, collective memory persists tenaciously like ineradicable love in *Eternal Sunshine*. While *Eternal Sunshine* represents different dimensions of love (and the resulting joy and torment), with the hope of retaining the authenticity of personal memory, *Be Kind Rewind* employs reflexive aesthetics by demonstrating the process of memory-making and further evokes our memories of film history and popular culture in a post-modern American context. That premise of reflexivity is epitomized by the scenes where the characters collectively make their own adaptations of Hollywood movies, paying homage to filmmakers that have inspired them to be creative—on behalf of the real director of this film. That is, *Be Kind Rewind* is comprised of Gondry's memories and adaptations of Hollywood movies. Therefore, casting Mia Farrow as Miss Falewicz also reflects Gondry's nostalgia and reflexive aesthetics. Farrow is the perfect advocate of imagination due to her role in *The Purple Rose of Cairo* (Woody Allen, 1985), in which she plays a waitress who watches movies to forget her stagnant life in New Jersey, until one day she falls in love with a character emerging from the screen. The subtle intertextuality may also bring to mind that another character in *The Purple Rose of Cairo* once commented: "In New Jersey anything can happen." Indeed, in *Be Kind Rewind*, characters project their fantasies of Hollywood onto DIY filmmaking, make their adaptations, create their memories, and transform Passaic, New Jersey, from a sleepy backwater into a fantastical space where anything can happen.

Figure 10.2 Miss Falewicz encourages Mr. Fletcher to create his memories of Fats Waller in Passaic, New Jersey, in *Be Kind Rewind* (New Line Cinema, 2008)

Be Kind Rewind, like *Eternal Sunshine*, is a loop story that begins with the future. It starts with clips from *Fats Waller Was Born Here*, with Mr. Fletcher and Miss Falewicz remembering Fats Waller's fabricated life, and ends with the communal screening inside and outside of the Be Kind Rewind building an hour before its midnight demolition. At this time, local people from Passaic gather at Be Kind Rewind to watch the movie in which all of them participated, as if their reverie of the democratic essence of moviemaking is the last resort in the resistance of destruction and escape from the boundaries of linear time.

In an interview, Gondry used a Möbius strip to explain the loop in his mind as follows: "You fold a 2-D space into a 3-D space. You create a depth that doesn't exist. It becomes something much closer to what's in your head."[18] The narrative structure of *Be Kind Rewind*, as Gondry planned it, is a 3-D space that folds the audience's viewing experience into time. In the film, during the script development process, the locals gather at Be Kind Rewind to discuss how to map out the storyline. Looking at the recorded cassette tapes on the table, Jerry plans to begin with Fats's birth but is criticized for lacking in originality. Mike proposes to start with his death instead, to which Alma replies, "It's like *Citizen Kane*. You're original." To imitate Orson Welles's film is not original, but the reference to *Citizen Kane* (1941) is authentic and it functions as the filmmaker's self-referential circuit that connects cinephiles with their cinematic memories. The storyline has to move backwards in this regard, for one needs to rewind the tape to remember the past and keep pre-digitalized personal memories intact.

In early 2008, Gondry installed the "Be Kind Rewind Film Club" exhibition at New York City's Deitch Projects, in which visitors were invited to make their own movies at the gallery in two hours, following the "Be Kind Rewind Protocol" designed by him. Gondry observed how his protocol would affect visitors' filmmaking, since they were asked to decide on film genre before conceiving the film title and storyline.[19] In retrospect, the protocol recalls how Mr. Fletcher learns efficient management from a local DVD rental store that categorizes stock items in only two genres. We see from his work how Gondry prioritizes the democratic essence in creative collaboration over the result of artistic distinction and how he embraces the liberating power of filmmaking like a lover of Hollywood. Just as Jerry in *Be Kind Rewind* promises to customize genre videos *à la carte*, gallery visitors would draw from their cinematic memory and imaginations to create their genre films à la Americana.

CONCLUSION

Both *Eternal Sunshine* and *Be Kind Rewind* pose anxieties about memory erasure and cultural amnesia, either through voluntary forgetting or unintentional removal, in late capitalist America. In *Be Kind Rewind*, the building is to be demolished and the magnetic tapes are to be destroyed, whereas in *Eternal Sunshine*, the memory of love is to be wiped away. The materials that trigger the emotional core of memory are mediated substitutes that are mixed with premature nostalgia and post-modern pastiche, be it a plastic memento or a re-recorded tape. Yet these two films also demonstrate that there is hope for change, whether exemplified by how the fictional Joel Barish in *Eternal Sunshine* makes up new memories to resist the erasure of *his* memories or how the fictionalized narrative of real-life Fats Waller in *Be Kind Rewind* epitomizes the creation of collective memory by a community out of digital time. As seen in both Gondry's *Eternal Sunshine* and his *Be Kind Rewind*, to resist the irreversible forgetting, one needs to re-remember the past.

NOTES

1. Roger Ebert, *The Great Movies IV* (Chicago and London: University Press of Chicago, 2016), 77. Anthony Lane, "Don't Look Back," review of *Eternal Sunshine of the Spotless Mind* by Michel Gondry, *The New Yorker*, March 22, 2004.
2. Chris Dzialo, "'Frustrated Time' Narration: The Screenplays of Charlie Kaufman," in *Puzzle Films: Complex Storytelling in Contemporary Cinema*, ed. Warren Buckland (Malden, MA, and Oxford: Wiley–Blackwell, 2009), 108.
3. Dzialo, "'Frustrated Time' Narration," 111.
4. Carol Vernallis, "Music Video, Songs, Sound: Experience, Technique and Emotion in *Eternal Sunshine of the Spotless Mind*," *Screen*, 49, no. 3 (Autumn 2008): 278, 286.
5. David Bordwell, "Film Futures," *SubStance*, 31, no. 1 (Issue 97, 2002): 92.
6. Thomas Elsaesser, "The Mind-Game Film," in Buckland, *Puzzle Films*, 14.
7. Charlie Kaufman, *Eternal Sunshine of the Spotless Mind* (New York: Newsmarket Press, 2004), 38.

8. Sigmund Freud, "A Note upon the "Mystic Writing-Pad,"" *Theories of Memory: A Reader*, eds Michael Rossington and Anne Whitehead (Baltimore: Johns Hopkins University Press, 2007), 117.
9. Fredric Jameson, *Postmodernism, or The Cultural Logic of Late Capitalism* (Durham, NC: Duke University Press, 1991), 16.
10. Jameson, *Postmodernism*, 17.
11. Alexander Pope, "Eloisa to Abelard," in *The Major Works*, ed. Pat Rogers (Oxford and New York: Oxford University Press, 2008), 143.
12. Andrew M. Butler, *Eternal Sunshine of the Spotless Mind* (London: Palgrave Macmillan, 2014), 68.
13. Beck, "Everybody's Gotta Learn Sometime," track 9 on *Eternal Sunshine of the Spotless Mind* original soundtrack, Hollywood Records, 2004, compact disc.
14. For further discussion of *Dave Chappelle's Block Party*, please see this volume's ninth chapter: "The Reel and Surreal of Race in America: Michel Gondry and the African–American Identity Crisis of Dave Chappelle," by Monique Taylor.
15. Michel Gondry, *You'll Like This Film Because You're in It: The Be Kind Rewind Protocol* (Brooklyn: PictureBox, 2008), 14.
16. For further discussion of *The Science of Sleep*, please see the first three chapters of this volume: "'We Can Change the Whole Narrative': Crafting Play and Nostalgia in Michel Gondry's *The Science of Sleep* and *Mood Indigo*," by Danica van de Velde; "In Dreams and in Love There are no Impossibilities: Michel Gondry's Cinema and the Aesthetics of the Oneiric," by Bruno Surace; and "I Am Collecting Beautiful Objects: Michel Gondry's Taxidermy of Emotions," by Jenny Pyke.
17. Jameson, *Postmodernism, or The Cultural Logic of Late Capitalism*, 309.
18. Jennifer Hillner, "*Be Kind Rewind* Director Michel Gondry Forgoes Dreamy Plots for Straight-Up Comedy," *Wired* (December 24, 2007). Available at <https://www.wired.com/2007/12/ff-gondry/> (last accessed February 26, 2020).
19. Gondry, *You'll Like This Film Because You're in it*, 51.

CHAPTER 11

Playing with Superheroes: Genre, Aesthetics, and Deconstruction in *The Green Hornet*

Jennifer Kirby

In a scathing one-star review, Roger Ebert described Michel Gondry's *The Green Hornet* (2011) as "an almost unendurable demonstration of a movie with nothing to be about."[1] Ebert criticizes the film for its one-dimensional portrayal of its only female character, Lenore Case (Cameron Diaz); its reliance on outlandish action sequences; and the unlikableness of its main protagonist, Britt Reid (Seth Rogen), an infantilized "spoiled little rich brat."[2] Such vitriolic criticism is characteristic of the general response to the film, which has a score of only 39 on review aggregation website Metacritic.[3] This response, however, fails to acknowledge the extent to which the film can be read as a deconstruction of the generic codes and aesthetics of the superhero genre from an outsider's perspective. Just as incompetent playboy Britt Reid plays at his childhood ambition of being a superhero in the film, European auteur Michel Gondry plays with the conventions of the "quintessentially American genre"[4] of the superhero movie.

As a director well known for his "quizzical dreamscapes"[5] in films such as *Eternal Sunshine of the Spotless Mind* (2004) and *The Science of Sleep* (2006), Gondry was perhaps not widely expected to helm a big-budget superhero film for Sony Pictures. A loose adaptation of the character from a popular children's radio show, *The Green Hornet* follows Britt, a narcissistic and immature young man, who adopts a superhero alter ego after the death of his disapproving father, newspaper editor and millionaire James Reid (Tom Wilkinson). As Britt is largely incompetent, he enlists the help of his father's barista, engineer, and mechanic, Kato (Jay Chou), to provide him with strategy and weaponry, and they settle upon a plan to pretend to be criminals in order to get closer to their enemies. Britt and Kato must now battle the crime lord, Chudnofsky (Christoph Waltz), and fool District Attorney Scanlon (David Harbour), who is revealed to be corrupt. The film features a number of the hallmarks of the American superhero film: "alternate identities,"[6] heroes and sidekicks, supervillains, and a coming-of-age story in which a male character learns to be a man and a hero at the same time.[7] It is also one of the few English-language Gondrian productions that does not have any French funding, but rather is embedded in the Hollywood system.

Despite these formulaic elements and an American generic sensibility, Gondry expressed his commitment to incorporating his own aesthetic into the film, as quoted in *Variety*: "There are recipes that the studios apply that make successful movies, but there's also a pretty strong unknown factor, and in this unknown area is where I could play and bring more personal stuff."[8] These intentions were largely dismissed by critics, who disputed Gondry's claim that he had maintained his integrity as an auteur in the face of studio interference. For example, *The Guardian*'s Peter Bradshaw noted that Gondry's aesthetic:

> only surfaces in one sequence, a brief action montage with wacky cut-out impressions . . . I'd bet that there was far more of this kind of thing in Gondry's original conception, weeded out and blandified by the studio.[9]

Bradshaw's assessment, however, ignores the strong continuities in the film with Gondry's previous work. In particular, the film emphasizes play, deconstruction, and reconstruction in common with his previous works, such as the better-received *Be Kind Rewind* (2008), which centers on the DIY recreation of classic movies after a videotape library is accidentally wiped in a small town. This earlier film highlights the power of "unorthodox imagination" and displays the degree to which remaking existing texts provides an opportunity to find one's own voice in a form of play and mimicry that mirrors the process that children go through as they imitate adults they know, and then later other people encountered through mediated images.[10] In *The Green Hornet*, Britt locates his sense of identity via his childlike play at being a superhero, and the film emphasizes this notion through the use of drawings and childhood toys in its aesthetic and iconography. On a textual level, in *The Green Hornet*, Gondry similarly plays with the genre of the superhero movie by dismantling and recreating its conventions. He carries out this deconstruction on the levels of narrative and characterization by undercutting the genre's predominant "fantasies of morally just, heroic white men, gifted with incredible powers and personal resolve"[11] through his depiction of an incompetent fool in the lead role. This level of deconstruction proves itself to be less convincing or consistent, however, than the aesthetic deconstruction in the film. Gondry enacts a project of DIY reconstruction by utilizing analogue special effects in place of CGI at crucial moments, wherever possible,[12] thus subverting the genre's well-documented reliance on computer-generated technology.[13] In this way, Gondry works with genre codes and motifs, but remakes them from analogue resources almost as if they were produced by children recreating superhero narratives from cardboard and cellophane. If Britt plays at being a superhero, Gondry plays at producing an American-style superhero film, but retains his idiosyncratic analogue aesthetic.

"WE COULD BE HEROES": INTERTEXTUAL HUMOR AND GENERIC REVISION

In *The Green Hornet*, Britt and his assistant, Kato, decide to become superheroes and design their own costumes, vehicles, and so on accordingly, based on their knowledge of superhero media; the film similarly expects its audience to be familiar with these conventions and to recognize the playful subversion of these elements. The film thus exhibits what Justin S. Schumaker describes as "super-intertexuality," which occurs "when intertextuality offers metatextual commentary on genre and mythic structures."[14] Through a comparison of the *Spider-Man* franchise (Sam Raimi, 2002–7) and *Kick-Ass* (Matthew Vaughn, 2010), Schumaker argues that when one film references another, there is an opportunity to provide a critical perspective not only on the film referred to but also on "the narrative moments and mythic tropes" the film invokes.[15] *The Green Hornet* enacts a similar process by parodying core elements of superhero films, and using irreverence to undermine generally serious moments and thus lampoon the moral pomposity of the superhero genre. As Jeffrey A. Brown notes, parodies of superhero films

> effectively ridicule the genre's presentation of ridiculously ideal bodies, of the hero's ability to easily win every fight, of clearly demarcated lines between good and evil, and the levels of seemingly bloodless violence portrayed as normal in the mainstream films.[16]

Indeed, Britt is depicted as an oversized child, whose transformation into a superhero only highlights his inadequacies. For example, when presented with a newly produced green gas gun that is to be his trademark weapon, he accidentally shoots himself in the face. Similarly, the film uses irreverent subversions of other key aspects of the superhero genre like the elaborate machinery and vehicles utilized by the more serious superheroes, such as Batman. Early in the film, Britt brings a woman home to his mansion. He opens the garage, revealing numerous luxurious cars in various colors, recalling the extensive car collection of Bruce Wayne (aka Batman). In typical Gondrian speeded-up motion, Britt and the young woman kiss on each of the cars, defying the seriousness usually associated with vehicles in the superhero film. Furthermore, the audience soon realizes that the car collection belongs not to Britt but to his father when Britt's father scolds him like a naughty child for his actions. Later, after his father's death, Britt learns that Kato has designed elaborate gadgets for his father, but rather than a weapon or costume, as Iron Man might require, Kato's signature creation is an elaborate, high-tech coffee maker. These revelations defy audience expectations and undercut the gravitas associated with the conventions of the superhero genre.

Gondry also consistently undermines Britt's status as a hero or leading man by presenting him as both physically and intellectually inferior to his Asian sidekick, Kato. In this way, the film depicts a crisis in white male privilege. For example, through cross-cutting, Gondry establishes Britt as less creative than Kato, while parodying one of the crucial turning points in adopting a superhero identity from other superhero narratives. Schumaker explains that the motif of an identity creation montage in films such as the *Spider-Man* franchise functions to draw a parallel between the transition from "boy to man and human to superhero," and often features recognizable tropes, such as the design of a costume which will come to signify the superhero identity.[17] In *The Green Hornet*, Gondry cuts between Kato making weapons while Britt doodles aimlessly and colors in a magazine image. Here Britt is depicted as an eternal child, whose skills and abilities do not extend to properly designing a costume or car. Furthermore, the hallmarks of the superhero identity are created by the labor of Britt's assistant/sidekick, whose contribution is frequently not recognized by Britt. Ever petulant, Britt responds with hostility when Kato questions his actions or decisions, exclaiming that "Heroes beat sidekicks, period!" Following this exchange, the two fight in a comically exaggerated sequence in which they attack each other, destroying Britt's house in the process, complete with heightened sound effects to emphasize grunts, falls, punches, and so on. The sequence lampoons the pomposity of fight sequences in modern action films by demonstrating the chaos that ensues from petty arguments between friends, while simultaneously accentuating Britt's inferior skills. In such sequences, the film's mockery of white male superiority is inseparable from the parody of the superhero genre. Britt's sheltered lack of understanding of the world further surfaces in a sequence in which Kato and Britt drive off in their modified car, the Black Beauty, while aggressively nodding their heads and singing along to the rap song "Gangsta's Paradise," which plays on a record player installed in the car (a typical Gondrian contraption). They are full of macho bravado. Gondry cuts to a wide shot of the car, and then the record abruptly stops as the needle is lifted. Kato asks where they are going and Britt replies in his characteristic bumbling manner, "I thought you knew." The illusion is shattered as Britt realizes that he has no idea what he is doing and that he has appropriated heroism, much as he is appropriating African–American culture. Soon Britt muses, "I think we are in the hood, Kato." This line highlights Britt's naivety, in addition to his white privilege.

Yet, despite these attempts to undermine the genre's hyper-masculinity and Eurocentricity, *The Green Hornet* falls into a pattern identified by Brown in relation to other contemporary films centered on unworthy amateur superheroes, *Kick-Ass* and *Super* (James Gunn, 2010). In these films,

> while superhero parodies mock the genre they also, ultimately, reinforce its construction of hegemonic masculinity . . . for all of their comedy and their condemnation of superheroes as ridiculous, both films allow their foolish titular heroes to defeat the bad guys and get the girl of their dreams. Rather than undermining the premise of superheroes as aspirational models of hegemonic masculinity, *Super* and *Kick-Ass* suggest that even the least likely man can become a hero by putting on a costume and beating up criminals.[18]

In *The Green Hornet*, Britt ultimately triumphs over his enemies while winning over his love interest, secretary Lenore Case (Cameron Diaz). Furthermore, Britt proves himself worthy of the legacy of his father when he exposes and defeats corrupt District Attorney Scanlon, after refusing to submit and allow Scanlon to control the news media, thus demonstrating Britt's newfound sense of moral and ethical righteousness. Britt therefore conforms to a second archetype in American superhero films—prominent examples include the titular characters in both the *Batman* and *Spider-Man* films—in which a literal or figurative boy becomes a superhero in order to live up to the example set by a dead or missing father figure, whose influence "gives him his sense of morality and justice."[19] This emphasis on patriarchal legacy produces what Kara M. Kvaran calls "a specifically American pattern of gender relations and ideology . . . thereby emphasizing heroics as masculine and homosocial stories about men as most essential."[20] In the final estimation, then, *The Green Hornet* remains fairly generic and conservative, ideologically. Perhaps the greatest challenge to the conventions of the superhero genre posed by the film is not in its characterization, but rather in its aesthetic, which consistently validates and glorifies analogue effects and a handmade style that resembles children's play objects more than contemporary seamless CGI Hollywood special effects.

ANALOGUE ANTICS AND CUT-OUT COLLAGES

Superheroes have a complex relationship with technological and industrial progress. Aldo J. Regalado argues that Superman—famously introduced as "faster than a speeding bullet" and "more powerful than a locomotive"—and "most of the superheroes created to follow in the wake of his success were . . . defined by their oppositional or transcendent stance towards indices of American power and progress. At their genesis, therefore, superheroes are cultural responses to American modernity."[21] Superheroes such as Superman, Batman, and Captain America tackled the problems of the corrupt American industrial city while re-affirming their strength and traditional value of self-sacrifice for the community in hostile urban environments.[22] Yet despite this emphasis on bodily and character strength, cinematic superheroes are also frequently augmented technologically in some way, whether by mechanical or computerized equipment or by radioactivity (in the case of Spider-Man). For example, Lisa Gotto analyzes the depiction of Tony Stark's suit in *Iron Man* (Jon Favreau, 2008), which possesses "a self-contained environment consisting of various communication arrays and sensors that turn Tony into a technologically enabled superhero."[23] Because the viewer is often placed inside Tony's perspective in the suit, the viewer inhabits not the character's body but his enhanced viewpoint.[24] Iron Man's primary weapon is his costume, which further functions as an extension of his body/senses; this costume is also physically intertwined with Stark's vital systems, as it is powered by the reactor that keeps him alive. Kvaran notes that the superhero film represents an updating of Robert Jewett and John Shelton Lawrence's concept of the American monomyth, originally exemplified by the western genre, in which a lone outsider utilizes violence to resolve a conflict or threat that the town's institutions and officials have failed to squash.[25] In the superhero film, the guns, hats, and horses from the western are replaced "with special effects and capes," reflecting how "science and technology helped move American exceptionalism away from older narratives of individualism toward newer forms of the same ideology."[26] No longer does the hero have the fastest gun, but rather the most advanced technological weapons.

It follows, then, that the superhero film provides ample opportunities "for the deployment of perceptual forms and effects" in its depiction of individuals with "supernatural skills."[27] In the twenty-first century, digital effects therefore dominate the superhero film. Regalado argues that this effects technology "has enabled Hollywood to produce live-action and computer-generated superhero adventure movies that approximate the visual style and grandeur of comic books," resulting in a "superhero movie renaissance."[28] Larrie Dudenhoffer similarly suggests that there is an inherent ontological connection between contemporary digital effects and the superheroes born from comic books that they remediate because

> much as the comic nests a fantastic element, the superhero, into an otherwise ordinary milieu, so too does the digital film nest a "fantastic" or rather a completely non-indexical element, the CG animation, into footage taken of actual actors, objects, and settings.[29]

Some critics and academics have, however, criticized the reliance of the genre on digital effects, cementing a cultural perception of superhero films as pure entertainment lacking thematic and narrative depth. Furthermore, Scott Bukatman questions the assumption that digital technologies reproduce the aesthetic and effect of the comic book image, arguing that the digital sheen and ostentatious computer effects of the superhero film reduce the stakes of the action and result in a loss of the sense of corporeal engagement with the environment depicted.[30] In *The Green Hornet*, the special effects appear to explicitly disavow the polished digital aesthetic of the majority of superhero films, often resembling a child's handmade approximation of a comic book instead. In this way, Gondry blends his own preoccupation with craft and the analogue with the superhero genre's emphasis on fantastical spaces that draw attention to their mediation and to the way in which superheroes function both "as mediating figures and figures of mediation."[31]

In *The Green Hornet*, the environments inhabited by Britt and Kato frequently look as though they have been pasted together or produced using children's toys. The film in fact emphasizes play from its very first moments, in which a young Britt holds a superhero action figure out the window while being driven to his father's office, where James chastises young Britt for getting into a fight and takes the head off the toy. This motif of toys and childhood play structures the film's visual aesthetic. When Kato fights, the film employs a technique to represent "Kato-Vision," in which slow motion shows Kato's mastery of the situation, and a red radar, accompanied by a rudimentary warning sound, zooms in on important elements to emphasize Kato's thought process. This red radar resembles the lights and sensors of mechanical toys, rather than a sophisticated computer imaging system like the one inside Iron Man's suit. The film's cinematographer, John Schwartzmann, describes how, whenever the Green Hornet has his enemies lined up against a wall, he "replaced the car's headlights with Barco HD projectors, which produced disorienting green and black patterns Gondry designed."[32] These flashing lights again recall the noisy, garish effects produced by toy cars and weapons. In the film's most bravura sequence, Britt mentally reconstructs the events leading up to his father's death. After Scanlon reveals that he in fact killed Britt's father through an overdose of the toxin found in bee stings, the camera zooms into Britt's eye, or perhaps his mind's eye, and his father enters the soundtrack in a voiceover instructing Britt to think. Britt slowly pieces together how his father, Scanlon, and Chudnofsky were connected, and a series of events linked by cause and effect are depicted, with each new element that Britt understands appearing as if onto a paper collage, pasted on. For example, white, hollow dead body shapes, which look like cardboard cut-outs of crime scene outlines, appear over the image from Britt's memory of Lenore recounting how the *Daily Sentinel* has become soft in its crime coverage over the last couple of years. The body outlines also waver slightly as if hanging by strings. This visual collage accompanies the voiceover in which Britt realizes how Chudnofsky managed to commit crimes under the radar after killing a crime reporter, thus scaring James Reid into temporarily stopping the newspaper's coverage of crime. The sequence uses numerous analogue metaphors, such as a newspaper front page spreading across the screen as if it were crinkling out. These evocations of analogue materials give the film a sense of tangibility and draw attention to traces of the film's construction. This aesthetic effect is substantiated by accounts of the film's production. The film undoubtedly does utilize computer-generated effects, evident particularly in sequences like those that use elaborate, continually dividing split-screens to replicate comic book panels.[33] However, Schwartzmann recounts that computer-generated effects were used only in cases where it would have been unsafe or impossible to produce the effect physically.[34] Gondry often preferred old-fashioned optical tricks instead.[35]

In addition to the use of non-computerized special effects, the film embeds a narrative of the failure of digital technology and the triumph of the physical into its plotline. After meeting Scanlon in a bar, where the latter confesses to killing Britt's father, Britt triumphantly shows Scanlon that he has recorded the conversation with a recording device, attached to a USB, in the shape of a piece of sushi. When he later attempts to play back the recording, however, the USB drive is empty and there are no data. In the final fight, Kato and Britt overcome their enemies, in part by hurling the remnants of their car, the Black Beauty, out of the window to physically crush Scanlon. It is a material fight, notably taking place in the offices of a newspaper complete with printing press, that allows the Green Hornet to triumph, not the use of digital technology.

CONCLUSION

In *The Green Hornet*, the protagonist, Britt, often fails or brings ridicule upon himself. It takes him several attempts to become a successful superhero; in fact, even his initial alter ego choice, "the green bee," is laughed off by journalists who compare the name to a knitting store or energy bar. Yet Britt eventually discovers that his point of difference from other superheroes—that nobody knows that he is a good guy—is, in fact, his advantage. In many respects, Gondry's film also fails in conforming to the conventions of an American superhero film, yet these supposed inadequacies appear crucial to the film's project of deconstruction. Reading *The Green Hornet* in the context of Gondry's other films and his preoccupations with themes such as childhood wonder, play, and DIY recreation provides a valuable perspective on the film, but the context of genre should not be discounted. *The Green Hornet* can be productively considered as not so much a rejection of the superhero genre, but a (re)negotiation of this largely American genre and of the filmmaking practices and aesthetic conventions of the contemporary Hollywood blockbuster.

NOTES

1. Roger Ebert, "The Green Hornet," last modified January 11, 2011. Available at <https://www.rogerebert.com/reviews/the-green-hornet-2011> (last accessed February 26, 2020).
2. Ebert, "The Green Hornet."
3. "The Green Hornet Reviews-Metacitic," Metacritic. Available at <https://www.metacritic.com/movie/the-green-hornet> (last accessed January 3, 2019).
4. Jeffrey A. Brown, *The Modern Superhero in Film and Television* (New York and London: Routledge, 2017), 13.
5. Anthony Kaufman, "Lord of the Strings: Gondry Balances Studio, Style in 'Hornet,'" *Variety* (January 3–11, 2017), 6.
6. Justin S. Schumaker, "Super-Intertextuality and 21st Century Individualized Social Advocacy in *Spider-Man* and *Kick Ass*," in *The 21st Century Superhero: Essays on Gender, Genre and Globalization*, eds Richard J. Gray II and Betty Kaklamanidou (Jefferson, NC, and London: McFarland, 2011), 130.
7. Schumaker, "Super-Intertextuality and 21st Century Individualized Social Advocacy in *Spider-Man* and *Kick Ass*," 132.
8. Kaufman, "Lord of the Strings," 6.
9. Peter Bradshaw, "The Green Hornet—review," last modified January 13, 2011. Available at <https://www.theguardian.com/film/2011/jan/13/the-green-hornet-review> (last accessed February 26, 2020).
10. Myke Bartlett, "Imitation as Inspiration: DIY Filmmaking in *Son of Rambow* and *Be Kind Rewind*," *Screen Education*, 51 (2008): 36.
11. Brown, *The Modern Superhero in Film and Television*, 5.
12. Iain Stasukevich, "Masked Men," *American Cinematographer* (February 2011): 27.
13. Scott Bukatman, "Why I Hate Superhero Movies," *Cinema Journal*, 50, no. 3 (2011): 120.
14. Schumaker, "Super-Intertextuality and 21st Century Individualized Social Advocacy in *Spider-Man* and *Kick Ass*," 130.
15. Schumaker, "Super-Intertextuality and 21st Century Individualized Social Advocacy in *Spider-Man* and *Kick Ass*," 133.
16. Brown, *The Modern Superhero in Film and Television*, 14.
17. Schumaker, "Super-Intertextuality and 21st Century Individualized Social Advocacy in *Spider-Man* and *Kick Ass*," 132.
18. Brown, *The Modern Superhero in Film and Television*, 14–15.
19. Kara M. Kvaran, "Super Daddy Issues: Parental Figures, Masculinity, and Superhero Films," *The Journal of Popular Culture*, 50, no. 2 (2017): 218.
20. Kvaran, "Super Daddy Issues," 219.
21. Aldo J. Regalado, *Bending Steel: Modernity and the American Superhero* (Jackson: University Press of Mississippi, 2005), 4.
22. Regalado, *Bending Steel*, 8–9.
23. Lisa Gotto, "Fantastic Views: Superheroes, Visual Perception, and Digital Perspective," in *Superhero Synergies: Comic Book Characters Go Digital*, eds James N. Gilmore and Matthias Stork (Lanham, MD: Rowman & Littlefield, 2014), 50.
24. Gotto, "Fantastic Views," 50.
25. Kvaran, "Super Daddy Issues," 222.
26. Kvaran, "Super Daddy Issues," 222–3.
27. Gotto, "Fantastic Views," 47.
28. Regalado, *Bending Steel*, 226.
29. Larrie Dudenhoffer, *Anatomy of the Superhero Film* (Cham: Palgrave Macmillan, 2017), 2.

30. Bukatman, "Why I Hate Superhero Movies," 120.
31. Gotto, "Fantastic Views," 56.
32. Stasukevich, "Masked Men," 28.
33. Gotto, "Fantastic Views," 57.
34. Stasukevich, "Masked Men," 27.
35. Stasukevich, "Masked Men," 27–8.

PART V

Multi-Media: Music Video and Television

CHAPTER 12

"It Would Not Be Just visual, It Could Have Words and a Story": Performance and Narrative in the Music Video Oeuvre of Michel Gondry

Daniel Klug

"SOUNDS LIKE YOU": MICHEL GONDRY AND AUDIO-VISUAL EXPERIENCES

In a 2014 interview, Michel Gondry evaluates his career as a music video director: "I've been pleased with my music videos, but a few of them don't succeed, but at least I've tried something new each time."[1] Gondry's claim in this statement, which emphasizes his ambition for narrative and cinematic innovation over success, reminds us that he is one of the most influential music video directors in the history of the medium. Indeed, through his pioneering work on the music video, Gondry—together with other directors such as Anton Corbijn, Chris Cunningham, Jonathan Glazer, Spike Jonze, Mark Romanek, Floria Sigismondi, and Hype Williams—has helped establish the reputation of this genre beyond popular culture.

Along with his music videos, Gondry also directed highly praised commercials, such as "Sounds Like You" (2017), for music streaming service Pandora, in which he re-uses narrative features and aesthetic modes similar to those in his music videos. In "Sounds Like You," a woman runs, to the beat of New Order's "Blue Monday" (1983), through oversized iconic album artworks, which smoothly merge into infinite scenery. She starts at The Doors' *Morrison Hotel* (1970) and runs up to a motorcycle. The lights darken, and another woman steps out of a yellow-lit entrance, which, together with the motorcycle, forms the cover of *Purple Rain* (1984) by Prince. She passes through the white crosses of *Master of Puppets* (1986) by Metallica, jumps over the red helmet heads of Devo's *Freedom of Choice* (1980), or dives through a baby-in-the-pool replica of Nirvana's *Nevermind* (1991). Then, she runs past a tree; the camera turns 90 degrees, and the tree crown forms the afro hair of a boy against a blue sky, revealing the cover for *Nothing Was the Same* (2013) by Drake. She continues through the black-and-white trees of The Cure's *A Forest* (1980) and the white-on-black radio waves of *Unknown Pleasures* (1979) by Joy Division. After stopping in David Bowie's *Blackstar* (2016) cover, she eventually ends up back at the *Morrison Hotel* façade but, from the left, neon-lit garage scenery slides in and forms the cover of *I Decided* (2017) by rapper Big Sean. The camera then zooms out, and the screen turns into the display of the Pandora app on a smartphone. The song "Moves," from Big Sean's *I Decided*, starts to play, and we see the woman exercising on a treadmill in a gym.

In "Sounds Like You," Gondry establishes a dreamlike, emotional experience for the viewer, based on album covers as visualizations of different musical genres and decades. It exemplifies how Gondry translates musicality into visual elements in his work. Alternating between running through and lingering on the album covers produces a visual flow and dynamic interaction with the beat of "Blue Monday," through which the numerous cuts become unnoticed. Gondry most prominently creates an illusion similar to morphing, merging, and turning the album covers featured in "Sounds Like You" in the music video for "Let Forever Be" (1999) by The Chemical Brothers. Here, digital manipulation of the image, visual effects, and dance collages merge into kaleidoscopic optical illusions to depict nightmares of the female protagonist, as well as to visualize the rhythmic structure of the song.

Since around 2009, Michel Gondry has focused more on directing feature films than music videos, as well as his first television series as a producer, *Kidding* (2019), for Showtime, for which he reunited with Jim Carrey, who starred in Gondry's film *Eternal Sunshine of the Spotless Mind* (2004). But, as Gondry's oeuvre ranges from music videos to commercials, short films, films, and television shows, all of his works, according to each genre, carry a characteristic aesthetic and narrative signature that is obvious yet hard to point out.

This chapter examines key aspects of Gondry's music video oeuvre in relation to his films. First, it discusses the general characteristics of music video audio-vision and its relation to film. Second, the chapter analyzes the audio-visual surplus in performance music videos directed by Gondry. Third, in contrast to performance, it looks at Gondry's narrative music videos and examines the complex visual storytelling concerning lyrics and musical structures in Gondry's music video for "Everlong" (1997) by Foo Fighters.

THE AUDIO-VISION OF MUSIC VIDEOS: MICHEL GONDRY AND GENRE REFERENTIALITY

Although Gondry's "Sounds Like You" commercial features New Order's "Blue Monday," it is not a (or the official) music video because it does not feature the full-length song. Music videos are short(er) audio-visual forms that combine different (moving) images with a musical piece.[2] They present artists and bands as performers, establish visual styles based on rhythm or musical patterns, or illustrate the lyrics with various aesthetic and narrative elements.[3] The foundation of music videos is the subsequent editing of (moving) images according to the linearity of the pre-existing song.[4] Therefore, they are characterized by audio-visual rhythm (images arranged to the musical beat), visual interpretations of the lyrics ("filmic" or narrative enhancement), or illustrations of the overall musical atmosphere.[5] Music videos are then commonly defined as either musical performances, chronological narratives, situative sequences, or illustrative elements. However, they are usually combinations or alterations of types, which means that "music videos can be described as generic hybrids, drawing from two or more categories in a more or less self-conscious way."[6]

Compared to film, the audio-vision of music videos is music-based. All visual material is usually created solely to visualize the song and does not have any validity otherwise.[7] Therefore, audio-visual coherences or congruencies are intentional and rooted in the musical structure of the song. But music and (moving) images do not enter a causal relation; especially in performance videos, the visible action does not create the audible sound and vice versa.[8] In music videos, musical and visual elements, previously unconnected, are coupled to form an artificial and technically originated audio-visual media product.

Music videos are hybrid audio-visual artifacts. Like commercials, they serve to advertise the song and the artist(s) in a pop cultural media context. They additionally adapt aesthetic and conceptual elements of experimental film and contemporary video art, such as technical modification of the image, or reduction of images to forms and backgrounds to visualize sound and rhythm.[9]

The work of Michel Gondry demonstrates the interdependencies of music videos and film. Music videos commonly draw inspiration from the imagery and narrative styles of film: "Tonight, Tonight" (1996) by the Smashing Pumpkins (Jonathan Dayton and Valerie Faris) adapts Georges Méliès's silent movie *A Trip to the Moon* (1902); "Last Cup of Sorrow" (1997) by US rock band Faith No More (Joseph Kahn) re-enacts the acrophobia scenes from Alfred Hitchcock's *Vertigo* (1958); and "California Love" (1995) by 2Pac feat. Dr. Dre (Hype Williams) adapts the apocalyptic imagery of *Mad Max Beyond Thunderdome* (George Miller and George Ogilvie, 1985). Gondry's films, conversely, include various references to his music videos. In fact, he even created the music video for "Light & Day" (2004) by The Polyphonic Spree from scenes from his film *Eternal Sunshine of the Spotless Mind*. In the music video, Gondry pastes lead singer Tim DeLaughter's mouth on the characters' faces, using them as vehicles to "sing" the song; however, because the song is part of the soundtrack, it also functions to advertise the film.

Furthermore, Gondry's films feature recurring subjects from his music videos. Gondry's film *Human Nature* (2001), similar to the video Gondry directed for Björk's song "Human Behavior" (1993), deals with the relation of animals to humans. *Eternal Sunshine of the Spotless Mind* is, as Carol Vernallis analyzes, a music-video-influenced *potpourri* of Gondry's visual strategies for distorting time and constructing a second narrative through "telling" with music.[10] Gondry's film *The Science of Sleep* (*La Science des rêves*, 2006) is the compressed film version of his dreamscape music video imagery. For example, *Science* reuses the giant hand sequence from Foo Fighters' "Everlong" (1997), and reversed narratives similar to the music videos Gondry directed for the songs "Sugar Water" (1996) by Cibo Matto and *Deadweight* (1997) by Beck.[11] In his feature film *Be Kind Rewind* (2008), Gondry focuses on his characteristic handmade-scenery aesthetic, which he frequently uses in his music videos to visualize childhood and re-enchantment.[12] Examples in which this aesthetic appears in Gondry's music videos include the hand-painted scenery in "Love Letters" (2014) by Metronomy; the surreal hospital setting of a giant Operation game board in Radiohead's "Knives Out" (2001); and the group of kids knitting props and instruments in Steriogram's "Walkie Talkie Man" (2004). The latter resembles the "sweded" look of Jerry and Mike's homemade videos in Gondry's *Be Kind Rewind*.[13]

"CITY LIGHTS," "GO," "CRYSTALLINE": MICHEL GONDRY AND THE RHYTHMIZATION OF SOUND AND IMAGE

The music video work of Michel Gondry is often approached from an auteur and authorship perspective and considered artistry beyond the appealing visualization of a song. Rather than by genre or date, his music videos are characterized by recurring visualization techniques, such as the merging and morphing of moving images, illustrations, or backgrounds; the frequent use of sequence shots; and generally, the synchronization of musical, rhythmical, and visual elements to create synesthetic relations.

Numerous Gondry-directed music videos deal with the "reconciliation of nature and technology,"[14] and are typically received as a "profilmic creation of fairytale dreamscapes in front of the camera often in real time."[15] Effects that look digital are frequently produced analogously and realized with handmade materials, a mathematical mind, and references to the *art brut* tradition.[16] Though many of Gondry's music video concepts imply comparisons to the special effects employed by early filmmakers, his recent videos demonstrate that he "made low-tech his stylistic signature."[17] "City Lights" (2016) by The White Stripes is a sequence shot of a person drawing sketches that match the lyrics of the song on the inside of a steamy glass shower door. Together with the acoustic guitar, the gentle rattling of an egg shaker percussion, and singer Jack White's high-pitched voice, the briefness of the fading watery sketches on top of each other creates a form of audio-visual immediacy. The volatility of "City Lights" is an intimate moment between the viewer, an unseen person, and their natural visual associations with and interpretations of the song. In contrast to the illustrations of the lyrics in "City Lights," the music video for "Go" (2015) by The Chemical Brothers is a typical Gondrian visualization of musical rhythm. Seven women, all dressed in the same black and grey skirts and helmets, synchronously march in a line through the brutalist architecture of the Paris Front-de-Seine neighborhood. They carry two large bars, which they move around in synch with the melodic and harmonic elements of the song. In a making-of-video, Gondry explains that the bass line of "Go" reminded him of a "moving train,"[18] and that the constructivist architecture of the setting and "research on mechanics and movement"[19] inspired the marching choreography. The humanized rhythms and patterns of the song, the minimalist dance movements, and the alignment of musical elements to architecture are typical elements that Gondry previously used in his earlier music videos: for example, "Around the World" (1997) by Daft Punk, or "Star Guitar" (2001) by The Chemical Brothers. For "Crystalline" (2011) by Björk, from her multimedia app album *Biophilia*, Gondry picks up the album's theme of the relationship between music, technology, and nature.[20] With every verse, a meteorite shower, coming from a blinking sphere with Björk's face on it, hits the surface of a planet and creates different craters, colors, and materials, alternating with kaleidoscopic illustrations in the sky. "Crystalline" features Gondry's typical handmade stop-motion animation aesthetic, in which all visual objects are carefully arranged as if they would produce the sound to which they are synched.

The examples given include essential features that Gondry established in music videos to present and visualize music with performative elements. "City Lights" was filmed as a live illustration of the lyrics and the music; "Go" is a humanized mechanical performance of the musical rhythm; and in "Crystalline," objects, lights, colors, and shapes "perform" to the music.

MULTIPLICATION AND OBJECTIFICATION: THE PERFORMANCE MUSIC VIDEOS OF MICHEL GONDRY

Performance in a music video can be anything from bad acting to simulating music-making, dancing, or close-up lip-synching.[21] Usually, performance means that the artists in some way present their musical parts of the song, as well as themselves, according to the mimic, gestural, habitual, emotional, and so on repertoire linked to the musical features and the genre of the song. Performance then usually describes the ways in which musicians pretend to sing or to play their instruments, referring to a non-filmed live performance.[22] As Railton and Watson point out, most performances either are part of a "pseudo-documentary" on the apparent life of the musicians or are staged solely for the music video.[23] Few performance music videos show only the artist or band performing the song without adding other visual elements or montage to it. Gondry's notable music videos for "Around the World", "Come Into My World" (2002), "Fell In Love with a Girl" (2002), "Star Guitar", and "The Hardest Button to Button" (2003) all include staged performances in artificial locations, according to the plausible presentation of the song. In addition, these music videos demonstrate different visual adaptions of musical elements to create audio-visual performances. As a result, the physical body of the artist as performative authority gradually vanishes and is replaced by objects.

"Come Into My World," by Australian singer Kylie Minogue, is, like many other of Gondry's music videos, inspired by his childhood dream worlds—more precisely by magic tricks and optical illusions—and based on the visual duplication and circular repetition of musical time. The music video translates the repetitive structure of the pop song into visual multiplication around Kylie's performance, an idea that Gondry previously used for his video for "Feel It" (1997) by Neneh Cherry. In "Come Into My World," Kylie is walking around a lively urban street scene while lip-synching the song's lyrics. Up to minute 1:07, which spans the intro, first verse, and first bridge of the song, the music video is a sequence shot of a fixed, rotating camera placed in the middle of the scene. With the first chorus, Kylie completes her first round, and her duplicate enters the scene out of the same house that she did previously. For the second verse, Kylie and her clone both walk the next round. The original Kylie takes a slightly different route than her clone, while all other people and objects in the background multiply. This visual technique creates "optical traces,"[24] and repeats twice more, according to the formal structure of the song. Gondry explains that "[t]he fact that Kylie will always come back to the same starting point echoes the hypnotic repetitiveness of the track."[25] In the end, four Kylies are walking through the street setting, visualizing the four repetitions of verse and chorus. While "Come Into My World" visualizes the song's formal structure, Gondry's music video for "Ride" (2004), by The Vines, adapts visual multiplication to a staged rock performance to visualize the changing musical intensity in the chorus. At first, the band plays its instruments in an empty auditorium, but with the start of heavier drums and guitars in the chorus, numerous other bands instantly appear and perform along.

"The Hardest Button to Button" for The White Stripes is all about the visual multiplication of instruments, an idea that Gondry had already employed briefly in his video for "How the West Was Won" (1992) by Energy Orchard, where, in two scenes, the drummer plays amid myriad drums. The shape and the pattern of "The Hardest Button to Button" inspired Gondry to visualize the song's rhythmical structure by manually arranging identical drum sets and amplifiers in different street settings and in the subway. Stop-motion technique is used to create the impression that, with every beat of the song, the musicians move through time and space from one set of drums and amplifier to the next, and so on. The music video is an example of how visualization can embody musical rhythm "through camera movement or the movement of elements within the frame."[26] It produces a visual equivalent to the linearity and predictability of the song structure because the visible line of drums and amplifiers represents the previous and upcoming beats. "The Hardest Button to Button" also symbolizes the transience of music, of every drum kick and every guitar strum that vanish as quickly as they appear.

However, performance in music videos does not ultimately have to involve the depiction of the artist(s) or any other person or character miming or re-enacting the musical production or presentation of the song. Performance can be artificial, such as by the lookalike puppet band in Gondry's video "Anysound" (2006) for The Vines. Objects, forms, shapes, and colors can also become the "performers" of the song, based on its musical parameters.

"Fell in Love with a Girl" by The White Stripes, one of Gondry's most iconic music videos, best demonstrates the visual artificialization of a musical performance. Following Railton and Watson, it could be considered an art music video.[27] But "Fell in Love with a Girl" perfectly illustrates an artificialized performance because it is a stop-motion LEGO animation that simulates a performance (video) by the band. It shows that Gondry's dedication to analogue is deeply rooted in his goal of finding new, creative ways to make objects perform in synch with the music. In "Fell in Love with a Girl," this ambition is manifested in a skillful and carefully fabricated manual animation which brings immobile LEGO blocks to life.

In his previous music video for "Around the World" by Daft Punk, Gondry already exemplifies the transition between human and object performance, and how synching characters (or objects) and their movements to the musical track generates audio-visual surplus.[28] "Around the World" symbolizes the repetitiveness and circularity of the dance-pop track and, in particular, deals with the "humanization" of sound. Five groups of people—athletes, robots, skeletons, mummies, and female swimmers—each represent a musical element of the song and its rhythmical structure in a piece of circular choreography.[29] Gondry later advanced this idea in the video for "Open Your Heart" (2010) by Mia Doi Todd, in which people in different-colored shirts perform choreographies and create color ranges based on musical rhythm. In "Around the World," the translation of musical into visual elements builds, as Chion calls it, a continuous "synchresis"[30] and a form of "reversed visual mickeymousing"[31] because the music precedes the images. This music video also indicates the thin line between performance and illustration, between human, or identifiable, performers and rhythmed abstract objects. "Around the World," representing Gondry's oeuvre, prototypically shows how "[m]usic videos can create moments of punctuation through both music and image."[32]

Similarly, "Star Guitar" by The Chemical Brothers builds synchresis on the linearity of sound, paired with the movement of time, by placing the first-person viewer behind the window of a moving train. "Star Guitar" visualizes the song with landscapes and repetitive objects, such as power poles, smokestacks, factory buildings, and bridges that synchronize to the musical elements and the rhythm of the song.[33] These strong audio-visual bonds blur the analytical categories of music videos: while sound and objects meet in synch to 'perform together' following musical linearity, they are nevertheless 'only' illustrating the beat, rhythm, and texture of this instrumental song.

BLENDING, BLURRING, CRAFTING: THE NARRATIVE MUSIC VIDEOS OF MICHEL GONDRY

The previous examples demonstrate that music videos rarely fall into a single category. Performance elements, in particular, can be part of visual storytelling in predominantly narrative music videos, or alternate with situative depictions. For example, Gondry's music videos for Björk's "Human Behavior", "Army of Me" (1995), and "Bachelorette" (1997) all feature completed storylines, but Björk always acts as the main character and mimes the lyrics. These videos also all include performance elements. Other Gondry music videos illustrate further options of combining narrative or situative elements with partial performance of the artist(s). In Gondry's video for "Heard 'Em Say" (2005) by Kanye West, kids stay overnight in a shopping mall, while West and co-singer Adam Levine impersonate a homeless person and a mall security guard, and lip-synch the lyrics in between scenes. The music video by Gondry for "Winning Days" (2004) by The Vines—similar to Gondry's earlier video for Stina Nordenstam's "Little Star" (1995)—combines the band's performance in a wintry forest with nature imagery, such as creeks, cairns, burning wood, and growing plants shot in time-lapse to symbolize the lyrics' ambivalence between despair and confidence. In Gondry's eerie video for "No One Knows" (2002) by Queens of the Stone Age, the band hits a deer with a truck; the deer then comes back to life, overpowers the band, and in the end, hangs their heads as trophies in his home. These scenes alternate with a traditional rock'n'roll band performance in a black space.

Performance sequences or elements are usually easy to identify within a narrative. It is more difficult to distinguish between narrative music videos and those with single situations that are strung together and primarily connected by the flow of the song. The latter applies to Gondry's music videos for "Close But No Cigar" (1992) by Thomas Dolby, "Lucas with the Lid Off" (1994) by Lucas, and "Protection" (1995) by Massive Attack. All of them use M. C. Escher-like illusions of fluidly blending perspectives and dimensions into each other, a concept Gondry later perfected in his Smirnoff "Smarienberg" (1997) commercial. The three music videos listed above do not tell linear or completed stories. They rather portray several thematically related situations along with the musical and lyrical continuity of the song. For example, in Gondry's video for "Protection," "we peer through cubbyhole-type apartment windows à la Hitchcock's *Rear Window* (1954) and see characters floating among 1950s and 1960s bric-a-brac while they play cards, throw balls, and so on."[34] At some point, situative sequences in all three music videos show the artist lip-synching the lyrics, and therefore these videos also include performance elements.

Complete audio-visual narratives are quite rare in the short form of the music video.[35] In general, narrative music videos are "forms of visual narration that, on the one hand, variously illustrate, complement or extend the lyrical content of the song, or, on the other hand, function independently of it."[36] But the visual narrative of music videos can also relate to the music. The visual style of narrating can illustrate rhythmical elements, amplifying and enhancing the meaning of the song, and visuals can also act as disjuncture to the musical feel or the lyrical content.[37]

Many of Gondry's narrative music videos show his characteristic aesthetics of handmade settings and his surreal touch. His narrative videos often "follow the irrepressible logic of reverie—objects shrink and grow without warning, perspectives suddenly shift, and, most essentially, the fundamental rules of reality are subtly tweaked."[38] Some of Gondry's music videos are little gems of children's-book-like stop-motion adventures with a subtle meaning. For example, in his video for "High Head Blues" (1995) by The Black Crowes, tiny people in flying saucers transform the singer into a mechanical being, or in "Snowbound" (1993) by Donald Fagen, little half-robot, half-human worker drones revolt against their leader in a dull futuristic space city. In more recent music videos, such as "Dead Leaves and the Dirty Ground" (2002) by The White Stripes, Gondry experiments with visual superimposition. Singer Jack White walks through his destroyed home, and the images become the canvas for another simultaneous but transparent visualization. As a background story, the transparent layer depicts the events of a party that took place earlier in the house and led to its now visible destruction. This adds a second meaning to the story and creates complex audio-visual narratives with rather simple filmic methods. In this way, as Gondry explains in a 2007 interview, "in the same space, you see the cause revealed as you're revealing the effect."[39]

"EVERLONG": LUCID DREAMING IN COMPLEX NARRATIVES

In what follows, I analyze Michel Gondry's music video for "Everlong" (1997) by American rock band Foo Fighters. "Everlong" is a prime example of how Gondry constructs a short but complex narrative according to the lyrics and the musical progression of the song, using dreamlike visuals and filmic references in his characteristic aesthetic style.

"Everlong" starts out as a soft guitar riff establishing a B/Dm/G-chord harmony before distorted guitars and actuating hi-hats push the song into its melodic drive, with high-pitched vocals in the verses and an intense outburst of sound and vocals in the choruses. "Everlong" is rumored to be a post-breakup love song; the lyrics are vague, yet powerful and emotional enough to paint memorable metaphors that are open for personal interpretation. The polysemantic nature of the song's lyrics is similarly evidenced in Foo Fighters' live performance of "Everlong" at the end of the final episode of *Late Show with David Letterman* on May 20, 2015. About thirty seconds into the performance, a six-minute-long montage shows scenes from Letterman's TV career to the live sound of the band. We learn that "Everlong" is Letterman's favorite song and helped him recover from heart surgery in 2000, which, together with the lyrics and harmonic progression of the song between ballad and rock, creates an audio-visual intensity around the emotional farewell to Letterman.

"Everlong" is one of Gondry's best-known and most accomplished music videos. Like his later film, *The Science of Sleep*, "Everlong" is inspired by Gondry's weird childhood dreams.[40] Overall, it is his most consequent, thorough, and philosophical examination of the subject of "dream" in his entire oeuvre. "Everlong" is a surreal, complex, and intertwined narrative, yet the story of two parallel dreams progresses to a logical conclusion along linear narrative patterns that follow the formal structure of the song.

The video starts with two men (played by band members Nate Mendel and Pat Smear) breaking into the home of a couple (played by male band members Dave Grohl and Taylor Hawkins as the wife), who are asleep in their bed. The intruders come up the stairs along a wall decorated with the couple's photographs, seen from a subjective camera perspective, and into their bedroom. This narrative exposition matches the instrumental guitar and hi-hat intro. With the start of the full instrumental song, the camera zooms into sleeping Dave's face, symbolizing the two intruders subconsciously entering his dream. The first verse then coincides with the first part of Dave's dream, in which the two men watch for him and threaten him in a bathroom. Dave, dressed as a punk rocker, then enters a room of dancing and partying people, only to find the two men harassing his wife. In this scene, Dave's lip synching ties the ambiguous lyrics to this threatening dream situation.

The tranquility of the vocal performance of the song's first lyric soon visibly changes with Dave's angry face when he sees his wife being bullied. The subsequent instrumental part again matches the entry into a subconscious dream world. The camera zooms back out to Dave sleeping in bed, visibly shaking with anger from his dream, and now, with the start of the second verse, zooms in on the wife. The intruders also entered into her dreamscape, in which she is trapped in a hut while they try to break in through the trapdoor. Meanwhile, Dave, now dressed as a neat-looking husband, is out in a forest collecting wood. From her screaming face, the story blends back into Dave's dream. There is no lip synching in these sequences, and the lyrics are fairly general. However, the lyrical emphasis of togetherness and the addressing of a counterpart correspond with Dave, who now saves his wife. His anger lets his hand grow and, in synch with the faster drum beat of the pre-chorus bridge, he beats up the two men. After intercutting to the sleeping Dave punching and kicking around in bed, the two bullies vaporize from his dream with the start of the chorus, only to appear in the dreamscape of the wife. The interrogative lyrics of the chorus address partnership in an unclear future based on the here and now. The chorus ends with demanding a commitment to this potential relationship. In this context, the nightmarish images provide a "what if" situation for Dave, in his subconscious state of mind, that he should support his wife in good times and bad times, including nightmares that seem too real. From now on, dream and reality narratives become more and more entangled. An oversized ringing telephone in Dave's dream wakes him up in reality, again matching the instrumental riff of the song, and this turns out to be his actual phone ringing, with his wife calling him from her dream.

With the second verse, we zoom back into her dream, where she is trying to save herself from one intruder who is approaching her hut with a large axe, and the other who is trying to get in through the trapdoor. Again, in this second verse, the lyrics deal with aspects of unity, solidarity, and eternity, this time using the immateriality of breath and air as a metaphor. In the wife's dream, Dave is still in the forest, unaware of the danger, while the two men, in synch with the pre-chorus drum roll, bang on the trapdoor and smack against a window of the hut. Desperate, she reaches out to Dave in reality by calling him from her dream during the chorus. This blurring of dream and reality adds new meaning to the chorus lyrics. First, "The only thing I'll ever ask of you" turns into her demand for Dave to save her in her dream; second, "You gotta promise not to stop when I say when" is Dave's plea for her to hold on.[41] Here, the music video creates outstanding audio-visual connections between reality and dream. In reality, Dave fails to wake his wife, grabbing her chin, which instead immediately transfers into her dreamscape and to the intruder simultaneously grabbing her.

In the quiet, moderate guitar interlude that follows, Dave tries hard to fall asleep to enter her dream but first dreams of making out with several women. He succeeds when—in the music video's most impressive scene—the legs of the women turn into the logs of wood that he previously collected and then into a nunchaku. The subdued main guitar riff starts, Dave runs to the hut, the drum roll fades in, Dave swings his nunchaku at the intruders, the pre-chorus sets in, his hand again grows, and with the chorus, he once more beats up the intruders. Afterwards, Dave and his wife throw their apparently dead bodies into a lake; they sink, and, for one last time, the camera now zooms out of their corresponding dreams and into their bedroom, where the two intruders are standing next to the bed watching the couple sleep. The song then, in contrast to the recorded version, rewinds for some seconds, and the actual musicians peel out of their dream-story costumes to perform the last chorus in blurry distorted imagery.

The music video for "Everlong" illustrates Gondry's philosophical and metaphysical approach to the mind, consciousness, and dreams. In "Everlong," due to the shortness of the song and therefore its music video, the narrative is much more condensed than in Gondry's films *Eternal Sunshine of the Spotless Mind* and *The Science of Sleep*. However, "Everlong" is almost an expressionist short film, based on the musical structure and harmonic progression of the song and on a loose interpretation of some passages in the lyrics, but it opposes standard filmic narration, especially within the limited time frame of a music video. Gondry borrows the uncanny aesthetics of iconic horror movies, such as *The Texas Chainsaw Massacre* (Tobe Hooper, 1974) and *The Evil Dead* (Sam Raimi, 1981), to visualize the surrealism of dreams and nightmares as potential physical threats in waking reality. People and objects enter an unclear in-between state. Are the intruders real or only imaginative? Does the phone conversation really happen or is it only a metaphor for a subconscious connection? Can you dream yourself into someone else's dream? Whose dream is it anyway? And is the entire music-video scenery "the" dream?

Any possible mystification is counteracted with opposing visual elements. The fact that the band members are acting as fictional characters, especially Taylor Hawkins in drag, contrasts with any serious horror. Instead, comedy aspects are added: for example, through the oddity of overly large objects, like the axe of the intruder, Dave's magically enlarging hand, or the overacted grin of love between Dave and his wife after they defeat the villains.

"Everlong" also narrates through its color scheme. The black-and-white reality sequences refer to well-known horror aesthetics. However, it especially functions to distinguish its blandness from the colored and lively dreamscapes.

In Dave's dream, strong colors contrast with the matte hues that match the threatening nightmare of the wife. Despite the somewhat gloomy undertone of the lyrics and the minor key harmony of the verses, the visual narrative ultimately makes "Everlong" a love story, though not with a traditional happy ending. The final band performance adds another layer to the question of what is supposed to constitute reality in this surreal narrative.

Along with their complexity, the visuals in "Everlong" manage to add meaning to the music and the lyrics, resulting in an overall audio-visual surplus. The song already provides a tonal climax structure, with a moderate progression from a clean melodic motif and driving hi-hats in the verses to powerful drum rolls and distorted guitars in the chorus. The lyrics follow a repetitive structure with a verse-spanning rhyme scheme. The final chorus line generates an openness that the visuals pick up to mark turning points in the narrative. After the first chorus, the giant telephone rings and wakes Dave up from his dream; after the second chorus, he forces himself back to sleep to save his wife in her dream; and after the third chorus, the combined dream ends and the intruders stand next to the couple's bed.

Overall, "Everlong" illustrates how much of Gondry's visual work is a cathartic processing of his lucid dream experiences. He projects his nonsense dreams as challenges to create reasonable realities, making them a creative inspiration. Gondry's music videos and films reveal how he is becoming his own oneirologist.

CONCLUSION: MICHEL GONDRY AND "AUDIO-VISUAL BIOGRAPHIES"

The discussion of the music video oeuvre of Michel Gondry demonstrates specific strategies of visualizing a song in various performances, whether by complex audio-visual storytelling or in hybrid combinations of these basic types. This chapter illustrates Gondry's unique filmic skills and audio-visual techniques in his creation of music videos that match his and the artists' idea of translating, extending, or advancing the song into a visual sphere. In this way, he designed "audio-visual biographies" for his frequent collaborators Björk, The White Stripes, and The Chemical Brothers in the form of music video corpora. However, Gondry's music video oeuvre is also his "audio-visual biography" as a director.

Gondry relies on a repertoire of film techniques, such as visual flow, infinite scenery, morphing images, zooming, or merging and flipping perspectives, angles, and objects to create entertaining illusions. His visual aesthetics are frequently characterized by analogue means, such as handmade sceneries or props, and foremost by analogue stop-motion animation.

In Gondry's music videos, rhythmic visualizations of musical elements are paired with skillful and comic features that, together with analogue aesthetics, complete his characteristic style of "telling" music with visuals. Occasionally, this causes amazement: for example, when we ask ourselves how he made Dave Grohl's hand grow in "Everlong." How did the camera fly into all the multi-floor settings in the "Protection" music video? How did he make four Kylie Minogues dance around the lamppost in "Come into My World"? Or, looking at Gondry's other videos, how did he solve the Rubik's Cube with his feet? (Spoiler: the video simply runs backwards.)

The music video examples discussed here demonstrate that Gondry's audio-visual composing is best seen in his performance videos. In synching objects to the rhythm or by visually multiplying the artist or instruments as the main sound source, Gondry creates visual surrogates for the invisible formal, rhythmic, and melodic structures of the musical time. Though many of his famous performance videos are based on complex audio-visual patterns, his recent low-key style can be understood as an advanced and innovative artistic approach with carefully reduced visual features, such as his short film *Detour* (2017), which he shot entirely with an iPhone.

Gondry's fascination with and inspiration from dreams is ever-present in his oeuvre, and the music video for "Everlong" is both the culmination of and the foundation for his later films. Starting out as a music video director, Michel Gondry grew to be an audio-visually focused filmmaker, or, in his own words:

> That is my dream, to use what I learned from music videos in feature films. [. . .] Each music video I did had a concept that would run through the music video [. . .]. It would not be maybe your typical movie, and it would not be just visual; it could have words and a story.[42]

NOTES

1. Ryan Lambie, "Michel Gondry Interview: Mood Indigo, Eternal Sunshine, Ubik," *Den of Geek!*, July 28, 2014. Available at <http://www.denofgeek.com/movies/michel-gondry/31451/michel-gondry-interview-mood-indigo-eternal-sunshine-ubik> (last accessed September 1, 2019).
2. Carol Vernallis, *Unruly Media: YouTube, Music Video, and the New Digital Cinema* (Oxford: Oxford University Press, 2013), 208.
3. Daniel Klug, "These Kind of Dreams: Dystopian Depictions of California in the Music Video Californication," in *A Dark California: Essays on Dystopian Depictions in Popular Culture*, eds Katarzyna Nowak-McNeice and Agata Zarzycka (Jefferson, NC: McFarland, 2017), 174–5.
4. Michel Chion, *Audio-vision: Sound on Screen* (New York: Columbia University Press, 1994), 165.

5. Andrew Goodwin, *Dancing in the Distraction Factory: Music Television and Popular Culture* (Minneapolis: University of Minnesota Press, 1992), 85.
6. Diane Railton and Paul Watson, *Music Video and the Politics of Representation* (Edinburgh: Edinburgh University Press, 2011), 61.
7. Jason Middleton, "The Audio-Vision of Found-Footage Film and Video," in *Medium Cool: Music Videos from Soundies to Cellphones*, eds Roger Beebe and Jason Middleton (Durham, NC: Duke University Press, 2007), 76–8.
8. Klug, "These Kind of Dreams," 174.
9. Henry Keazor and Thorsten Wübbena, "Rewind, Play, Fast Forward: The Past, Present and Future of the Music Video: Introduction," in *Rewind, Play, Fast Forward: The Past, Present and Future of the Music Video*, eds Henry Keazor and Thorsten Wübbena (Bielefeld: transcript, 2010), 7–31.
10. Vernallis, *Unruly Media*, 94–115.
11. Stephen L. White, "Michel Gondry and the Phenomenology of Visual Perception," in *Eternal Sunshine of the Spotless Mind*, ed. Christopher Grau (New York: Routledge, 2009), 103.
12. John Richardson, *An Eye for Music: Popular Music and the Audiovisual Surreal* (Oxford: Oxford University Press, 2012), 100.
13. Keazor and Wübbena, "Rewind, Play, Fast Forward," 16–18.
14. Saul Austerlitz, *Money for Nothing: A History of the Music Video from the Beatles to the White Stripes* (New York: Bloomsbury, 2008), 166.
15. Railton and Watson, *Music Video and the Politics of Representation*, 67.
16. Vernallis, *Unruly Media*, 269.
17. Vernallis, *Unruly Media*, 214.
18. Mathieu Rathery, "On Set with Michel Gondry," *Nowness*, 27 May 2015. Available at <http://www.nowness.com/story/michel-gondry-the-chemical-brothers-go-born-in-the-echoes> (last accessed February 26, 2020).
19. Rathery, "On Set with Michel Gondry."
20. Nicola Dibben, "Visualizing the App Album with Björk's *Biophilia*," in *The Oxford Handbook of Sound and Image in Digital Media*, eds Carol Vernallis, Amy Herzog, and John Richardson (Oxford: Oxford University Press, 2013), 687.
21. Vernallis, *Unruly Media*, 221.
22. Goodwin, *Dancing in the Distraction Factory*, 89.
23. Railton and Watson, *Music Video and the Politics of Representation*, 49–61.
24. White, "Michel Gondry and the Phenomenology of Visual Perception," 97.
25. Michel Gondry, "I've been twelve forever," *The Work of Director Michel Gondry* (Palm Pictures, 2003), DVD, Booklet.
26. Mathias Bonde Korsgaard, *Music Video After MTV: Audiovisual Studies, New Media, and Popular Music* (New York: Routledge, 2017), 66.
27. Railton and Watson, *Music Video and the Politics of Representation*, 54.
28. Korsgaard, *Music Video After MTV*, 65–9.
29. José Cláudio Siqueira Castanheira, "Timeline Philosophy: Technical Hedonism and Formal Aspects of Films and Music Videos," in *Music/Video: Histories, Aesthetics, Media*, eds Gina Arnold, Daniel Cookney, Kirsty Fairclough, and Michael Goddard (New York: Bloomsbury, 2017), 222–3.
30. Chion, *Audio-vision*, 63.
31. Giulia Gabriella, "An Analysis of the Relation between Music and Image: The Contribution of Michel Gondry," in *Rewind, Play, Fast Forward: The Past, Present and Future of the Music Video*, eds Henry Keazor and Thorsten Wübbena (Bielefeld: transcript, 2010), 104.

32. Carol Vernallis, *Experiencing Music Video: Aesthetics and Cultural Context* (New York: Columbia University Press, 2004), 181.
33. Allan Cameron, "Instrumental Visions: Electronica, Music Video, and the Environmental Interface," in *The Oxford Handbook of Sound and Image in Digital Media*, eds Carol Vernallis, Amy Herzog, and John Richardson (Oxford: Oxford University Press, 2013), 766–8.
34. Vernallis, *Unruly Media*, 270.
35. Vernallis, *Experiencing Music Video*, 4–13.
36. Railton and Watson, *Music Video and the Politics of Representation*, 55.
37. Goodwin, *Dancing in the Distraction Factory*, 85–9.
38. Austerlitz, *Money for Nothing*, 165.
39. Whitney Pastorek, "How Michel Gondry Earned his Music-video Stripes," *Entertainment Weekly*, May 18, 2007. Available at <http://ew.com/article/2007/05/18/how-michel-gondry-earned-his-music-video-stripes> (last accessed February 26, 2020).
40. Xan Brooks, "'It's Complexicated,'" *The Guardian*, February 14, 2007. Available at <http://www.theguardian.com/film/2007/feb/14/1> (last accessed February 26, 2020).
41. Foo Fighters, "Everlong," recorded February 1997, track 11 on *The Colour and the Shape*, Roswell and Capitol, 1997, CD.
42. Eric Kohn, "Michel Gondry Discusses His Affinity for Noam Chomsky and the Relationship Between His New Documentary and Music Videos," *IndieWire*, November 20, 2013. Available at <http://www.indiewire.com/2013/11/michel-gondry-discusses-his-affinity-for-noam-chomsky-and-the-relationship-between-his-new-documentary-and-music-videos-32812/> (last accessed February 26, 2020).

CHAPTER 13

Death and Pickles: Thinking through Gondry's Neighborhood

Lisa DeTora

INTRODUCTION: EVERYONE KNOWS UKE-LARRY!

In Dave Holstein's Showtime series, *Kidding* (2018–),[1] Jeff Piccirillo (Jim Carrey) plays Mr. Pickles, the universally beloved star of the television show *Mr. Pickles' Puppet Time*, who has now fallen on hard times. The viewer of *Kidding* first sees Mr. Pickles/Jeff as he is being introduced to Conan O'Brien (himself) backstage at *Conan*. An offscreen briefing informs O'Brien and the viewer that Jeff's son, Phil, died about a year ago, and that he should not mention the situation. Luckily, there are other topics to discuss. Jeff/Mr. Pickles has never seen *Conan*, and he does not understand what fellow guest Danny Trejo's (himself) "P-Dogg" necklace means. Trejo, reflexively, knows that the word "pussy" is not Pickles-friendly.[2] Thus, the programs—*Kidding* and *Conan*—each begin with a fundamental disjunction between adult life and *Puppet Time*, between embodied experiences, such as sexuality, and an idealized figment of childhood imagination.

A concerned O'Brien asks if Jeff/Mr. Pickles has ever seen *Conan*. He has not. It soon becomes clear why Jeff has agreed to make an appearance so far out of his afternoon-television-programming-for-children element: his wife Jill (Judy Greer) loves *Conan*. And the disconnect between off-color late night and afternoon edutainment is reciprocal. Although Mr. Pickles's antics and songs informed the upbringing of a generation—he has been on the air for thirty years—Conan reveals himself to be as ignorant of Pickle Barrel Falls, the setting for much of *Mr. Pickles' Puppet Time* as Jeff/Mr. Pickles is of *Conan*. This disconnect is made evident when Mr. Pickles reveals his friend, an animatronic/muppet ukulele: when Conan asks for an introduction, Trejo, delighted, says, "Come on! Everyone knows Uke-Larry!" Conan then watches, somewhat bemused, as the entire audience joins with Mr. Pickles's/Jeff's song for Jill: "You can feel anything at all/Anything at all/You can feel it/Happy, sad, big or very small/Anything at all/It's fine."[3] This scene sets out the core problem in Jeff's/Mr. Pickles's life and work, which is that the death of his son, Phil, highlights not only his failure to master adult life but also his continual conflation of himself and his television persona, his personal life and public performance. As the series progresses, it emerges that nothing is fine, and that feeling anything at all is much more of a problem than Mr. Pickles and Uke-Larry might think. Ultimately, *Kidding* presents a world in which many usual binaries—such as adult/child, life/death, fiction/reality, man/woman—are conflated while simultaneously so extremely divorced as to render both elements meaningless.

When considering *Kidding* within the context of Michel Gondry's larger body of work, it becomes evident that the questions about the immutability of personal identity and mutual attraction that play out in Gondry's earlier film *Eternal Sunshine of the Spotless Mind* (2004)[4] have undergone a profound shift. Unlike in *Eternal Sunshine*, in *Kidding*, characters are unable to self-identify or to clarify their desires because of a multiplicity of possibilities, whose reconciliation into a unitary, and thus coherent, identity has potentially catastrophic consequences. In effect, the characters are trapped in a version of the Schrödinger's cat thought experiment, in which a cat is trapped in a box with a vial of poison: until the box is opened, the cat is both alive and dead.[5] In *Kidding*, characters are trapped in a both/and, neither/nor situation that prevents any of them from realizing their full personhood so long as they remain associated with Mr. Pickles or *Puppet Time*.

MUTUALLY ASSURED DESTRUCTION

Identity in film and other visual media, like television, can be read through Laura Mulvey's 1975 essay "Visual Pleasure and Narrative Cinema," in which she identifies a gaze that constructs certain people, usually women, as objects of visual pleasure, and other people, predominantly men, as those doing the looking.[6] Mulvey's ideas about the fundamentally heteronormative construction of narrative film have been critiqued and revised many times since.[7] And Jean-Michel Rabaté observed that a crucial development in this "lucid critical polyphony" was "the very discourse of science facing gender"[8] discussed in "Life Finds a Way: Monstrous Maternity and the Quantum Gaze in *Jurassic Park* and *The Thirteenth Warrior*."[9] In that essay, I suggested that a "quantum gaze" created a new form of gendered monstrosity because certain films constructed visual narratives that destabilized gender in such a way as to make "Schrödinger's cat"—the animal that is both alive and dead until looked at—an apt model. It became unclear whether certain figures in these films were male or female, human or monster, until they entered an identifiable gaze. The result was that certain figures were rendered both male and female, or human and monster, until looked at. In the films I discussed, these figures each eventually became stabilized, which located the space of uncertainty in off-screen spaces, generally even outside the *mise-en-scène*. In *Kidding*, the viewer is trapped in these liminal spaces where questions of identity and looking remain in flux.

An added complication for the characters in *Kidding*—and hence its viewers—is the conflict between embodied and imagined experiences. Although traditional constructions of embodiment and corporeality begin with gender, foundational texts like Anne Fausto Sterling's *Myths of Gender* (1985), Judith Butler's *Bodies that Matter: On the Discursive Limits of Sex* (1993), Elisabeth Grosz's *Volatile Bodies: Toward a Corporeal Feminism* (1994), and Katie Conboy, Nadia Medina, and Sarah Stanbury's anthology, *Writing on the Body: Female Embodiment and Feminist Theory* (1997),[10] each call the biological and semiotic meanings of gender into question. These thinkers ultimately create a space for considering personal identity outside of heteronormative constructions, and *Kidding* does the same. In *Kidding*, however, embodied identities are called into question not only because male/female dichotomies fail to operate as they would in mainstream Hollywood cinema, but also because the show's construction conflates the puppets of Pickle Barrel Falls with human characters: every character in *Mr. Pickles' Puppet Time* has a diegetic real-life counterpart, and vice versa, except Jeff.[11] In effect, every character is trapped in a site of existential uncertainty that impedes access to embodied human experience. Jeff's situation is even more fraught because his own body stands in for a puppet, creating a site of essential uncertainty.

The central site of irreconcilable sameness and difference is located in Jeff himself, because his whole life is an overlapping milieu of family and work, and all the other characters are framed and defined in terms of their relationship with him. Jeff's father, Seb (Frank Langella), runs the business side of *Mr. Pickles' Puppet Time*, while his sister Deirdre (Catherine Keener) designs and makes all of the puppets.[12] Jeff, still grieving the loss of his son Phil, also questions the utility of a show about colors and instead wants to discuss serious topics. Seb, explaining why Mr. Pickles cannot do a show on death, comments that the audience is not comprised of Jeff's (or even Mr. Pickles's) friends, but rather, is composed of viewers and customers. Seb lays out the fundamental difference for his son/employee:

> You need to understand something. There's two of you. There's Mr. Pickles, the $112,000,000 licensing industry of edutaining toys, DVDs and books, that keep the lights on in this little charity of ours. And then, there's Jeff, a separated husband and grieving father who needs to hammer out a few dents in his psyche.

This separation, as Seb indicates, is essential, because an attempt to combine Jeff and Mr. Pickles would "lead to the destruction of them both." In fact, although "Jeff needs to heal, Mr. Pickles is fine."[13] Tension from the stress of maintaining a "just fine" persona in the wake of the loss of his son hinders not only all areas of Jeff's life—it is telling that Seb's construction of Mr. Pickles is essentially sexless—but also the lives of every other character in *Kidding*. The complications inherent in hammering out personal identities become increasingly evident in the face of Deirdre's inability to make a Mr. Pickles puppet. Usually, Deirdre makes puppets by seeing someone else's core being.[14] Deirdre cannot make a puppet of Mr. Pickles or of Jeff because she cannot see his true essence, which hints that perhaps Jeff lacks a core personality. However, the fact that Jeff's body does double duty as himself and a denizen of Pickle Barrel Falls may add to Deirdre's perplexity.

The remainder of the first season of *Kidding* represents Jeff's denthammering and its impact on his family, friends, and *Mr. Pickles' Puppet Time*. Although the season's trajectory seems to follow the path of a hero's journey/*Bildungsroman* in which Jeff matures to find his place in adult society, the show also highlights the inherent difficulties of establishing a personal identity simultaneously with the need to maintain distinct, mutually conflicting personae within a single body. In effect, the program enacts problems with embodiment, identity, and *techne* that underpin fundamental and irreconcilable questions about personal identity in society. Jeff/Mr. Pickles functions in *Kidding* in much the same way as nuclear weapons solidified the *détente* that characterized the Cold War: mutually assured destruction generates a situation in which personal identity, especially for Jeff/Mr. Pickles, depends not on positive attributes but rather on an ability to self-define only in contrast with some other. These others primarily include copies, or what Jeff considers to be bad copies, of Mr. Pickles, Pickle Barrel Falls, and *Mr. Pickles' Puppet Time*. Even more concerning, others and bad copies threaten to engulf and subsume the self, creating a space in which identity defies not only the ability of a gaze to identify it, but also embodiment to function at all. Ultimately, the hero's journey of *Kidding* reinforces the primacy of Mr. Pickles, as played by Jeff, over all the other possible permutations of Mr. Pickles (and possibly Jeff), only after just such a positive attribute is identified.

A PLETHORA OF PICKLES

Ironically, the means by which Jeff attempts to address the fissures in his identity is by rejecting the carefully curated image of Mr. Pickles, breaking out of civilized adult behavior, and sharing unpleasant information about death, loss, and failed parenthood on *Mr. Pickles' Puppet Time*.[15] Jeff's added challenge, and the one that propels the rest of the season, is to maintain control of the multimillion-dollar television and merchandise franchise empire, even as Seb ups the stakes by creating a multiplicity of bad copies of Mr. Pickles: a mass-produced merchandising doll; a live show of "Mr. Pickles on Ice" (featuring real-life Olympic Gold medalist ice skater Tara Lipinski), and an animated television program.[16] In fact, it appears that Seb, in responding to the real-life grief of his only son, concentrates first on protecting *Mr. Pickles' Puppet Time*, enhancing the multimillion-dollar edutainment franchise at the expense of his personal relationships. Central to these activities is "Mr. Pickles on Ice," an Icecapades-style romp populated by ice versions of all of the *Puppet Time* favorites, including Mr. Pickles (played by Lipinski, who is also a huge fan of Pickle Barrel Falls).[17] Deirdre's struggles to make a successful Mr. Pickles costume for Lipinski result in an ugly and deformed caricature of Jeff's face, rather than the more synthetic representations she produces to populate *Puppet Time* (for example, Seb rendered as a disembodied giant foot). This caricature recurs on the Mr. Pickles doll, while animated versions vary between an innocent, and officially authorized, rendition of Pickle Barrel Falls and a blood-soaked bootleg shoot-'em-up game.[18]

The myriad facsimiles of Mr. Pickles, which at first threaten to engulf Jeff, depriving him of his personhood, hold the key to the series' resolution. After many failed attempts to inject unpleasant realities—essentially, elements of embodied humanity—into *Puppet Time*, Mr. Pickles rebels at the national tree-lighting ceremony, claiming that he killed his son Phil with his failure to listen. Jeff's solution to this problem requires a further rebellion, which occurred behind the scenes at the voice-taping for the Mr. Pickles doll, which instead of emitting cheery slogans now says, "I am listening."[19] Both of these scenes are informed by Jeff's struggles with Will, Phil's twin and the remaining Piccirillo child, who wants Jeff to listen rather than "say[ing] the right thing." Will's rebelliousness, unlike Jeff's, centers on his demands to have access to Jeff, his father, and a unified entity rather than the amalgam of Jeff and Mr. Pickles, who is an unsatisfying parent.

Of course, Mr. Pickles is more than just a character: he is a franchise, and his brand at first appears threatened by Jeff's struggles. Yet, although the Public Broadcasting Service sees Jeff's/Mr.Pickles's rebellion as an end to the edutainment empire Seb fought for, the proliferation of products, including the violent war game, hints that the transition from public work to private profit will be in their financial interests.[20] In other words, *Kidding* depicts a transition from the innocent, childhood world of public television to a world of profit and adult intervention much more like *Conan*. The spontaneous outpouring of attention from thousands of children who line up outside the studio, Mr. Pickles dolls in hand, reinforces this likely success. Unfortunately, the solidification of Mr. Pickles as a good listener occurs at the cost of Jeff's relationship with Will. While the dead

Phil can be recuperated now as a denizen of Pickle Barrel Falls, Will remains troublingly embodied and outside the fantasy puppet world: Jeff only listens in his role as Mr. Pickles, and Will lacks any sort of privileged access in that setting. To Mr. Pickles's fans, Will is only another child. Ultimately, Jeff's inability to coalesce as himself renders his relationship with Will a source of "material" for Mr. Pickles's performances rather than genuine embodied presence.

The opening of *Kidding*—specifically, the confusion over what the "p" in "p-dogg" might mean—hints that Jeff's primary struggle is sexual, the need to become an embodied man capable of having an adult sexual relationship. Yet Jeff's—and Mr. Pickles's—gender troubles transcend the mere act of sexual congress. From the instant that Seb asks why the puppet Snagglehorse "smells like buggery"[21] to the moment that Jeff tells Jill's new boyfriend Peter ("Big P") that he is a good person,[22] sexual identity and performance remain fluid across the series. The depiction of Mr. Pickles by Tara Lipinski opens the door to these exchanges at the level of corporeal embodiment, particularly for puppets, and Mr. Pickles subsequently transgenders *Puppet Time*'s Astronotter. Yet sexual exchange is complicated in the "real" word as well: Deirdre's husband Scott gets into a same-sex entanglement,[23] and Jill and Jeff both start sexual relationships. Yet, for Jeff/Mr. Pickles, these issues are easily resolved, because ultimately, Seb is right that sex does not matter to him as much as love, friendship, and parenthood. As Mr. Pickles-san, the Japanese version of Mr. Pickles, illustrates, the male member can function simply as another appendage, such as when he uses his penis to control a puppet. Sexuality, then, is a less critical embodied function for Jeff than parenthood. The critical engagement—and failure—at stake for Jeff is his abject lack of ability to manage a successful relationship with Will, not because he does not listen, but because Will's access to Jeff is impeded by Mr. Pickles's attention to every child.[24]

The closing scene of Season One, when Jeff (I hesitate to conflate him with Mr. Pickles at this moment) hits Peter with the car, leaving him for dead, is precipitated not by Peter's sexual relationship with Jill, but by the revelation that Peter introduced Will to drugs.[25] And this scene illustrates another fundamental conflation in *Kidding*: good and bad parenting. Jeff, demonstrably a bad father because he confuses the fantasy world of *Puppet Time* with real-life relationships, was unable to intervene in Will's drug use, a task that fell to Seb's more pragmatic approach to life and relationships.[26] Peter's parenting ability is even worse, as he encourages Will to engage in adolescent pranks, undermining both Jeff and Jill's attempts to raise Will. Thus, while Jeff's unpredictable and uncontrolled rage erupts in the worst possible way, it is unclear exactly what he is angry about: Peter's drug use, the possibility that Peter encouraged Will to take drugs, or the fact that Jill's boyfriend is not working in her best interests. While it is tempting to say that Jeff reveals himself in the closing scene of Season One, the nature of *Kidding*, and its relentless undermining of any attempt to fix identity or truth, can only leave the viewer wondering. After all, every scene of rage follows on an act of almost beatific generosity. Jeff trashes Seb's office after doing a good deed for his ex-girlfriend, Vivian, who dumps him at a family party after he saves her life.[27] And that same family party reveals something critically important about the entire *Puppet Time* family: its foundations in repressed rage. When Vivian reveals that she has planned a trip alone, and that the family and Jeff are not invited, they scream and curse at Vivian until she flees. The scene is particularly uncomfortable in the light of Vivian's attempts to defer the conversation, her heartfelt apology in which she reveals that Jeff reminds her of death, Jeff's forgiveness, and the family's spontaneous, collective rage. And it is this tension, the connection between the saccharine world of *Puppet Time* and the underlying rage of the real-life Piccirillos, that presents the fundamental site of uncertainty for the program. The only thing that remains certain at the end of *Kidding*, as at its beginning, is that "anything at all" is certainly not fine.

NOTES

1. David Holstein, *Kidding* (2018; Los Angeles: Aggregate Films), Television Show.
2. *Kidding*, season 1, episode 1, "Green Means Go," written by David Holstein, directed by Michel Gondry, aired September 9, 2018, on Showtime.
3. *Kidding*, "Green Means Go."
4. Michel Gondry, *Eternal Sunshine of the Spotless Mind* (Anonymous Content, 2004), Film.
5. Lisa DeTora, "Life Finds a Way: Monstrous Maternities and the Quantum Gaze in *Jurassic Park* and *The Thirteenth Warrior*," in *Situating the Feminist Gaze and Spectatorship in Postwar Cinema*, ed. Marcelline Block (Newcastle upon Tyne: Cambridge Scholars, 2008), 2–26.
6. Laura Mulvey, "Visual Pleasure and Narrative Cinema," *Screen*, 16, no. 3 (1975): 6–18.
7. Marcelline Block, ed., *Situating the Feminist Gaze and Spectatorship in Postwar Cinema* (Newcastle upon Tyne: Cambridge Scholars, 2008).
8. Jean-Paul Rabaté, "Preface," in *Situating the Feminist Gaze and Spectatorship in Postwar Cinema*, ed. Marcelline Block (Newcastle upon Tyne: Cambridge Scholars, 2008), XIII.
9. DeTora, "Life Finds a Way"
10. Ann Fausto-Sterling, *Myths of Gender: Biological Theories About Women and Men* (New York: Basic Books, 1985); Judith Butler, *Bodies that Matter: On the Discursive Limits of Sex* (New York: Taylor and Francis, 1993); Elisabeth Grosz, *Volatile Bodies: Toward a Corporeal Feminism* (Bloomington: Indiana University Press, 1994); Conboy, Kate, Nadia Medina, and Sarah Stanbury, *Writing on the Body: Female Embodiment and Feminist Theory* (New York: Columbia University Press, 1997).
11. *Kidding*, season 1, episode 10, "Some Day," written by David Holstein, directed by Michel Gondry, aired November 11, 2018, on Showtime.
12. *Kidding*, "Green Means Go."
13. *Kidding*, "Green Means Go."
14. *Kidding*, "Some Day."
15. *Kidding*, "Green Means Go"; *Kidding*, "Some Day"; *Kidding*, season 1, episode 3, "Every Pain Needs a Name," written by Halley Feiffer, directed by Jake Schrier, aired September 23, 2018, on Showtime; *Kidding*, season 1, episode 5, "The New You," written by Cody Heller, directed by Michel Gondry, aired October 7, 2018, on Showtime.

16. *Kidding*, "Green Means Go."
17. *Kidding*, season 1, episode 9, "Lt. Pickles," written by Joey Mazzarino and Dave Holstein, directed by Michel Gondry, aired October 7, 2018, on Showtime; *Kidding*, season 1, episode 6, "The Cookie," written by Noah Haidle, directed by Michel Gondry, aired October 14, 2018, on Showtime.
18. *Kidding*, "Some Day."
19. *Kidding*, "Lt. Pickles."
20. *Kidding*, "Some Day."
21. *Kidding*, "Green Means Go."
22. *Kidding*, "Some Day."
23. *Kidding*, "Every Pain Needs a Name."
24. *Kidding*, "Some Day."
25. *Kidding*, "Some Day."
26. *Kidding*, "The Cookie."
27. *Kidding*, season 1, episode 8, "Kintsugi," written by Jas Waters, directed by Minkie Spiro, aired October 14, 2018, on Showtime.

Index

Adaptation (Jonze, 2002), 128
African Americans, 155, 157
album covers, 197–8
Alger, Horatio, 79
Allen, Woody, 124, 126, 127–8
amateurism/amateurs, 71, 78, 168, 176–9
ambivalence, 118, 128
Amélie (Jeunet, 2001), 73
Amenábar, Alejandro, 35
American culture/genre cinema, 103–4, 105, 109, 111
amour fou, 91–100
analogue special effects, 185–6, 188, 190
Anderson, Wes, 60, 66–8, 69–70, 73, 77–81, 82
animals, 50–2, 56, 61–2, 200
animation, 25, 89
Annie Hall (Allen, 1977), 124, 127–8
Archer, Neil, 103, 104–5
"Around the World" (1997), 201, 203–4
art films, 119, 127
art romantic comedies, 118, 124–9
Artaud, Antonin, 93

artisanal dream, 42–3
audience
   Eternal Sunshine, 137, 138–9, 146
   Mood Indigo, 74
   and romantic comedy, 125, 134
   Science of Sleep, 51, 55
   television, 117
auditory repetition, 170–1, 173
Auerbach, Erich, 143
authenticity, 117, 128, 139, 142, 146, 155
authorship, 118, 124

Bachelard, Gaston, 98–9
Badu, Erykah, 154
Bartlett, Myke, 28
Baumbach, Noah, 126
Be Kind Rewind (2008), 19, 28, 37–8, 154, 175–82
   artisanal dream in, 43
   DIY aesthetic, 69
   and music video, 200
Being John Malkovich (Jonze, 1999), 120, 127
belonging, 162, 163
Benjamin, Walter, 98

INDEX

Bernal, Gael García, 18, 51
Bey, Yasiin *see* Mos Def
Bildungsroman, 38–9, 216
Björk, 61–2, 200, 201, 204
Black, Jack, 37–8, 175, 176, 178
Black, Lisa, 50
black Americans *see Dave Chappelle's Block Party* (2005)
Bompoint, Jean-Louis, 90
Bonnie and Clyde (Penn, 1967), 104, 105
Bordwell, David, 119–20, 122, 127, 128
Bossi, Luc, 18, 30
Botz-Bornstein, Thorsten, 26
Bowman, James, 139–40, 144
Boym, Svetlana, 29
Bradforde, George, 49
Bradshaw, Peter, 185
Brennan, Neal, 155
Brereton, Pat, 19
Breton, André, 92–3
Brody, Richard, 80
Brooks, Mel, 157
Brown, Jeffrey A., 186
Buñuel, Luis, 90, 93

Cabiria (Pastrone, 1914), 46
Campora, Matthew, 26–7
capitalism, 148, 178
Carrey, Jim, 33–4, 198, 213
Carroll, Noël, 138
cave, allegory of the, 58
CGI, 20, 190, 191
Chappelle, Dave, 153–5, 157; *see also Dave Chappelle's Block Party* (2005)
Chappelle's Show, 154–5, 158
Chemical Brothers, 164, 198, 201, 204, 209
childhood, 20, 27, 30, 31, 62, 67–8
Chomsky, Noam, 58

"*cinéma-monde*," 111
cinematography, 34, 46–7, 90, 99, 190
  black-and-white, 128
  Block Party, 160–1
  Eternal Sunshine, 44, 122, 134–5
  see also special effects
Citizen Kane (Welles, 1941), 181
"City Lights" (2016), 201
cognitivism, 138–40, 142, 147
collective memory, *Be Kind Rewind*, 167–8, 177, 180
"Come Into My World," 202
comic books, 189–90
coming-of-age theme, 105, 109, 185
commercials, 132, 153, 159, 197–8
computer-generated imagery (CGI), 20, 190, 191
concert documentary *see Dave Chappelle's Block Party* (2005)
Conley, Tom, 106
conservatism, 118, 188
Conversation, The (Coppola, 1974), 46–7
Coppola, Francis Ford, 46–7
costuming, 21
craft aesthetic, 18–32, 185–6, 190; *see also* handmade objects
creative practices, 91
Crowe, Cameron, 35
"Crystalline" (2011), 201
curating, 58, 63

Daft Punk, 201, 203–4
Darjeeling Limited, The (Anderson, 2007), 70
Dave Chappelle's Block Party (2005), 153–65, 175–6
decorative collecting, 60–1
Deleuze, Gilles, 99
Diaz, Cameron, 184

digital technologies, 20, 43–5, 133, 189–90; *see also* CGI; special effects
displacement, 103, 106
DIY aesthetic, 25, 68, 69, 176–9
Do the Right Thing (Lee, 1989), 161, 176
documentaries
  MG's personal history, 17
  see also Dave Chappelle's Block Party (2005)
domestic space, 30
Dowd, A. A., 66, 72, 73
dreams and dreamers, 18, 33–47, 90, 93, 206
  in *Be Kind Rewind*, 37–8
  in *Mood Indigo*, 27
  in *The Science of Sleep*, 25–7
  and society, 41
  and surrealism, 92
  three typologies, 42
Duke Ellington, 36, 43, 94
Duris, Romain, 73–4

Easy Rider (Hopper, 1969), 105
Ebert, Roger, 184
economic themes, 77–8
editing, 44, 46, 96
  Block Party, 158–9, 164–5
  and dreams, 26
  Eternal Sunshine, 132, 134–6, 170
  Microbe & Gasoline (2015), 106
  Mood Indigo, 73, 75, 81
  music videos, 199
embodiment, 215, 216
empathy, 139
Eternal Sunshine of the Spotless Mind (2004), 26–7, 33–4, 35–6, 73, 95, 96–8, 198
  as art romantic comedy, 118
  and *Be Kind Rewind*, 176
  dream tautologies in, 43–5

editing, 122
ending, 129, 146–7
  and music video, 200
  narrative structure, 121–2, 128, 132, 134–6
  protagonists' psychology, 91
ethical dilemmas, 144
"Everlong" (1997), 198, 200, 206–9

fairy tale/fable, 40–1
fantasy, 91, 123, 218; *see also* dreams and dreamers; play motif
Farrow, Mia, 176, 180–1
Fats Waller, 175, 177, 180, 181
"Feel It" (1997), 202
"Fell in Love with a Girl," 203
Film Factories, 71
Foo Fighters, 90, 198, 200, 206–9
Foucault, Michel, 40
framing, 107, 153, 162, 163
French film history, 89
French road movies, 102–13
Freud, Sigmund, 91, 93, 169
Fugees, The, 154, 164–5

Gainsbourg, Charlotte, 18–19, 22–4
gaze, 52, 159, 214–15
gender relations/ideology, 188, 214–15, 218
Ghostbusters (1984), 176, 179
"Gilded Age," 79
"Go" (2015), 201
Godard, Jean-Luc, 105
Gondry, Michel
  influences on, 89–91
  interviews with, 26, 52–3, 68–70, 76, 91, 181, 197
Gott, Michael, 102–3, 106, 110, 111
Graduate, The (Nichols, 1967), 119, 124

Grand Budapest Hotel, The (Anderson, 2014), 66, 67–8, 69, 70, 73, 77–81
   budget and box office, 69, 82
Green Hornet, The (2011), 27, 38, 39, 45, 184–91
Grierson, John, 95–6
Grindon, Leger, 118, 119, 120, 127
growth, personal, 144, 146–7

Haggins, Bambi, 155
handheld camera, 122
handmade objects
   haptic visuality of, 50–1
   in music video, 200
   in *Science of Sleep*, 51–3, 54–8
   see also amateurism; craft aesthetic
handmade stop-motion animation, 201
Hansen, Beck, 174
haptic visuality/hapticity, 5, 50–2, 63–4
Hill, Lauryn, 164–5
hip hop, 157
Hirschberg, Lynn, 159
Hitchcock, Alfred, 199, 205
Hollywood, 81, 82, 176; *see also* individual film genres
Holstein, Dave, 213
home, 103, 104, 109–10
Home Movie Factory, 71
Homeric style of narrative, 143
horror, 208
"Human Behavior" (1993), 61–2, 200, 204
Human Nature (2001), 33, 37, 41, 45–6, 132
hyper-reality, 164–5

identity
   French, 102, 109, 110–11
   in *Kidding*, 214–16
   and memory(ies), 140
   and postmodern art, 147
immigrants to France, 103
Inception (Nolan, 2010), 133, 134, 144, 148
independent/art films, and Hollywood, 81–2
intertextuality, 180, 186, 199
Is the Man Who is Tall Happy? (2013), 58
I've Been 12 Forever (2003), 17

Jameson, Fredric, 172, 180
jazz *see* Duke Ellington; Fats Waller
Jonze, Spike, 37, 122, 124, 128, 168

Kaufman, Charlie, 37, 120, 128, 134, 136–7, 141, 146
Kermode, Frank, 136, 140, 141, 143
Kick-Ass (Vaughn, 2010), 186, 188
Kidding (2018–), 198, 204, 213–19
kitsch, 168, 176–9
knowledge, and power, 40
Korgis, 174
Kvaran, Kara M., 188, 189

Laderman, David, 105, 109
Laine, Tarja, 135, 146, 147
L'Atalante (Vigo, 1934), 89, 95–6, 99
Lee, Spike, 161, 175–6
"Let Forever Be" (1999), 198
liminal space, 22, 215
Lost in Translation (Coppola, 2003), 125, 127, 129
"Love Letters" (2014), 200
love stories, 53, 72, 91–100
luxury brands, 69, 70, 82

McGinn, Colin, 47
McGowan, Todd, 137
made animals, 56, 61–2

magic realism, 18–19, 51, 55–6
make-believe, language of, 18;
    see also play motif
male bonding, 107–8
Marks, Laura U., 50, 64n
Masters, Patricia Anne, 28
Mazanti, Louise, 22
memorialization, 49
memory(ies), 17–18
    analogue, 176
    Block Party, 154
    Eternal Sunshine, 94, 97, 133, 169–71
    of film history/popular culture, 180
    and identity, 140
    and loss, 136–7, 138
    see also trauma
metanarration, 128
Microbe & Gasoline (2015), 38–9, 71, 102–13
Minogue, Kylie, 132, 202, 210
mise-en-scène, 19, 20–1, 134, 162, 179
mobility, 109–11
montage, 46, 47, 106
Mood Indigo (2013), 18–32, 36, 70, 93–4
    artisanal dream in, 43
    budget and box office, 69, 81–2
    critics on, 66, 72, 73
    editing, 73, 75, 81, 98–9
    funding, 76
    over-consumption in, 73–5
    protagonists' psychology, 91
    and surrealism, 96
    and trauma, 39
Moonrise Kingdom (Anderson, 2012), 67, 70
Mos Def, 37–8, 161–2, 175, 176, 178
moviemaking, democratic essence of, 179
Mulvey, Laura, 214

music videos, 18, 21, 61–2, 69, 71–2, 90, 163, 164, 174, 197–210, 202
narrative
    Homeric/linear, 143
    in music videos, 206
    parallel, 132, 134–6, 170
    Revelation, 143–5
Neal, Mark Anthony, 154
Neale, Steve, 118
Neill, Alex, 139
new wave culture, 71–2
Nietzsche, 172
Nolan, Christopher, 133, 134
Norris, Chris, 142
nostalgia, 17–18, 22, 29–31, 73, 176;
    see also childhood
nostalgia movies, 81
novels, 141

Oliver, Valerie Cassel, 22
omniscience, 54
oneirism *see* dreams and dreamers
Open Your Eyes (1997), 35
optical illusion, 21, 57, 191; *see also* magic realism
'origins' category, road movies, 103
otherness, 34
outlaw narratives, 104, 105, 107
outsiders, 109, 153

Parker, Tracey K., 146–7, 148
parody, 186–8
pastiche, 172
Pastrone, Giovanni, 46
performance videos, 199, 201–4
photography, as taxidermy, 49–50
photography, early, 49
Plato, 58
play motif, 22, 27–8, 29, 56, 57, 60, 185
postmodern art, and identity, 147

post-soul aesthetic, 154, 157
poverty, 78–9, 162
power relationships, 40, 41
private (feminine) space, 22
professionalism, 80
psychoanalysis, 91, 92, 138–9, 140
Purple Rose of Cairo, The (Allen, 1985), 180

queer cinema, 108
quest narratives, 105

race, commodification of, 154; see also *Dave Chappelle's Block Party* (2005)
racism, 155
realism, 94–5, 118, 128
reality television shows, and taxidermy, 60–1
Regalado, Aldo J., 188–9
"repair art," roadkill, 50, 62
retro objects, 29
Revelation, 141, 143–5, 147
reverie, 60
Richardson, Michael, 4–5, 92
road movies, 38–9
road movies, American, 103–4, 105, 109, 111
roadkill "repair art," 50, 62
Robbins, Tim, 33
Rogen, Seth, 2, 38
rogue taxidermy, 50–1, 61, 62
Roma, 106, 110
Romanek, Mark, 69
romantic comedies, 117–18, 120–1
  and art film, 119
  "new romances," 118
romanticism, 92–3
Royal Tenenbaums, The (Anderson, 2001), 67, 68, 80
Rush Hour 2 (Ratner, 2001), 177
Rushmore (Anderson, 1998), 80

Schatz, Thomas, 125, 128
Schilt, Thibault, 102–3, 106, 111
Schumaker, Justin S., 186, 187
Schwartz, Alexandra, 72
Schwartzmann, John, 190–1
Science of Sleep, The (2006), 18–32, 34–5, 51–60, 63–4, 90, 177
  artisanal dream in, 42–3
  and music video, 200
  and trauma, 39
Scott, A. O., 53
script, 134, 136, 146
Sedgwick, Eve Kosofsky, 57, 63
self-reflection, 146
self-reflexivity, 107, 128
Showtime series see *Kidding* (2018–)
Sideways (Payne, 2004), 127, 129
Society of the Crossed Keys, The, 77
"Sounds Like You" (2017), 197–8
space, 22, 215; see also time and space
special effects
  and dream typologies, 42–6
  The Green Hornet, 185–6, 190, 191
spectacle, 147
Sperb, Jason, 81
Spider-Man films, 186, 187, 188
Spitz, Marc, 67, 68
"Star Guitar" (2001), 201, 202, 204
Steele, Jamie, 102
Stewart, Susan, 60
"Sugar Water" (1996), 200
Super (Gunn, 2010), 188
superhero genre, 27, 184–91
surrealism, 4–5, 51, 90, 155–6, 205
  l'amour fou, 91–4
  and realism, 94–5
  and romanticism, 92–3
Suskind, Alex, 70
"sweding," 19, 28

taxidermy, 50–3
  and MG's objects, 60–4
technology, and human will, 148

television *see* Kidding (2018–)
"The Hardest Button to Button," 203
The We and the I (2012), 71, 163
time and space, 60, 96, 132, 141; *see also* space
Tokyo (2009), 35
touch, 21, 49–50, 57; *see also* haptic visuality
transport, modes of, 109–10
trauma, 39, 40, 41–2, 144
Trilling, Lionel, 117
tweeness *see* whimsy

Vanilla Sky (2001), 35
Varda, Agnès, 109
Vian, Boris, 30, 72–3
 L'Écume des jours/ Froth on the Daydream, 18, 20
Vigo, Jean, 89–90, 95–6
Vines, The, 202, 203, 204
vintage technology, 29
visual effects
 Block Party, 160–1
 Mood Indigo, 98–9
 see also special effects

Waiting for the Midnight Express (Anonymous, 1911), 46
Waller, Thomas "Fats" *see* Fats Waller
Warner, Marina, 27
Washington Post, 161
water, as metaphor, 98–9
Wattstax (Stuart, 1973), 154
Weaver, Sigourney, 179
Weekend (Godard, 1967), 105
Wenders, Wim, 105
West, Kanye, 164, 204
western genre, 189
whimsy, 67–74, 75, 107
White, Jack, 205
white male privilege, 187
White Stripes, The, 201, 203, 205, 209
Wilder, Billy, 117, 126
Willis, Holly, 159, 164
wish fulfillment, 91, 93
Witham, Kimberly, 50, 62

Yates, Kimberly, 157

Zweig, Stefan, 77–8, 80–1

EU representative:
Easy Access System Europe
Mustamäe tee 50, 10621 Tallinn, Estonia
Gpsr.requests@easproject.com

www.ingramcontent.com/pod-product-compliance
Lightning Source LLC
Chambersburg PA
CBHW071831230426
43672CB00013B/2816